DSE212
Mapping Psychology

Book **2**

We would like to dedicate this course to the memory of Brenda Smith, Psychology Staff Tutor and member of the course team, who died during the final year of the course's production. She had been a Psychology Staff Tutor since 1995, first in Scotland and then most recently in Ireland, but her close association with the Open University stretches back much further than this. She was an Open University student herself and then later returned to teach and was a tutor who enthused and supported very many students throughout their social science studies. At her funeral one of these students spoke very movingly of her warmth and energy and of the fact that she had really 'made a difference' to their lives. She certainly also made a difference to our DSE212 course team, where her commitment to education for mature students was clear in everything that she said and did, and her immensely hard work influenced many of our plans for the teaching and learning strategy of the course and the content of the texts. She contributed enormously at both a professional and personal level, particularly to the early work of the course team, and we hope that her influence on the course will shine through, helping it in turn to 'make a difference' to the lives of all the students who will study it in the coming years.

DSE212
Mapping Psychology

Book **2**

Edited by Troy Cooper and Ilona Roth

This publication forms part of an Open University course DSE212 *Exploring Psychology*. Details of this and other Open University courses can be obtained from the Student Registration and Enquiry Service, The Open University, PO Box 197, Milton Keynes MK7 6BJ, United Kingdom: tel. +44 (0)870 333 4340, email general-enquiries@open.ac.uk

Alternatively, you may visit the Open University website at http://www.open.ac.uk where you can learn more about the wide range of courses and packs offered at all levels by The Open University.

To purchase a selection of Open University course materials visit http://www.ouw.co.uk, or contact Open University Worldwide, Michael Young Building, \Walton Hall, Milton Keynes MK7 6AA, United Kingdom for a brochure. tel. +44 (0)1908 858785; fax +44 (0)1908 858787; email ouwenq@open.ac.uk

The Open University
Walton Hall, Milton Keynes
MK7 6AA

First published 2002. Second edition 2007.

Edited and designed by The Open University.

Typeset by Pam Callow, S & P Enterprises (rfod) Ltd.

Printed and bound in the UK by Charlesworth Press, Wakefield.

ISBN 978 0 7492 1629 0

2.1

DSE212 course team: production

Open University staff

Dr Dorothy Miell, Senior Lecturer in Psychology, Faculty of Social Sciences (Course Team Chair)

Dr Paul Anand, Lecturer in Economics, Faculty of Social Sciences

Peter Barnes, Senior Lecturer in Centre for Childhood, Development and Learning, Faculty of Education and Language Studies

Pam Berry, Key Compositor

Dr Nicola Brace, Lecturer in Psychology, Faculty of Social Sciences

Dr Nick Braisby, Lecturer in Psychology, Faculty of Social Sciences

Maurice Brown, Software Designer

Sue Carter, Staff Tutor, Faculty of Social Sciences

Annabel Caulfield, Course Manager, Faculty of Social Sciences

Lydia Chant, Course Manager, Faculty of Social Sciences

Dr Troy Cooper, Staff Tutor, Faculty of Social Sciences

Crystal Cunningham, Researcher, BBC/OU

Shanti Dass, Editor

Sue Dobson, Graphic Artist

Alison Edwards, Editor

Marion Edwards, Software Designer

Jayne Ellery, Production Assistant, BBC/OU

Dr Linda Finlay, Associate Lecturer, Faculty of Social Sciences, co-opted member of course team

Alison Goslin, Designer

Professor Judith Greene, Professor of Psychology (retired), Faculty of Social Sciences

Celia Hart, Picture Researcher

Professor Wendy Hollway, Professor of Psychology, Faculty of Social Sciences

Silvana Ioannou, Researcher, BBC/OU

Dr Amy Johnston, Lecturer in Behavioural Neuroscience, Faculty of Science

Dr Adam Joinson, Lecturer in Educational Technology, Institute of Educational Technology

Sally Kynan, Research Associate in Psychology

Andrew Law, Executive Producer, BBC/OU

Dr Martin Le Voi, Senior Lecturer in Psychology, Faculty of Social Sciences

Dr Karen Littleton, Senior Lecturer in Centre for Childhood, Development and Learning, Faculty of Education and Language Studies

Dr Bundy Mackintosh, Lecturer in Psychology, Faculty of Social Sciences

Marie Morris, Course Secretary

Dr Peter Naish, Lecturer in Psychology, Faculty of Social Sciences

Daniel Nettle, Lecturer in Biological Psychology, Departments of Biological Sciences and Psychology

John Oates, Senior Lecturer in Centre for Childhood, Development and Learning, Faculty of Education and Language Studies

Michael Peet, Producer, BBC/OU

Dr Ann Phoenix, Senior Lecturer in Psychology, Faculty of Social Sciences

Dr Graham Pike, Lecturer in Psychology, Faculty of Social Sciences

Dr Ilona Roth, Senior Lecturer in Psychology, Faculty of Social Sciences

Brenda Smith, Staff Tutor, Faculty of Social Sciences

Dr Richard Stevens, Senior Lecturer in Psychology, Faculty of Social Sciences

Colin Thomas, Lead Software Designer

Dr Kerry Thomas, Senior Lecturer in Psychology, Faculty of Social Sciences

Dr Frederick Toates, Reader in Psychobiology, Faculty of Science

Jenny Walker, Production Director, BBC/OU

Dr Helen Westcott, Lecturer in Psychology, Faculty of Social Sciences

Dr Clare Wood, Lecturer in Centre for Childhood, Development and Learning, Faculty of Education and Language Studies

Christopher Wooldridge, Editor

External authors and critical readers

Dr Koula Asimakopoulou, Tutor Panel

Debbie Balchin, Tutor Panel

Dr Peter Banister, Head of Psychology and Speech Pathology Department, Manchester Metropolitan University

Clive Barrett, Tutor Panel

Dr Kevin Buchanan, Senior Lecturer in Psychology, University College, Northampton

Dr Richard Cains, Tutor Panel

Professor Stephen Clift, Tutor Panel

Linda Corlett, Associate Lecturer, Faculty of Social Sciences

Victoria Culpin, Tutor Panel

Dr Tim Dalgleish, Research Clinical Psychologist, Brain Sciences Unit, Cambridge

Dr Graham Edgar, Tutor Panel, Research Scientist, BAE Systems

Patricia Fisher, Equal Opportunities critical reader

David Goddard, Tutor Panel

Dr Dan Goodley, Lecturer in Inclusive Education, University of Sheffield

Victoria Green, Student Panel

Dr Mary Hanley, Senior Lecturer in Psychology, University College, Northampton

Dr Jarrod Hollis, Associate Lecturer, Faculty of Social Sciences

Rob Jarman, Tutor Panel

Dr Hélène Joffe, Lecturer in Psychology, University College London

Dr Helen Kaye, Associate Lecturer, Faculty of Social Sciences

Professor Matt Lambon-Ralph, Professor of Cognitive Neuroscience, University of Manchester

Rebecca Lawthom, Senior Lecturer in Psychology, Manchester Metropolitan University

Kim Lock, Student Panel

Patricia Matthews, Tutor Panel

Dr Elizabeth Ockleford, Tutor Panel

Penelope Quest, Student Panel

Susan Ram, Student Panel

Dr Alex Richardson, Senior Research Fellow in Psychology and Neuroscience, Imperial College of Medicine, London, also Research Affiliate, University Laboratory of Physiology, Oxford

Dr Carol Sweeney, Tutor Panel

Dr Annette Thomson, Associate Lecturer, Faculty of Social Sciences

Dr Stella Tickle, Tutor Panel

Carol Tindall, Senior Lecturer in Psychology, Manchester Metropolitan University

Jane Tobbell, Senior Lecturer in Psychology, Manchester Metropolitan University

Martin Treacy, Associate Lecturer, Faculty of Social Sciences

Professor Aldert Vrij, Professor in Applied Social Psychology, University of Portsmouth

External assessors

Professor Martin Conway, Professor of Psychology, Durham University

Professor Anne Woollet, Professor of Psychology, University of East London

DSE212 course team: update

Open University staff

Dr Nicola Brace, Senior Lecturer in Psychology, Faculty of Social Sciences (Course Team Chair)

Lesley Adams, Course Manager, Faculty of Social Sciences

Melanie Bayley, Media Project Manager, LTS Media

Dr Esther Burkitt, Lecturer in Developmental Psychology, Centre for Childhood, Development and Learning, Faculty of Education and Language Studies

Dr Jovan Byford, Lecturer in Psychology, Faculty of Social Sciences

Sue Carter, Staff Tutor, Faculty of Social Sciences

Lisa Collender, Assistant Print Buyer

Lene Connolly, Print Buyer

Dr Troy Cooper, Staff Tutor, Faculty of Social Sciences

Karen Hagan, Staff Tutor, Faculty of Social Sciences

Paul Hillery, Graphics Media Developer, LTS

Dr Martin Le Voi, Senior Lecturer in Psychology, Faculty of Social Sciences

Dr Helen Lucey, Lecturer in Psychology, Faculty of Social Sciences

Jo Mack, Sound and Vision Producer, LTS

Margaret McManus, Media Assistant (Rights and Picture Research), LTS Media

Professor Dorothy Miell, Professor of Psychology, Faculty of Social Sciences

Marie Morris, Course Secretary, Faculty of Social Sciences

Dr Johanna Motzkau, Lecturer in Psychology, Faculty of Social Sciences

John O'Dwyer, Media Project Manager, LTS Media

Professor Ann Phoenix, Professor of Social and Developmental Psychology, Faculty of Social Sciences

Dr Graham Pike, Senior Lecturer in Psychology, Faculty of Social Sciences

Alvaro Roberts, Media Assistant, LTS Media

Dr Kathy Robinson, Lecturer in Psychology, Faculty of Social Sciences

Dr Lynne Rogers, Lecturer in Psychology, Faculty of Social Sciences

Dr Ilona Roth, Senior Lecturer in Psychology, Faculty of Science

Emma Sadera, Editor, LTS Media

Dr Jim Turner, Lecturer in Psychology, Faculty of Social Sciences

Howie Twiner, Graphics Media Developer, LTS Media

Dr Helen Westcott, Senior Lecturer in Psychology, Faculty of Social Sciences

Christopher Wooldridge, Editor

External authors and critical readers

Elizabeth Barnes, Associate Lecturer, Faculty of Social Sciences

Dr Susan Cave, Associate Lecturer, Faculty of Social Sciences

Dr Helen Clegg, Lecturer in Psychology, University of Northampton

Linda Corlett, Academic Consultant, Faculty of Social Sciences

Dr Tom Dickins, Principal Lecturer in Psychology, University of East London

Dr Graham Edgar, Senior Lecturer in Psychology, University of Gloucestershire

Dr Linda Green, Associate Lecturer, Faculty of Social Sciences

Dr Brenda K. Todd, Lecturer in Psychology, City University

Julia Willerton, Associate Lecturer, Faculty of Social Sciences, co-opted member of course team

External assessor

Dr Judi Ellis, Head of School, University of Reading

Contents

Introduction

In Book 2, we present three challenging topics in contemporary psychological research. The chapters cover discussions of development as a capacity which continues throughout the lifespan (Chapter 1), the nature of language (Chapter 2) and the complex question of the factors which influence our emergence as men or women (Chapter 3). In discussing these topics, we build on perspectives, theories and themes which you have already encountered in the course. We introduce new ideas and frequently juxtapose approaches which challenge one another. In Book 1, a key theme was the extent to which psychology can explain what makes us distinctive as individuals – as similar to, or different from other human beings. The topics of Book 2 were chosen with a related question in mind: are there aspects of our behaviour and experience in which we are essentially distinct from other animals? Each chapter deals with an area of functioning which is either unique to humans or which, arguably, takes on a distinctive form in humans.

The chapters also weave in the second and third key themes from Book 1. For example, Chapters 1 and 3 return to the second theme of fixity and change in a discussion of human development across the lifespan. We, like other animals, develop physically and in terms of behaviour and capability during our early lives – but does that early development then determine our behaviour and capability in later life to the large extent that it does for other animals? Or is there evidence that the development of advanced social and cognitive skills represents a degree of change?

All three chapters in this book illustrate the third theme of 'nature–nurture' by evaluating the contributions of both biological and social influences to human distinctiveness. The focus in Chapter 1 ranges from organismic approaches which assume set paths or patterns of development and change throughout life, to contextual development approaches which focus on the social and individual experiences which influence development. Discussion in Chapter 2 ranges from the evolutionary origins of language as a species-specific characteristic to the role of social interaction and context in determining meaning. Chapter 3 addresses sex and gender, an area in which there is heated debate about the nature of attributes which mark humans out as qualitatively distinct from one another and from other animals.

You should already be familiar with the notion that different perspectives fit together in various ways. They may conflict (where the contrasting claims of different perspectives are mutually exclusive and cannot be resolved), or be complementary (where contrasting claims are mutually compatible and can be accommodated within a common explanatory framework). They may also coexist (when particular perspectives, even in the same topic area, have no real point of contact: they neither conflict nor complement one another).

Book 1 introduced the shorthand notion of the 'three Cs' to refer to these relationships between theories. In Book 2 we highlight areas where these interrelationships take particularly challenging forms and try to examine more closely where the three Cs might apply differently to perspectives depending on whether you look at the focus of investigation, the method or the background assumptions. For example, in Chapter 2, the cognitive and social constructionist perspectives make conflicting assumptions about communication. The cognitive perspective embraces a view of language as an exchange of individually created meanings between individuals. The social constructionist perspective views language as creating meaning between people as they negotiate their different goals and purposes. Sometimes the question of how perspectives relate to each other in terms of the 'three Cs' is open to debate. This offers you opportunities to consider the ways in which different perspectives interrelate. Throughout this book it is important to think about whether particular perspectives can do no more than coexist because they make no shared assumptions about the phenomena under consideration.

One challenging issue which may occur to you is how such a diversity of perspectives can all fall within the subject area of psychology. This is perhaps most apparent in relation to the diversity of methods used by different perspectives. In the first chapter of *Exploring Psychological Research Methods*, you encountered both subjective and objective approaches to methodology, and a discussion of their philosophical assumptions and of the particular methods favoured by each approach. As you read about the very different types of research conducted from different perspectives, you might begin to wonder how such striking differences in what is accepted as a legitimate means of investigation and valid evidence can prevail within one subject area. This diversity is a key feature of psychology in the twenty-first century as the boundaries of psychology shift and change to encompass new methods and perspectives. It is this dynamism that helps to make psychology a vibrant, exciting discipline. We hope that you enjoy learning about approaches which reflect this diversity as you work through this book.

Meeting the challenge

Below are summaries of key features of chapters in this book. The summaries focus on the perspectives with which you should already be familiar from Book 1, and show which theories and studies from the chapter belong to them. You will encounter new approaches and concepts in this book which will build on those from Book 1. You may therefore wish to use these summaries as a basis for adding your own notes and observations as you read the chapters.

Chapter 1
Lifespan development

Perspectives

- The evolutionary perspective informs the notion that development fulfils adaptive functions for the species.
- Cognitive and psychometric perspectives inform studies of intellectual functioning in later life.
- The psychoanalytic perspective partly underpins attachment theory.
- The humanistic perspective underpins Erikson's theory.
- The sociocultural perspective informs work on friendship and collaborative learning.

Themes

The chapter focuses on the theme of fixity and change, and the extent to which human beings are determined by their early developmental experiences, or have autonomy and the capacity for change. It also considers how, and in which areas, development continues over the lifespan, and what may be gained rather than lost in older age. The chapter explores the issue of the interaction in development between biology, cognition, the environment and physiology through experience and learning, and how the balance may shift throughout the human lifespan.

Chapter 2
Language and meaning

Perspectives

- The evolutionary perspective informs theories of the human species-specific development of language.
- The cognitive perspective underpins theories of how language is processed and understood by communicating individuals.
- The social constructionist perspective underpins discursive psychological theories of meaning as emerging from context and interaction.

Themes

The chapter looks at whether language is a specific form of communication that distinguishes human beings from other animals. It examines what form that distinctiveness takes and how it might have come about. Part of the discussion of that distinctiveness concerns the place of rules and operations within language, and whether what distinguishes language from other forms of animal communication is its ability to create highly developed social interaction. It also focuses on the place of language in relation to cognition, the creation of meaning, and the debate about the relationship between language as reflecting or creating our perception and understanding of the world.

Chapter 3
The psychology of sex and gender

Perspectives

- The biological perspective offers theories of the relationship between genetic and physiological aspects of sex, and their implications for gender.
- The evolutionary perspective underpins theories that sexual behaviour and sexual partner choice are determined by behaviours and dispositions that have been selected for in evolutionary history.
- The psychoanalytic perspective underpins theories that the earliest relationships with parents and other significant individuals determine progression through a series of psychosexual stages and consequent sex- and pleasure-seeking behaviours.
- The social constructionist perspective underpins theories that the construction of meaning through language and social practices has produced current gender-differentiated patterns of behaviour, cognition and emotional response.

Themes

The central debate of the chapter is around the terms 'sex' and 'gender': what the different perspectives construe those terms to mean and the differing priority they give to each term in explaining patterns of difference between men and women, boys and girls. Each perspective presents its own account with little evaluative comment or critique from other perspectives. The chapter raises issues and debates relevant to comparing and evaluating the four perspectives.

Some of these topics may have personal relevance to you as a student. In a study of Open University (OU) psychology graduates, many spoke of attaining long-cherished goals for intellectual and personal development, of challenging expectations of them based on traditional sex roles or disabilities, or of achieving heightened consciousness of self and others as a result of acquiring the language and concepts of psychology (Barrett *et al.*, 1999). You will undoubtedly encounter material that challenges you to think about your own life history and the ways you view the world. We hope that it will enable you to reflect creatively on what you think, experience and do in your personal life. In bringing that reflection to bear in evaluating the academic subject matter of psychology, we hope that you will begin to formulate your own challenging psychological issues.

Reference

Barrett, C., Roth, I., Barnes, P. and Woodley, A. (1999) 'The aspirations and achievements of Open University psychology graduates and diplomates', Open University Working Paper.

CHAPTER **1**

Lifespan development

Clare Wood, Karen Littleton and John Oates

Contents

Aims

This chapter aims to:

- discuss the role of peer relations in social and cognitive development
- introduce the notion of 'attachment' as one explanatory device for understanding human relationships
- discuss evidence for psychological development throughout the lifespan
- describe and contrast different perspectives and theoretical approaches to human development.

1 Themes in lifespan development

Lifespan psychology, also referred to as developmental psychology, is concerned with the way our psychological characteristics change and develop throughout life, from conception to old age. This includes:

- how our personality develops
- how we learn to interact with others
- how our cognitive capacities change as we mature
- how changes in our biology can affect us psychologically, for example during puberty.

Developmental psychology encompasses a wide variety of the psychological perspectives that you have studied in the first course book (*Mapping Psychology*) and examines the way they interact. For example, as we mature biologically this can influence our cognitive and social development; our social development influences our cognitive and self-development, and so on. In other words, a developmental change in just one aspect of our psychology will have an impact on some or all of the others.

The idea that psychological changes occur during adulthood has not always been addressed by developmental psychology. For a long time it was primarily concerned with the changes that occur during childhood, with some theories suggesting (by omission) that adulthood was a time of psychological stability – the 'product' of developmental processes – until old age, when the trend turned towards psychological decline. Evidence now suggests that these ideas are not necessarily sound. This is why some psychologists prefer the term 'lifespan psychology', which indicates that we no longer accept such assumptions.

This chapter will introduce you to key ideas and research areas from within lifespan psychology. This first section will revisit the psychological perspectives that you encountered in the first course book and show how discussions of human development are influenced by a variety of perspectives. One theme that emerges from such discussions is the important influence that our relationships with others have on our psychological development. To illustrate this point, we have selected research and ideas relating to two important sources of interpersonal influence: our peers and our parents. Section 2 examines sibling and peer relationships and how they contribute to our development. Section 3 introduces you to the concept of 'attachment' and the way our early relationships with our parents may affect the way we interact as adults with others and with our own children. A second theme addressed by this chapter is that of change throughout the lifespan. This includes a re-evaluation of the idea that adulthood is the expression of all that we have acquired during childhood and that ageing in adulthood equals deterioration. In Section 4 we will present material that has begun to address the relative lack of research into adult development. The chapter concludes with an explanation of the historical development of lifespan psychology and how ideas from different perspectives have contributed to this area of psychology.

1.1 Thinking about perspectives

In the first course book you looked at various psychological perspectives to understand how different psychologists might answer key questions that occur in everyday contexts. The key perspectives in psychology identified in the first course book were:

- behaviourism
- biological psychology (including neuropsychology)
- cognitive psychology
- evolutionary psychology
- experimental social psychology
- humanistic psychology
- psychoanalytic psychology
- psychometrics
- social constructionism.

As you can see from this list, when we talk about psychological perspectives we are referring to different 'styles' of psychological explanation. They also tend to have a historical tradition that underpins their ideas and methods. It is easy to think of these perspectives as being in opposition to each other. Certainly there are some perspectives that do have some conflicting ideas, such as behaviourism and cognitive psychology. However ideas from different perspectives are often complementary, and can overlap. For example, both biological and cognitive psychologists try to explain memory processes. Their methods and explanations differ, but they often draw on research from each other's perspective in formulating their theories (see Chapter 8 in the first course book).

Developmental psychology is a good example of a psychological perspective that draws heavily on other psychological perspectives. This is because one of the key ideas in lifespan psychology is that human development is the result of *multiple influences* including individual psychological and physiological differences (**internal influences**), as well as historical and cultural factors (**external influences**). In order to acknowledge these multiple influences it is necessary to draw on a variety of psychological perspectives in our discussions of development throughout the lifespan. As you will see in Section 5, approaches to developmental psychology have been informed by evolutionary theory (Darwin in particular) as well as biological, psychodynamic, psychometric, social and cognitive perspectives.

Internal influences
Potential influences on development that are part of the individual, such as physical or psychological variables.

External influences
Potential influences on development that are not part of the individual, such as the immediate context, culture or history.

1.1　Revisiting the 'three Cs'

One of the things that you will notice about this course book is that it is impossible to give an account of the topics in each chapter without drawing on two or more psychological perspectives. The commentaries in the first course book highlighted the fact that when we consider two or more perspectives we need to reflect on the 'three Cs': whether they are *complementary, coexisting or conflicting*. This type of reflection will help you to develop your own critical awareness of psychology when you write your assignments. Whenever you start to learn about a new topic in psychology, or begin to write an assignment about that topic, do the following:

- explicitly acknowledge which perspectives have relevance to the topic area
- identify areas of commonality and compatibility between ideas, methods and findings relevant to that topic
- acknowledge any areas of conflict, and show that you understand why these conflicts are difficult to resolve
- offer an evaluation of which perspectives provide the most compelling explanations to you, as a student of psychology.

You can see that psychology does not present a neat, coherent picture in which all ideas from all perspectives are seen as valid and complementary. Accounts of psychology often highlight longstanding conflicts in areas of research and as a student it is important that you understand them, are aware of the research that the ideas are based on, and can begin to evaluate the nature of the evidence presented to you.

1.2 Thinking about relationships

We will now begin by reflecting in a very simple way on one of the themes of the chapter: the importance of relationships in human development. Modern developmental psychology embraces the idea that we are able to shape our own personal development, while acknowledging that development occurs within, and is therefore subject to, the influence of different social and cultural contexts. Our relationships with others are an important social context for development.

Activity 1.1

Take a moment to consider the ways that a close friend and one of your parents have influenced your development. How do you think they influenced you? In which of the following aspects have you been most influenced?

- personality
- cognitive development
- social development
- biological development
- other

At first, you may find it difficult to say whether you have been influenced in any of these ways. Or you may find that there are some areas where your parents influenced you more than your friends. Similarly, you may feel that your friendships helped you to develop in ways that your relationship with your parents did not. However, how do you know that your parents and friends have influenced you? What evidence are you drawing on? How would you go about 'testing' such claims? These are exactly the questions that developmental psychologists working in this area are faced with. This chapter will take you through some theories that make claims about the influence of siblings, parents and friends on social and cognitive development, and describe some of the evidence that supports them.

1.3 Thinking about adulthood

The other theme of the chapter is a reflection on some of the assumptions that psychologists have made about adulthood. One assumption is that adulthood is the product of childhood – that, psychologically at least, we do not really change a great deal: our mental capabilities, our personalities, our interpersonal style, and so on are all 'fixed' by the time we are adults. The only scope for change in adulthood is assumed to be negative, such as the loss of memory.

Activity 1.2

Take a few moments to reflect on whether you agree with the types of claims made above. Thinking about yourself, to what extent would you say that the person you are today reflects the experiences that you had as a child? Can you think of any ways that you have developed, either positively or negatively, during your adult years?

Comment

Many people can think of connections between their experiences as a child and aspects of themselves as adults. This is a notion that has been popularized in Western cultures over the last 100 years or so, originally due to the ideas of Sigmund Freud. You will recall that Freud's theory suggests that the (psychosexual) experiences we have as children impact on the development of our adult personalities. However, you may have also been able to think of ways that you have developed during your adult years. You may have come up with quite a long list of ways that you have developed positively during adulthood, perhaps in response to major changes in circumstance, such as entering or leaving a committed relationship, parenthood, becoming a student, taking a new job or acquiring a new friendship. At the same time you may have noted that some of your adult attempts at learning seem quite effortful when compared to those of a child (e.g. learning about a computer!). You may also find it quite difficult to say for certain when adulthood really began for you, as often it is culturally, rather than chronologically, defined (e.g. when you get your first job or leave home).

While development in childhood is dramatic and significant, positive psychological change continues throughout our adult lives, although we know relatively little about the processes involved. The notion of when adulthood begins is a complex one. We will return to these issues in Section 4. We will begin by looking at research that has attempted to explain how our relationships with our siblings and peers can impact on our psychological development, both in childhood and in adulthood. We will consider some ideas relating to the influence of our parents in Section 3. As you read on, keep notes on what psychological perspectives are being reflected in the research described to you.

Summary Section 1

- Lifespan psychology acknowledges and draws on multiple psychological perspectives.
- Development during the lifespan is the result of many interacting influences, both internal and external.
- One important influence on our development throughout the lifespan is the relationships we have with others.
- For a long time the idea that we continue to develop psychologically during adulthood was neglected.

2 Sibling and peer relationships

In this section we focus on the importance of sibling and peer relationships for development across the lifespan. First however, it is helpful to understand the distinction that is often made between 'horizontal' and 'vertical' relationships.

2.1 Horizontal and vertical relationships

Horizontal relationship
A relationship between people of equal status and/or power.

Reciprocity
Refers to the principle of 'give and take' – that if one person 'gives' in some way, there will be a similar gesture made by the recipient at some point.

Vertical relationship
A relationship which involves one person who has more knowledge or power than the other person in the relationship.

A **horizontal relationship** is characterized by **reciprocity** and egalitarian interactions and expectations. This is because such relationships are formed between individuals with similar knowledge or social power. A typical example of a horizontal relationship would be a friendship between peers of the same age.

A **vertical relationship** involves an attachment to someone who has greater knowledge or social power – a typical example is a child's relationship with a parent or a teacher. The interactions on which a vertical relationship is based are characterized by the *complementarity* of roles such as a child asking for help and a teacher offering it. Whilst the roles of the people involved are inextricably interwoven, the behaviour patterns demonstrated by each one differ markedly.

The distinction between horizontal and vertical relationships is not an absolute one. As Schaffer (1996) notes, a relationship with an older sibling may contain both complementary and reciprocal elements. Occasionally there are also circumstances when a relationship with a peer or peers can assume some of the functions more typically associated with an adult–child relationship (Freud and Dann, 1951). However, the distinction between horizontal and vertical relationships is a useful one as it captures the essence of two different types of relationship, each of which contributes to the development of the individual. Vertical relationships provide the child with protection and security, and enable the child to gain knowledge and acquire skills (Schaffer, 1996). But horizontal relationships also represent important contexts for development and learning and their significance should not be underestimated. In the sub-sections that follow we will illustrate the significance of sibling and peer relationships by drawing on research which highlights their importance for the development of social and cultural understanding, and a sense of self. We will also consider the opportunities for learning afforded by working with a peer.

2.2 Living together, playing together

As Schaffer (1996) notes, siblings have a significant influence on each other, which should not be underestimated. They spend substantial amounts of time in each other's company, watching each other interacting with other people and sharing experiences. Moreover, as any parent will testify, their relationship with each other is often highly emotionally charged. Observational studies of siblings (e.g. Abramovitch, Corter, Pepler and Stanthorpe, 1986) have revealed that their interactions are diverse and multi-faceted. Whilst there is certainly evidence of 'sibling rivalry', there is more to sibling interactions than competition and conflict. In most cases their interactions can be characterized as being positive, with clear evidence of cooperation, sharing, support and assistance.

Observations such as these, which highlight the complexity of sibling interactions, emphasize the need to understand the developmental significance of sibling relationships. Sibling relationships are notably different from the parent–child relationship. Work focusing on children's conversations throws this into stark relief. Caretaking activities represent an important topic of conversation when the child is interacting with the mother. In contrast, when a sibling is the partner, humour and playfulness predominate. Furthermore, while mothers have a tendency to focus on the child's feelings during their interactions, siblings typically emphasise their own (Brown and Dunn, 1992). As Schaffer explains:

> *Each conversational partner ... fulfills a different function: in one case supporting the child's attempts to understand and come to terms with his or her own feelings; in the other drawing the child's attention to another individual's inner life.*

> *(Schaffer, 1996, p.265)*

Judy Dunn's work also emphasizes the distinctive developmental contribution made by sibling interactions. Her naturalistic observational studies revealed that issues of fairness and justice are paramount and are heatedly discussed, contested and debated between siblings (Dunn, 1988). It is also evident that joint play brings with it the need to construct shared meaning and establish collective goals in accordance with mutually negotiated rules. Schaffer summarises the distinctiveness of sibling relationships as follows:

> *What does distinguish sibling relationships in general is that they are characterized by a mixture of* complementary *and* reciprocal *features ... Complementary features are most evident in the parent-child relationship, where the older individual plays a role that is different from but interrelated with that of the younger one. Reciprocal features are found in peer interaction: both individuals play similar, matching parts. Among siblings there is a difference in knowledge and power, yet that difference is not so great that the two children cannot sometimes play and talk together on the same level. It is this combination of features that makes sibling relationships potentially so influential: on the one hand the older child can act as teacher, guide and model to the younger; on the other hand, however, both children share interest and competence to a sufficient degree to tackle jointly the task of social understanding.*
>
> *(Schaffer, 1996, pp.266–7).*

The developmental significance of playfulness and play between children has been discussed by many psychologists, and we will turn to this next.

2.3 Pretend play and development

Activity 1.3

If you are able to, observe two or three young children engaged in **pretend play** together. Pay particular attention to what is said and how it is said. What strikes you about the children's talk and joint activity?

Pretend play
Refers to play that involves the use of imagination where a person 'pretends' to be someone or something else, or uses an object as something else for the purposes of play.

As adults we are often captivated by the richness and diversity of young children's social pretend play. However, we usually take the occurrence of such play for granted and do not consider its function in the development of social and cultural understanding. Neither do we fully appreciate the skill with which even very young children negotiate shared understanding and meaning while engaged in pretend play together.

Göncü (1999) argues that social pretend play is a complex activity that involves negotiating shared meaning on different planes simultaneously. Göncü maintains that children engage in social pretend play to share and explore emotionally significant experiences with their peers. Göncü notes that while successfully establishing a mutual pretend focus is necessary, it is not a sufficient condition for social pretend play:

> *It also must be communicated that a pretend message is to be interpreted as such, rather than a literal message. Bateson (1955) refers to such communication as metacommunication ... The metacommunication*

indicates the changing form of interaction from play to non-play, and provides ... an interpretative frame for the activity. Used effectively this metacommunication conveys a desire to have fun by playing with representations.

(Göncü, 1999, p.124)

To understand both the complexity of pretend play and what is meant by metacommunication consider the extract of a video transcript reproduced below. This is an edited sequence of young children in a London nursery playing 'doctors and patients'. Girl 1 is the 'doctor' and Girl 2 is the 'patient'.

(1) Girl 1: Here's a drink of water

(2) Girl 2: OK, there – drink it. I got lots of ... on my laster band [elastic band?]

(3)   [To third child]   Oh, don't do that to me

(4) Girl 1: Don't do it to the doctor. Go huh huh huh huh

(5) Girl 2: You're hurting its cold

(6) Girl 1: In your ears

(7) Girl 3: My baby's not very well

(8) Girl 2: OK

(9) Girl 3: Yeah, I think he's got spots. Know what? My baby's got spots

(10) Girl 1: Wait

(11) Girl 2: That's not for your tummy. Is that for your tummy?

(12) Girl 1: No what's it for?

(13) Girl 2: It's for going like this – this

(14) Girl 1: Yeah – and what do you have to do like that? And what do you have to do like that?

(15) Girl 2: Look like that

(16) Girl 1: No

(17) Girl 2: OK, like that, have that one, that's much better. What's that for?

(18) Girl 1: Snapping your tummy

(19) Girl 2: Snapping your tummy – ouch, it's hurting, that hurts

(20) Girl 1: And now, so you can breathe

(21) Girl 2: Not my mouth!

(22) Girl 1: What do you have to do then?

Source: Faulkner *et al.*, p.48

Göncü would argue that the girls in this extract are able to establish a joint theme based on past experience (and presumably past play), where both have implicit knowledge of appropriate roles and narratives. But more than this, they must also negotiate their non-play relationship as friends in a nursery, surrounded by other children and adults, within the framework of daily routines and expectations about what is and what is not acceptable behaviour. The extraordinary feature of pretend play is the capacity of very young children to switch apparently effortlessly from one level of representation and mode of communication to another.

At the start of the sequence, the two girls have already established a joint pretend focus and themes for their play (Line 1). There is a brief negotiation with a boy (also playing a doctor) (Line 3), and shortly afterwards Girl 3 tries to initiate an interaction within the play theme (Line 7). She offers an appropriate entry bid: 'My baby's not very well'. Girl 2 (the patient) acknowledges Girl 3's overture, saying 'OK' (Line 8), but neither Girl 1 nor Girl 2 encourages Girl 3 to join in. At line 11, there is a shift in the joint focus of the girls' attention from play to non-play signalled by the patient's comment: 'that's not for your tummy', referring to her friend's 'misuse' of a toy syringe. Between lines 11 and 16 the children are actually negotiating what a toy syringe is used for. This continues to line 17, where Girl 2 reverts to her 'patient' role.

In short, the children shift from playing out an asymmetrical relationship (dominant doctor/passive patient) to negotiating within their symmetrical friendship relationship (discussing how to use a syringe). It is important to note the subtlety of the metacommunicative signals between play and non-play. The shift (at 11) is most clearly signalled by the 'patient's' challenge to the 'doctor' – 'That's not for your tummy'. Perhaps her voice tone shifts a little along with her facial expression. But in circumstances like this it is often difficult for a researcher to pinpoint exactly which cues the children are using. This is in itself interesting, as it draws attention to the importance of taking account of the shared play history of play partners, both separately and as a pair – as a general rule, the more they share in common, the less they will need to make their metacommunication explicit.

Boundary markers of metacommunication in children's play are sometimes made much more explicit for example, at transition points, at the beginnings and ends of play, and especially if a child is no longer sure the game is fun. Note there is a hint of ambiguity when Girl 2 comments on the 'snapping' of the syringe on her skin 'ouch its hurting, that hurts' (19). Is she expressing pain within the communicative frame of 'play' or 'non-play'?

Such complex interactions in social pretend play can be seen in children as young as 18 months and it is through play that children begin to explore role relationships at a 'pretend' level. This enables them to acquire social skills, perspectives and cultural roles that are well in advance of their actual abilities:

> *In play a child always behaves beyond his average age, above his daily*
> *behaviour; in play it is as though he were a head taller than himself. As in the*
> *focus of a magnifying glass, play contains all developmental tendencies in a*
> *condensed form and is itself a major source of development.*

(*Vygotsky, 1978, p.102*)

In most play situations, children are not bound by the normal rules of
interaction, but they experiment with them. In their pretend world, the
meanings of words, objects and actions are not strictly defined as they are in the
'real' world. Cardboard boxes can symbolise ships or cars, rugs can be islands
and children can become adults or animals. Meanings, rituals and roles are
more important than reality (Shotter, 1974). This illustrates how the capacity to
function symbolically is important developmentally and we see how pretend
play allows children to learn about roles and interaction by experimenting with
them. What is done in a conscious, deliberate and exaggerated form in play is
often taken for granted in real life.

A good example of this was given by Vygotsky. As reported by Damon
(1983), Vygotsky observed two young sisters aged five and seven years who
decided to play at being sisters. As they did so, their behaviour changed
dramatically from their normal sisterly conduct. For example, it became stylised
and self-conscious as they acted out stereotypes of sisterhood roles by dressing
alike and always holding hands. Vygotsky commented that the 'vital difference
in play is that the child in playing tried to be a sister' (Damon, 1983, p.107).
According to Vygotsky, instead of behaving as real sisters they are intending to
be sisters and are conscious of each other's aims:

> *In life the child behaves without thinking that she is her sister's sister ... except*
> *perhaps in those cases where her mother says 'Give in to her'. In the game of*
> *sisters playing at 'sisters', however, they are both concerned with displaying*
> *their sisterhood; the fact that the two sisters decided to play sisters makes them*
> *both acquire rules of behaviour ... only actions which will fit these rules are*
> *acceptable to the play situation.*

(*Vygotsky, 1933 quoted in Damon, 1983, p.107*)

Vygotsky argues that play affords children unique opportunities to manipulate
and test out rules of social interaction. He also makes the important point that in
play, children are able to substitute symbols for the real world. When a box is
used as a ship, it is a symbol for the ship. In the same way, the exaggerated
sisterly behaviour is a symbol for real sisterly behaviour. Symbols are in fact
representations of what is going on in the real world. It is only through the
shared meanings of symbols that concepts about the self, personal roles and
behaviour of others can develop. Language provides the most potent symbols,
as we shall see in the next chapter.

2.4 'Others' and the development of self-concept

Through increasingly complex social relations children gain awareness of other people's points of view. They learn that these might be different to their own and must be taken into account in planning their own course of action. By imitating the role of adults during their pretend games, children acquire the ability to see objects, other people and themselves from a different perspective. Thus they become more socially aware and also begin to form and clarify their own self-concepts. So, pretend play is also one of the principle means through which children can explore their sense of self in relation to others. Play allows children to imagine themselves as another, thereby clarifying or consolidating aspects of the self which are either similar to or different from other people. It is through this process that children gain a sense of their own unique distinctive identity and develop a coherent sense of self (Fein, 1991). (You will remember that the topic of identities and diversity was discussed in detail in Chapter 1 of the first course book.)

Symbolic interactionism
A theoretical approach which emphasizes the significance of social interaction and the use of 'symbols' within these interactions.

The idea that self-concept develops through social experience and social interaction is a position broadly based on **symbolic interactionism**, which stresses the importance of social interaction in human life and of symbols or meanings that exist between people in their interactions. Symbolic interactionism views the development of the self as inextricably bound up with the development of the person as a social being.

According to the symbolic interactionists, the self-concept develops through the internalisation of interactions with parents, siblings, teachers and peers. So whilst peer interaction is not the only form of social interaction important for the development of the self, sibling and peer interactions nevertheless represent an important context for development. They are part of the rich and complex social world in which the child participates. To give you a flavour of the symbolic interactionist stance, the ideas of one of its key proponents, George Herbert Mead, are presented in Box 1.2.

1.2 Mead on 'Self'

I
A theoretical construct which refers to the conscious, decision-making part of a person's self-concept.

Me
A theoretical construct which refers to knowledge about oneself, and is suggested to be another part of the self-concept which can reflect the views of others.

George Herbert Mead (1934), following James (1892), saw the self as being divided into two parts: the '**I**' and the '**me**'. The 'me' consists of what can be known about the self, such as physical descriptions of ones own body, clothes, possessions, one's manner of thinking, moral and religious values, roles, social identity, reputation and behaviour ('self as object'). The importance placed on these aspects is influenced by other people's attitudes. Thus we can suggest that the influence of the social context upon the self-concept is felt mainly on the 'me' part of the self-concept.

The 'I' is the active process of experiencing. The 'I' represents the basic capacity for conscious awareness. This part of the self-concept enables individuals to be free from relying absolutely on other's views for their sense of self. Whilst the 'me' represents the perceived attitudes and perspectives of other people, the 'I' is free to reject or change these views. The 'I' is the 'self as subject', the part that acts and reacts to circumstances creatively and spontaneously.

Mead believed that we experience and reflect on ourselves in the same way that we experience and reflect on other people around us. In order to achieve this however, we have to be able to role-take, to put ourselves 'in the role of' the other person, to anticipate their responses, imagine how we appear to them and adjust our responses to come into line with theirs.

Taking the role of the other in interaction is not an easy task, and we gradually master it throughout life. People vary in their capacity to do this and some people never master it. In particular, many people with autism seem unable to understand any point of view different from their own. Mead argued that it is not until we can gain an understanding of other's reactions to ourselves that we can reach an understanding of ourselves. He did not believe that chronological age was of paramount importance in determining the ability to take the role of other. Instead, Mead stressed that social meaning arose in *interactions with other people*. Thus a very young child who had experience in many varied interactions might show greater role-taking ability than an older but less experienced person.

Internalising the 'generalized other' into the 'me' of the self-concept allows children to participate competently in social interaction. This early development is called primary socialization. Mead also suggests that adults continue to adapt to new roles and new relationships as they encounter them throughout their lives in what he calls secondary socialisation. New perspectives on the self are encountered through relationships with other people and this changes the self by adding to and changing the 'me'. Thus the self is not fixed and continues to evolve and change throughout our adult lives as different reflections of and views on the self are encountered.

What counts as a developmental theory? Mead's approach offers a general theoretical perspective on the central function of social role-taking in the development of the self. But Mead's concept of what is meant by role-taking is abstract and ill-defined, and details of the processes by which such role-taking abilities might develop are unspecified. In practice, the social and cognitive skills implied by the capacity to take another person's point of view are exceedingly complex, and a 'developmental theory' which fails to address this complexity is, at best, incomplete. A possible consequence is that Mead's theory over-emphasizes the importance of role-taking as the main route to self-development. As we shall see in a later chapter, children with autism have great difficulty in 'taking the role of another', and while this may mean that they have a different sense of self, it does not follow that they have none. In summary, Mead's theory has been useful to more recent researchers in developing ideas and theories which have then been investigated or explored through empirical research (see Selman, 1980) but it has not been itself the basis of empirical investigation. Its main value is as a broad conceptual framework, rather than as a set of specific claims about the developmental process.

We can summarize Mead's view on the related development of self and of perspective taking as follows:

- Through their use of language, their games and their play, young children begin to take the perspective of other persons towards themselves, and in doing so, become capable of reflecting on themselves.
- As a result of the process of taking the role of the other, the reactions of a 'generalized other' are internalised into the 'me' aspect of an individual's self-concept to allow him or her to make comparisons and judgements about how other people would react, even when no other people are actually present.

Another important result of the ability to take the role of the other is that individuals are able to find agreement between the meanings that they and others place on the various actions and events, in other words, they establish shared meanings. For Mead human society rests upon shared meanings between people, upon shared understandings about each others' intentions and upon being able to interpret each other's behaviour. To be a social being, we must therefore be capable of putting ourselves in the position of the other person. To understand his or her meaning we have to be able to imagine how they might react to us. We acquire a sense of self by being able to see ourselves from the perspective of another person. By being able to anticipate the interpretation that the other will place on something, the individual can adjust his or her behaviour to ensure that the intended meaning is conveyed, and that communication is effective. This is what Mead meant by symbolic dialogue, which is, in his view, the basis of both social interaction and personal identity.

2.5 Working together

So far we have talked about horizontal relationships as important contexts for *social development*. However, collaborative interaction between peers can also constitute an important context for cognitive development and learning.

The influential developmental psychologist Jean Piaget saw children as actively constructing their own understanding and identified peer interaction as being particularly important for progress (Piaget, 1932). According to Piaget, the young child cannot treat adults' ideas on their own merits because of the differences of status involved. However, disagreements with other children serve to highlight alternatives to the child's own point of view much more effectively. The alternatives can be considered 'on equal terms' and since the resulting conflicts of opinion demand resolution, the children involved are effectively prompted towards higher level solutions which incorporate the partial insights reflected in their varying initial positions.

Inspired by Piaget's ideas, Doise and Mugny (1984) and Perret-Clermont (1980) undertook studies which demonstrated that individual progress in understanding could be fostered by **socio-cognitive conflict**; that is, exposure to the conflicting ideas of peers during paired or small group problem solving. The typical design adopted in their studies involved individual pre-tests and post-tests, separated by a period of practice on a task undertaken either individually (the 'control' condition) or in pairs or groups (the 'experimental' condition). A recurrent finding was that children who had the chance to work on the task with others made greater individual progress at post-test than those who had not.

Socio-cognitive conflict
The experience of being aware of conflicting ideas held by peers, which forces a re-examination of one's own understanding of that idea.

Activity 1.4

Work by Doise and Mugny (1984) and Perret-Clermont (1988) suggests that exposure to conflicting perspectives is important for cognitive development. Can you think of any other explanations for why working with a peer might be beneficial?

Comment

In thinking about this you may well have remembered some of the work discussed as part of the socio-cultural perspective on learning in Chapter 3 of *Mapping Psychology*. That work suggested that there is a key role for collaborative as well as conflictive processes. The emphasis was on the negotiation of meaning and processes of joint construction of understanding. We saw how primary school children could work together jointly to construct understanding and knowledge. Moreover, we saw how, by exploring each other's ideas, the children in Mercer's study were able to create a new collective outcome, such that personal meanings and understandings were 'created, negotiated and enriched within interpersonal exchanges' (Crook, 1999, p.369). These exchanges were situated in the particular institutional context of the school. The group, rather than the individual, was the focus of analysis, and the emphasis was placed on the socially constructed properties of interaction, rather than, as here, on individual performance on pre- and post-tests.

Whilst there is compelling evidence to suggest that in some circumstances working with peers can be beneficial, there are a number of factors which impact on the productivity of interaction. These involve:

- the age of the learners
- the difficulty of the task
- personality of the learners
- the level of interpersonal acquaintance.

These factors are likely to interact in complex ways. Consider for example, the issue of friendship. To date there is little consistent evidence concerning the impact of friendship on the processes and outcomes of collaborative work. For example, Berndt, Perry and Miller (1988) found no difference in the cognitive gains made by friends and non-friends working together, while Azmitia and Montgomery (1993) did find benefits for 'friendship pairs' as compared with 'acquaintance pairs' on at least some of the scientific reasoning tasks they studied. Following a review of a number of studies addressing the issue of friendship, Azmitia concludes that the nature of the task is crucial and its 'difficulty may mediate differences in the processes and outcomes of the collaborations of friends and acquaintances' (Azmitia, 1996, p.151). In particular, she notes that those studies which appear to lend support for the cognitive benefit of working with a friend had employed particularly challenging tasks or tasks which drew heavily on so called 'meta-cognitive skills' involving activities such as planning, monitoring and evaluating evidence. Thus, peer interaction is not an educational panacea and careful thought needs to be given to how best to support effective group-work.

In addition to evidence suggesting that children can benefit from peer interaction, there is increasing evidence to suggest that adults also benefit from opportunities to work collaboratively on problems and learning tasks (see Joiner, Littleton, Faulkner and Miell, 2000) and there is much ongoing work considering how we can optimize and resource such collaborations.

1.3 The effect of revision materials on students' discussions

If you think back to Chapter 3 of the first course book, you will remember the idea that human cognitive activity is mediated by tools and artefacts. The implication is that the nature of the tools and artifacts provided impact on the ways in which learners engage with a task. A study by Crook (2000) provides a striking demonstration of this. Crook studied undergraduate students revising for a finals examination on a particular lecture course. These students were invited to form pairs in order to take part in some informal revision sessions and they were assigned to one of two different conditions. In the first condition the students engaged in discussion of their own personal notes from lectures. In the second, the students were provided with a set of cross-referenced web pages constructed from the lecturer's own notes for these sessions. The students clearly had the same purpose, which was to revise for the examination and were oriented to the same syllabus. They had similar resources available to them – textual notes on the lecture course. However, Crook found that the interactions that occurred in the two sessions were distinctively different. Those students who were asked to talk around their own notes engaged in more exploratory and creative talk in which they oriented towards key disciplinary themes. Talk around the web-notes was characterized by discussions of 'what was expected' and comparisons within the pair regarding what each of them knew. The web-notes seem to invite the learners to learn them, as they represent the lecturer's expectations. The personal notes, however, invite a more exploratory and open-ended form of use.

Crook did not go on to report how well these two groups did in the subsequent examination. Nevertheless, these sorts of findings highlight the crucial need to understand the role of tools and artefacts in shaping and supporting joint activity.

A note on culture and society

The account of horizontal and vertical relationships developed in this section has not addressed the issue of whether the nature and extent of sibling and peer relationships are influenced by the specific social and cultural contexts within which a child is developing. This is a significant omission as there is evidence to suggest that the time spent in the company of parents, siblings, peers, grandparents and friends, for example, varies from culture to culture (Schaffer, 1996). These observations remind us of the importance of not over-generalizing from patterns of relationship observed in a particular society at a particular historical moment in time, using particular methods. We must be careful not to turn descriptions of particular relationship patterns into prescriptions for healthy development. We need to develop an understanding of the processes of development that respects the plurality of psychologically adequate pathways from infancy to maturity.

One influential topic area that has developed within developmental psychology and illustrates the need for this kind of sensitivity is known as *attachment theory*. The theory offers an account of how our early relationships with our parents may impact on our relationships with others later in life. We will turn to this topic next and consider the contribution of a variety of perspectives to the theory, and evaluate the evidence it is based upon.

Summary Section 2

- Relationships with peers and siblings are important contexts for development and learning.
- Relationships with siblings and peers contribute to the development of social understanding and contribute to a developing sense of self.
- Opportunities for interaction with peers can often promote learning.
- We must guard against turning descriptions of particular patterns of interactions into prescriptions for development.

3 Attachment and the development of the individual

A central issue in developmental psychology is whether our experiences during childhood – our vertical relationships with our parent figures (child–adult), in some way shape the patterns of our later, adult, horizontal relationships (adult–adult). It is perhaps easy to conclude from the research presented in Section 2 that children's peer relationships have some kind of primary importance in this respect. What role do parents play in influencing their children's development? Do they contribute at all? In *The Nurture Assumption*, Judith Rich Harris (1999) argues that parents do not influence their children in the way that has culturally been assumed and that it is peer groups that are the major influence in determining how children will grow up. This conclusion has been the source of much controversy. However, there are theories that suggest that vertical relationships during childhood have an equally significant impact on how we develop. In this section we will introduce you to **attachment theory** as an example of one such theory.

Attachment theory
Bowlby's theory that children have a drive to feel secure by forming an emotional bond with a primary care giver.

Continuities
Connections between experiences at one point in life and behaviour at some later time.

The study of human development seeks to explain influences on people as they develop in terms of 'internal' as well as 'external' factors. It also seeks to identify **continuities** – consistent connections between experiences at one point in life and behaviour at a later point. Given the complexity of such influences, it is unlikely that developmental psychology could ever be able to specify such continuities as absolute laws in the way some theories suggest, but rather that some connections will emerge as more valid and likely to occur than others.

What if it was possible to state with absolute certainty how early childhood experiences (with peers or adults) determine adult behaviour? What would this mean? Would it rule out the possibility of an individual making a difference to how their life turns out?

In some areas of psychological development it appears that there may be certain developmental pathways along which individuals are likely to travel. The key word here is 'likely'. Starting on a particular path does not absolutely guarantee that you will arrive at a particular destination, it just makes it more probable, and the further down a specific path you go, the greater this probability becomes. Such an approach is therefore not **deterministic** but rather, **probabilistic**.

Many lifespan psychologists find it helpful to think of development as a **transaction** between the individual and their environment, with each influencing the other and in turn affecting the developmental path followed. One only needs to think about how differently one might react to a crying and to a smiling baby to realise the power that a person has to affect what happens to them. This highlights the role that people can play in determining their own environments. This is one reason why the so-called nature–nurture distinction is a particularly problematic one in developmental psychology.

Deterministic
An approach that assumes that a particular outcome is fixed and inevitable.

Probabilistic
An approach that assumes that outcomes are more or less likely to occur.

Transaction
Refers to the idea that individuals affect their environments, that environments can affect individuals and that the combination of these influences affects development.

To make this point a little clearer consider the following example: babies vary in how responsive they are to external stimuli. In itself this is neither a desirable nor undesirable characteristic, and it is probably influenced by genetic factors. Yet the effect of this trait (responsiveness) on the baby's development depends in part on how it affects the baby's environment. First, imagine that a baby who is highly responsive to external stimuli is cared for by someone who interprets the baby's responsiveness as a sign of irritability or hypersensitivity. Next, imagine that the baby is cared for by someone who, in contrast, sees this responsiveness as a sign of engagement and liveliness. It is likely that each of these two carers will provide different environments, for example by controlling the level of exposure to external stimuli according to their belief about the cause of the baby's responsiveness. Thus, we can see in this example a genetic factor actually affecting the baby's environment, through (mediated by) the mother's reaction. Processes like this, which show how difficult it can be to talk about genes and environments as if they are separate, are usually called 'transactional' effects.

Intimate social relationships, such as mother–infant relations and romantic partnerships, are intrinsically bound up with how two people mutually affect each other. An increasingly important area of modern developmental psychology deals with issues surrounding the ways in which close relationships are formed and continue in early infancy along the way to adulthood and through the rest of the lifespan.

3.1 What is 'attachment'?

Attachment
A strong, ongoing emotional bond between two people.

Attachment is the concept used to describe relationships that are ongoing and involve emotional bonds. Attachment theory sets out to explore the nature of the different ways in which people can become attached to each other and the processes involved in the formation of these bonds. For most of us, the special relationships that we have with a small number of other people are very important to us. They may be with a partner, children, parents, close relations or friends. What singles out these special relationships is often a combination of a feeling that we mean something to these others and that they mean something to us. We usually think of these relationships as enduring over time. We expect them to continue even when we are not physically present, so that the relationship is ongoing. When we do meet again after an absence of a day, a week, or more, we expect to be able to 'pick up where we left off'. Indeed, we have many expectations of the particular others to whom we become attached; expectations of how they will behave towards us and how we will behave towards them. We tend to expect that their feelings towards us will stay much the same, as will our feelings for them. To use the language of psychology, these 'significant others' have become part of our mental life and contribute to our feelings of well-being and being valued. For many people, what they are is defined in a very real sense by their relationships with their significant others. But it is not just being able to think about 'the other' that is important for us; we also feel drawn to be with our significant others. In other words, we find it rewarding to spend time with them and we feel motivated to do so when we are apart. Using terms from attachment theory, we 'seek proximity' to them and can use them as a 'secure base'.

Of course, many people also have difficult relationships with others. It may be that we do not get on as well as we would like with our children or we feel that a friend has let us down in some way. Problems in relationships can trouble us and affect the way that we feel about ourselves. Often, when this happens, it can affect other aspects of our lives as well, for example our productivity at work. Perhaps the most frequent reason why people seek some form of psychological help, such as counselling or therapy, is that they are experiencing difficulties in their relationships with others. This shows that there is something which is central to our psychological well-being, that is to do with our ongoing connections with others. Attachment theory is an arena within which psychologists from a number of different backgrounds are seeking to explain this central aspect of human life and experience.

Attachment styles

There are two key assumptions in attachment research:

- individuals tend to have characteristic styles (or stances) in relationships that are reflected in the way they behave towards others
- these styles have their origins in peoples' previous relationships, most particularly in their first relationships, as infants with their caregivers.

Activity 1.5

The following is an adaptation of part of a 'love quiz' that was printed in the US newspaper *Rocky Mountain News* by two attachment researchers (Hazan and Shaver, 1987) to gather a large amount of data on people's attachment styles in romantic relationships:

These questions are concerned with your experiences in romantic love relationships. Take a moment to think about these experiences and answer the following questions with them in mind.

Read each of the three self-descriptions below (A, B, and C) and then place a checkmark next to the single alternative that best describes how you feel in romantic relationships, or is nearest to the way you feel. (Note: The terms 'close' and 'intimate' refer to psychological or emotional closeness, not necessarily to sexual intimacy.)

(A) I am somewhat uncomfortable being close to others; I find it difficult to trust them completely, difficult to allow myself to depend on them. I am nervous when anyone gets too close, and often, others want me to be more intimate than I feel comfortable being.

(B) I find it relatively easy to get close to others and am comfortable depending on them and having them depend on me. I don't worry about being abandoned or about someone getting too close to me.

(C) I find that others are reluctant to get as close as I would like. I often worry that my partner doesn't really love me or won't want to stay with me. I want to get very close to my partner, and this sometimes scares people away.

(Hazan and Shaver, 1987)

Comment

Although this is a very simple 'quiz' it illustrates what many attachment researchers believe to be characteristic of three different stances which people can take towards relationships with others. A distinction is made between 'secure' and 'insecure' styles, with style B called secure, and styles A and C called 'insecure'. Style A is described as an *anxious–avoidant* style, and C as an *anxious–ambivalent* style.

You may have found it difficult to characterize your own attachment style from these three options. For example, you might feel that there are ways in which two, or even all three, of the statements describe you to some extent, or that none of them really captures your 'style'. You might feel that sometimes you are closest to one option and at other times closer to others, or that you are different with different people. These possibilities highlight some potential problems with this approach. These issues are in part methodological, concerning aspects of the validity of the underlying concepts and problems with using such measures in research.

We can ask whether these three styles are:

- exhaustive (do they describe all possible styles of relating?)

- mutually exclusive (can people only fit one category at a time?)

- stable (do people shift from one to the other over time?)

- context-dependent (is 'style' affected by whom one is with, and the setting?)

- accurate (are people able to introspect in the way this approach assumes?)

- biased (do people give responses that they think will show them in a good light?)

Different approaches to describing attachment

Note that the approach mentioned above is a *categorical* one; it sets out to assign (classify) people to one of a number of *categories* (classes). In Chapter 5 of the first course book, you were introduced to a contrasting approach: *trait* theories of personality, in which a person can be located along one or more *dimensions* (e.g. extravert–introvert). Some attachment theorists have adopted a trait approach and they have suggested that adults' attachment styles can be described by using two dimensions: approach–avoidance and autonomy–dependence (Bartholomew, 1990).

Table 1.1   **Attachment styles using two dimensions**

		Model of self	
		Autonomy	Dependence
Model of other	Approach	Secure	Preoccupied
	Avoidance	Dismissing	Fearful

Activity 1.6

Try to find a match between trait and category descriptions of adult attachment by thinking about how each of the cells in Table 1.1 could be linked to one of the three attachment styles (A, B and C) introduced in Activity 1.5.

Comment

Clearly, the B classification fits the 'Secure' cell. The style A classification fits quite well with the 'Dismissing' cell. The C classification seems to fit both the 'Preoccupied' and 'Fearful' cells. The labels used for the theoretical constructs in attachment can evoke evaluative associations; the label 'secure' may evoke positive associations, while the labels 'insecure (anxious–avoidant)' and 'insecure (anxious-ambivalent)' may appear negative. The same dimension of positivity–negativity might be evoked by the four-way classification shown here. There is a risk that the concepts in attachment theory may seem to pathologise some styles of attachment while presenting others as 'normal' or even 'ideal'. Psychologists working in the attachment field argue strongly that these labels are not intended to be evaluative and you should certainly refrain from applying them in this way to yourself. For instance, the assumption that high dependency is problematic for an individual can be seen as a cultural value. Remember too that the attachment approach rests on the assumption that there *are* consistent attachment styles across different social situations and relationships. The arguments and evidence presented in this section indicate several ways in which this assumption needs to be questioned.

Correlates of attachment classifications

Hazan and Shaver received over 1,200 replies to the 'love quiz' after it was published. More than half of the respondents (56 per cent) classified themselves as 'B' (secure), 25 per cent classified themselves as 'A' (avoidant) and 19 per cent as 'C' (ambivalent). As well as the three questions on attachment style, the article also included numerous other questions on current and past relationships. The researchers were interested in finding out whether other aspects of people's relationships were correlated with their attachment style (as measured by the three-item set). 'B' respondents reported that their relationships with their partners had lasted twice as long as for the insecure respondents, but one of the highest correlations was found with how people described the quality of their relationships with their parents. The study was repeated with a sample of 108 college students and very similar results were found.

Activity 1.7

The 'love quiz' (see Activity 1.5) is a **self-report measure**. What are the limitations of self-report measures and what implications might they have for the results of Hazan and Shaver's study?

Self-report measure
A measure that relies on the participant in the research making judgements about him or herself.

Comment

Two things that may affect people's responses to self-report measures are:

i)   The tendency to give 'socially-desirable' responses. This could mean that people are less likely to report themselves as (for example) being uncomfortable with closeness.

ii) Such measures depend on people being sufficiently self-reflective to be able to give a good account of their feelings. This is not always the case!

3.2 The adult attachment interview

The way in which a person describes their previous and current relationships with their parents has turned out to be an important, core feature of their attachment style.

Mary Main, working in the US in the 1980s, developed a way of studying attachment in adults by conducting a standardized form of interview (Main, Kaplan and Cassidy, 1985). This follows a predetermined structure, with a set of questions exploring how adults describe their childhood experiences with their parents. Importantly, the focus of analysis of the tape recording of the interview is not on the content of what the person says, but on the way in which they talk about it. The person coding the interview looks particularly at the structure and amount of detail in the individual's account, its internal consistency (the extent to which it contains contradictory statements) and its coherence (the degree of linking between points in the narrative).

Main described three basic positions which people take in talking about their relationships during the interview:

i)   Insecure: dismissing

A *dismissing* narrative is one in which the person asserts that what happened in their childhood is not important. They may say for example, 'my father shut me up in the cellar when I was naughty, but I didn't really mind, and anyway, it's in the past now. No, I didn't get upset, it didn't bother me at all. In fact, I've forgotten about it'. The person gives the impression that personal relationships are not of much significance. The narrative is sparse, with little detail, and events and people are recalled in a rather bland, unemotive way, even where the content suggests that emotions would have been felt. The past is not described as having an influence on the self.

ii) Secure: autonomous/free to evaluate

An *autonomous* narrative is one in which the person acknowledges the importance of relationships to them, both in the present and during their childhood and talks freely and in some depth about past and present attachments. Richly described examples are given of both positive and negative experiences, and the person shows a capacity to integrate these. Insight is shown into the motives and feelings of others, and into influences on the self.

iii) Insecure: preoccupied/enmeshed

A *preoccupied* narrative is lengthy and without a clear structure. The link from one statement to another is often not apparent; points may be repeated. The person acknowledges the significance of past experiences, but does not seem to have resolved these and moved on from them. Past events are talked about with feeling; the person seems to re-experience the feelings in the interview. The person seems to be 'stuck' in unresolved issues from the past.

You will see the similarities between the adult attachment classifications described by Main and the style A, B and C classifications of Hazan and Shaver mentioned in Section 3.1.

Earned security

In relation to the secure, autonomous type, it has been found that this is not necessarily associated with a generally harmonious and happy childhood as described by the person. Some people appear to have had difficult childhoods, but have nevertheless come to terms with them and have moved on. Often, this is associated with strong and positive marital relationships (Rutter, Quinton, & Hill, 1990). This type of autonomous adult attachment has been called *earned secure* (Main and Goldwyn, 1984).

The 'earned secure' classification questions the idea that childhood attachment styles are enduring states that will inevitably *affect future relationships in designated ways. Clearly there are other factors that can influence the way we learn to interact with others. For example, the experience of good relationships in adolescence and adulthood seems to make a difference, and psychotherapy may also be able to bring about significant changes. By the same token, negative life experiences may have a detrimental effect on attachment style: arguably if there is an 'earned secure' style of attachment, there should also be special labels for styles which involve a move from secure to insecure status. In Section 3.5 we will look more specifically at the evidence of how other factors besides early relationships influence attachment style, and the extent to which attachment styles are stable or not over the lifespan.*

3.3 Internal working models and attachment theory

The evidence that there may be something which happens between parents and their children during childhood which has effects extending well into adulthood brings us to one of the central ideas of attachment theory: the concept of *internal working models*. The idea of 'internal objects' and the notion that one can usefully think of an 'internal world' with its own dynamics and elements, was first proposed by the psychoanalytical theorist, Melanie Klein (see Chapter 9 in Book 1, *Mapping Psychology*, for further discussion of her work).

John Bowlby, the key figure in the development of attachment theory, placed this concept centre-stage in attachment theory. He began his work on the theory in the 1940s. This was a time of quite exceptional creativity in psychodynamic theorizing, and indeed in psychology more generally. Bowlby read widely across many scientific disciplines and it was this eclecticism that made his theory so rich and productive. He drew on numerous sources, the main ones of which were:

- Psychoanalytic theory: Bowlby was himself psychoanalytically trained. Although Freud devoted little attention to early infancy, he did state that the relationship between infant and mother figure was effectively the prototype for all future love relationships. This is one of the central concepts that Bowlby took up and elaborated.

- Systems theory and cybernetics: showing ways of understanding how complex organisms and mechanisms could maintain stability in changing environments. In particular, Bowlby made use of the concepts of *feedback* and *homeostasis* from systems theory.

- Ethology: this was describing and explaining behavioural patterns in different animal species. From this field, Bowlby drew the ideas of *critical* and *sensitive periods* in development, and of *imprinting*, whereby the young chicks of some bird species become very strongly attached to the first moving object they see.

- Neuroscience: this was beginning to find out how networks of neurons in the brain could store complex information about the environment. From this field, attachment theory incorporated the notion of *mental representations* or *internal models* of things and events outside the person.

- Primate research: experimental studies with young monkeys were beginning to show that what motivates them to cling to their mothers is not only, or even primarily, the source of food, but rather their mothers' provision of comfort. From this, Bowlby drew the concept of *security* as a primary motive.

- Object relations theory: this was exploring the psychodynamics of early human infancy and explaining the processes by which an infant develops *internal objects* out of relations with their mother figure. Bowlby used this idea in his concept of *internal working model.*

- Developmental psychology: which was discovering that exploration and curiosity seem to be things that young children like to do, for their own sake. Bowlby added *exploratory behaviour* to *security* as another primary motive in human behaviour.

Bowlby's central idea was that human infants have a biological drive to achieve security through a particular form of relationship to what he called 'the mother figure' (since a person other than the biological mother could equally provide such a relationship, in Bowlby's view). This **primary attachment relationship** depends on the infant coming to represent the mother figure as a *secure base* from which exploration is possible, in the knowledge that the mother figure can be returned to if the demands of the environment become too great, and that the mother figure will reliably be *available* as a source of comfort and security. Bowlby saw this as happening through the infant building up an **internal working model** of herself and her mother figure, which is in the infant's mental world, even during times when the mother figure is not physically present. It is important to stress that this model is one of a *relationship* with three components: a model of self, a model of the mother figure and a model of the relationship between the two. Bowlby believed that the establishment of a 'healthy' internal working model is essential for later mental health, future relationships and socially responsible behaviour. He argued that this is a basic, biological process, much like imprinting in chicks, which happens during a critical period in early infancy. This, in essence, is the core of attachment theory.

Primary attachment relationship
An attachment to another person, normally a parent or other caregiver, formed by a child during early infancy. Is also used to refer to an older child's or adult's close relationship(s).

Internal working model
A set of expectations for how oneself and another person will relate to each other. According to attachment theory, this is established during childhood and affects later adult relationships.

Is the establishment of a 'healthy' internal working model during infancy essential for later mental health? As we have seen the existence of the earned secure *adult attachment type suggests that this is not necessarily the case. Moreover, as we shall see, what constitutes a 'healthy' internal working model is culturally defined.*

3.4 Mary Ainsworth and the 'Strange Situation'

Mary Ainsworth spent some years in the early 1950s working with Bowlby at the Tavistock Clinic in London, mainly researching the effects of 'maternal deprivation' (the lack of an adequate mother experience in infancy) on children's development. It was the results of this research that led Bowlby to believe he had found the main reason for juvenile delinquency: inadequate or non-existent 'mothering'.

In 1954 Ainsworth left for Africa and moved attachment theory forward through her observations of 28 mothers and their children in Uganda. She noted that although there were some important differences in how children behaved when they were separated from their mothers, it was during **reunions** after separations that differences between children's behaviour were most evident. She kept in touch with Bowlby and reported that she had identified three different types of attachment: secure, insecure and absent. She later moved to Baltimore, in the USA, and spent a long period closely observing and recording the behaviour of 15 infants and their mothers. It was during this time that she clarified her attachment categories by subdividing the insecure classification into two. She also developed a method for assessing attachment in infants aged around one year, the **Strange Situation**, which has become a standard experimental laboratory technique for attachment researchers (Ainsworth, Blehar, Waters and Wall, 1978).

Reunion
An episode in the Strange Situation when a child and mother (caregiver) are reunited after a brief separation.

Strange Situation
A standardized set of episodes involving a child, their mother and a stranger in a laboratory in a sequence of separations and reunions. A way of assessing attachment security.

1.4　The Strange Situation

This assessment is carried out in an observation laboratory, with video cameras strategically placed to record the behaviour of mothers and their infants.

- The laboratory contains two easy chairs, a play area, perhaps defined by a rug, and a set of toys.
- Once the mother and infant have settled, the mother sits reading a magazine and after about three minutes, a stranger enters and sits quietly on the free chair.
- After a minute or so, the stranger starts talking in a friendly way with the mother, and after another minute, moves to the floor and starts to play with the child.
- A minute later, the mother gets up and leaves the room, while the stranger stays with the child.
- After three minutes (or less if the infant becomes very distressed), the mother then enters the room and returns to her chair. The stranger leaves the room.
- After a further three minutes or so, the mother gets up and leaves the room, leaving the child alone.
- After three minutes (or less if the infant becomes very distressed), the stranger then enters, offers comfort to the child if necessary, and tries to play with the child again.
- Finally, the mother returns, the stranger leaves the room, and mother and child remain in the room for a few more minutes.

The video recording of the whole session is then coded by trained observers.

There have been three important criticisms of the Strange Situation procedure. First, the ethics of causing a child distress by separating them from their mother are questionable. Second, it has been argued that the test lacks 'ecological validity' in that it is indeed a 'strange situation', unlike other situations in a child's life. Finally, it has been argued that children's previous experiences of separation (e.g. if the mother works) will influence their reactions, making the test less reliable and valid. With regard to the first criticism, a researcher using the Strange Situation will typically follow an ethics protocol by which the mother or the researcher will respond rapidly if either feels that the infant is experiencing more distress than they can easily tolerate. With regard to the second criticism, a counter argument is that it is indeed the very 'strangeness' of the situation that evokes the infant's security-seeking behaviour, which is the focus of interest. Finally, it is indeed the case that an infant's previous experience of separation affects behaviour in the test, but it can be argued that this is because experiences of separation have an effect on attachment security, so the test is still a valid measure.

Infant attachment classification

Based on the behaviour observed in the Strange Situation, Ainsworth identified the three basic attachment types:

i) Type A: insecure, anxious avoidant

    This is when a child does not seek proximity on reunion and rejects the mother's attempts to calm or comfort.

ii) Type B: secure

    This is when a child seeks proximity on reunion and allows the mother to comfort him or her.

iii) Type C: insecure, anxious ambivalent

    This is when a child shows both avoidant and proximity-seeking behaviours, and may behave in apparently inconsistent ways towards the mother.

In current attachment research, each type is further subdivided.

Methodological criticisms notwithstanding, the infant attachment types mentioned above have been widely accepted as valid, sensitive measures of attachment. According to attachment theory, these types show the three main ways in which a child's internal working model can operate:

• A child with a Type A (insecure, anxious avoidant) attachment has a rather troubled attachment to her caregiver. She is often not upset at separation, and tends not to get close to her caregiver even when they are reunited after separation. Often, she turns away from, rather than towards, the caregiver. She seems to expect the caregiver's response to be inappropriate and the relationship to be difficult, and she seems to lack a solid sense of herself as worthy of affection.

- A child with a Type B (secure) attachment has an image of her caregiver as a secure base, who is available for comfort. She also has an image of herself as worthy of her caregiver's attention and love, and can gain some comfort from this when separated, having confidence that her caregiver will return. Her reactions to separation do not show panic; she has some capacity to contain them in the knowledge of her caregiver's availability. She is able to use her caregiver for comfort, and shows pleasure at reunion. She has an untroubled expectation of closeness and warmth between people, and this is also shown in her being able to accept some contact with the stranger.

- A child with a Type C (insecure, anxious ambivalent) attachment is likely to show distress at the separation, suggesting that the caregiver's presence is important to her. But she seems to lack a firm belief that her caregiver will return or that the caregiver will be able to comfort her effectively on return, and she thus fails to use her caregiver consistently as a source of comfort at reunion, sometimes showing both approach and avoidance towards the caregiver. She is not easily able to comfort herself, nor does she seem to feel herself worthy of affection from her caregiver. She rejects the stranger's attempts to console her. Her expectation seems to be a pessimistic one, that upset cannot be eased by another.

It can be seen from the above three types that each is associated with a different internal working model of the self, the other and the relationship. Bowlby's view was that the particular working model a child had formed has a major effect on how children approach subsequent relationships with other people. He argued that an individual's internal working model contains expectations about how others will behave and will thus mean that the individual will behave in ways consistent with these expectations. Someone with a Type B attachment for example, will approach a relationship with a degree of confidence that the other will respond positively, while someone with a Type C attachment will be hesitant and rather wary. How the relationship then develops will, of course, also depend on how the other person behaves and their attachment type. This is discussed again later in this section.

3.5   From infant attachment to adult attachment

According to attachment theory, if internal working models persist and continue to affect people's relationships after childhood, each type of infant attachment should be associated with a particular type of adult attachment.

Activity 1.8

Look at the following table. Work out which adult attachment type (secure; dismissing; preoccupied) you would expect to be associated with each of the infant attachment classifications, and write it in the appropriate cell.

Infant Attachment Type	Adult Attachment Type
A: Insecure, anxious avoidant	Dismissing.
B: Secure	Secure.
C: Insecure, anxious ambivalent	enmeshed / Preoccupied.

Comment

A logical set of predictions would be that a Type B infant attachment would lead to a secure adult attachment type (AAT); that a Type A infant attachment would be associated with a dismissing AAT; and a Type C infant attachment would go with an enmeshed/preoccupied AAT.

A good way to test out these theoretical predictions would be to conduct longitudinal research lasting for at least 17 years or so. It would be necessary to carry out Strange Situation assessments with a selected sample of infants and to then assess their AAT classification when they reached young adulthood, say 16 years of age. Some longitudinal studies of this sort have indeed been carried out. The Bielefeld longitudinal study for example, has been tracking the development of children in 49 families in Germany (Zimmerman et al., 2000). Forty-four children, whose attachment security was assessed when they were between 12 and 18 months of age, were later assessed for AAT classification at 16 years of age. Information was also systematically collected on the occurrence of various 'life events', such as divorce and death or illness of parents, in the intervening period between the two assessments. It was found that the Strange Situation type (SST) classification was not a good predictor of the adolescents' AAT; what emerged as a significant influence was, instead, the life events, particularly divorce and parental serious illness, which had happened during childhood. However, another study (Hamilton, 1994) of 30 adolescents in California, did find a strong correspondence between SST and AAT classification. This study also collected data on intervening events and experiences. A careful analysis of these data showed that the correspondence was largely found for children where their family circumstances had remained stable over the 16-year period between the SST and the AAT assessment. This was true for both secure and insecure type classifications on the two measures. Those children who changed from a secure to insecure classification (or vice-versa) were much more likely to have experienced major changes in their family circumstances.

Taking these two sets of results together suggests that there is some support for the link between infant and adult attachment status, but that life events are also a potent factor in influencing AAT. In a stable childhood, SST may be a predictor of AAT, but in a less stable developmental pathway through childhood, other events can have a major effect, both positively and negatively. Again, this illustrates the argument that no single factor can reliably account for developmental change, albeit in one narrowly defined area of psychology.

Adult attachment's influence on infant attachment

It has been much easier for researchers to look at the way that a mother's AAT might influence their infant's SST typing. A large number of studies have been carried out looking at how mothers with different AAT classifications behave towards their infants, and what types of attachment their infants show. Three consistent findings have emerged from these studies:

- Mothers' AAT is predictive of their infants' SST types, particularly for secure attachment. But the prediction is not 100 per cent accurate; for secure versus insecure classifications, it is around 75 per cent. For the two types of insecure attachment, it is weaker, at around 40 per cent.
- AAT is also predictive of how mothers behave towards their infants: secure mothers are more likely to behave sensitively towards their infants, responding to their bids for attention, comfort and communication. However, AAT is a rather inaccurate predictor of this, too. Only about 35 per cent of the variation in sensitivity is predicted by AAT.
- Maternal sensitivity does predict infant attachment, but it only explains about 33 per cent of variation.

These findings are drawn from a large-scale *meta-analysis* of attachment research (van IJzendoorn, 1995). The second of these findings is of particular interest, since they point to one route by which attachment security might be transmitted from mother to child. The so-called 'intergenerational transmission' of attachment has been a major concern of researchers for some years, in part because it has been felt that intervening in the process might be of major benefit to children who would otherwise suffer from the difficulties associated with insecure attachment.

1.5 FEATURED METHOD

Meta-analysis

This is a statistical technique of growing importance in psychology, especially in developmental psychology, where it is particularly difficult to set up large samples of participants. Meta-analysis is the analysis of analyses; it is a way of putting together the results from a number of different studies on the same topic. Through meta-analytic techniques, it is possible to gain a more reliable estimate of the true effects being investigated. Since studies vary in their sample sizes, adjustments are made for these and the analysis is based on the **effect sizes** found in the studies, which typically vary to some extent. These are measures of the strength of association(s) found between the variables being examined in each study. The end result of a meta-analysis is an estimate of the true effect size underlying the effects found in the different contributing studies.

Effect size
How strongly two variables are associated. Often assessed by a beta coefficient, which can range from -1 to 1.

3.6 Reflecting on attachment theory and relatedness

So how does Bowlby's theory stand up in relation to the various pieces of evidence discussed above? There is some support for parts of the theory: it does now seem that infant attachment is related to adult attachment in *certain conditions*. It also appears that adult attachment style may explain *some* of the differences in how mothers behave towards their infants. And research has also illuminated some of the processes by which attachment *type* may be transmitted. But it has also shown that this is only part of the picture; that life events may, in some cases, have an equal or greater effect. Generally, as in much psychological theorizing, Bowlby's seminal ideas have led to a great deal of fruitful research and some important modifications to his theory.

Relatedness and relationships

It appears that the concepts of attachment styles and their origins in early childhood do have some validity, along with the idea that there is not a permanently fixed style arising from these early experiences but rather that life events play a part as well. But it is worth reflecting on the factors that come into play when we enter into relationships with others. Clearly the specific form that the relationship takes is the outcome of the complex 'chemistry' between two people: we all know, for example, how one mistimed word or gesture can set off a whole chain of interpersonal negotiation. Given this, a person's attachment style is just a starting point for an interplay with the other's attachment style. You might find it helpful to think about what sorts of starting points various combinations of Type A (insecure, anxious avoidant), B (secure) and C (insecure, anxious avoidant) classifications might give. What would a Type A person be like with a Type C person, for example? Or, how might a Type C person's relationship with a Type B person begin and then develop so that Type C becomes 'earned secure'?

Relatedness
The capacities a person has to relate to another; the qualities of their approach to a relationship.

It is worth distinguishing **relatedness** (which is what our attachment style gives us as more likely ways of relating with another person) and *relationship* (which is what results from the interplay between the two people's attachment styles). Attachment theory can tell us which qualities of relatedness come easily to us and those that we find less easy to engage in. It also sheds some light on how we come to have these particular propensities, how they have origins in earlier relationships and how they may be perpetuated through later ones.

The two explicit assumptions highlighted within the introductory account of attachment theory in Section 3.1 were:
- individuals have a specific style of approach to attachment which is a consistent characteristic of them as individuals
- these 'styles' have their origins in previous relationships, particularly those which infants have with their care-givers.

However the arguments and evidence reviewed in this section has shown that:
- attachment styles may not generalize across different situations nor across the different people with whom an individual has relationships
- attachment styles may be affected by positive or negative experiences across the lifespan as well as by the infant's earliest relationships with carers.

In this section we have also noted a more implicit suggestion of attachment theory, that secure attachment is somehow a 'good thing' and a type B style is a desirable goal. But we have suggested that the traits or attachment styles characterized as 'secure' are not the only beneficial attachment styles, and that attachment theory makes subtle culturally-biased judgements about what constitutes 'good' relating and what does not. For example, some other cultures place much less value on 'closeness' than Western culture, and indeed there are many where even trance states and high levels of disengagement from others are highly valued. We should not forget that views about the desirability of 'secure' attachment are located within, and arose from historically specific social and economic conditions which allow this kind of attachment behaviour. For example, a century ago in Great Britain, working class mothers in industrial cities with young children would have found it much more difficult to provide the conditions in which secure attachment was fostered. Different forms of child-rearing have become valued during different historical periods in the West, and it is also worth reflecting on the great diversity of ways of relating that there are in different cultures and ethnic groups around the world.

Summary Section 3

- Attachment relationships can play an important part of our lives.
- Researchers have described adults' attachment styles using both categorical and trait approaches.
- Secure, insecure/avoidant and insecure/ambivalent classifications have been used to describe both infant and adult attachment.
- The concept of internal working models was developed by John Bowlby as a way of explaining how infants' relationships affect their adult attachment.
- There is some evidence that Bowlby's theory has some validity, but life events are also important.

4 Development in later life

So far you have been introduced to the idea that social relationships have an impact on our psychological development throughout life and this theme continues in this section, which deals exclusively with development in late adulthood. The idea that we continue to develop throughout adulthood was neglected until relatively recently, but is an important area in lifespan psychology. In this section we will consider the way psychologists have changed their characterization of adulthood and critically examine the question of whether later life really is a time of loss and decline.

4.1 Defining 'age'

You may have observed how frequently our concept of 'age' needs readjustment. Young children appear to engage in behaviours that we did not do 'when we were their age'. Similarly, our view of later life alters as some people live longer and enjoy better healthcare. Age can be characterized in a number of different ways (Hayslip and Panek, 1993):

- *Chronological age* is the length of time since birth and it forms the basis of many people's judgements of whether they are 'old' or 'young'.
- This can be contrasted with *biological age*, which is the physical age of one's body. If healthy diet and exercise habits are maintained, bodily organs and processes may appear to be those of a much younger person.
- *Social age* is defined by the habits, behaviour, interests and attitudes of a person. For example, people in their 60's may share the attitudes and interests of their children and identify with people who are aged 20 or 30 years. However, there is an implicit emphasis on 'acting your age' and some behaviours are culturally or legally forbidden until an appropriate age has been reached (e.g. sexual relations).
- Finally, *psychological age* refers to our 'adaptive' behaviours (the way we cope with situations) such as problem solving and intelligence.

Trying to describe age is, in some ways, a subjective process. An attempt to arrive at some form of objective measure has resulted in the concept of *functional age*. Functional age is obtained by measuring performance on a range of measures or tasks that reflect the various social, biological and psychological aspects of ageing. Functional age may be a useful way of thinking about age as it defines individuals in terms of their actual ability rather than how long they have been alive. However, it also assumes that better ability is a feature of 'youth'. As you will see, this is not always the case.

Activity 1.9

Think about the characteristics and behaviours that you associate with both being young (e.g. under 20 years), and becoming older (e.g. over 65 years). Write them down in two lists, and carefully consider whether you regard each aspect to be positive or negative.

Based on your list, would you say that you have a broadly positive or negative view of ageing? Does this contrast with your characterization of being young? When you compiled your list of features associated with being young, it is unlikely that you included increased tendencies towards certain types of disease (yet for example you are more likely to contract meningitis when young). However, it is likely that you listed some health-based characteristics of growing old. It is useful to make a distinction between 'age related' and 'ageing related' conditions. That is, not all 'disorders' are an inevitable consequence of growing old (ageing-related); they are simply more prevalent in older populations (age related). How many of the features you compiled are genuinely features of growing old and how many are simply 'increased risks'?

The characterization of later life as a time of illness and decline has, until recently, even been apparent in psychological textbooks (Pennington, 1999). However, as we shall see, ageing is characterized by both growth *and* decline in ability, and the social context of ageing is an important influence on this.

While adulthood has been a neglected area in developmental psychology, this is not the case in other areas of psychology, where adult samples have been used to study cognitive, social and biological psychology to name but a few. However, what was lacking in these 'static' accounts was a sense of the developing adult. Moreover, it is only relatively recently that attempts have been made to consider the broader social, historical and cultural influences on such data.

4.2 Characterizing later life

We will now consider how psychologists have characterized late adulthood, it being a particularly stereotyped and under-represented area of developmental psychology. One attempt at describing psychological development in later life is that of Erik Erikson (see Chapter 1 in *Mapping Psychology*). He devised a theory of psychological development, where each stage of a person's life is seen as requiring the resolution of an 'issue' as part of that person's ego development. The way each person resolves these issues will result in the acquisition of a 'virtue' – an ego 'strength' or special quality (see Table 1.2).

1.6 Summary of Erikson's (1950) eight stages of psychosocial development

Trust versus Mistrust (birth to one year of age)

The quality of parental care in meeting basic physical and psychological needs largely determines whether the child learns to view the world and people as safe and dependable.

Ego Strength: Hope

Autonomy versus Doubt (one to three years)

Parental responses to children's growing physical and mental abilities and their need to do things for themselves produce either a sense of self-government and self-sufficiency or self-doubt.

Ego Strength: Will

Initiative versus Guilt (three to six years)

Children given ample opportunity to initiate motor and intellectual activities learn to be self-starters, capable of planning and responsibility. Non-responsive and derisive parents foster guilt.

Ego Strength: Purpose

Industry versus Inferiority (six to eleven years)

Children who are encouraged to make, build, and do things and who are rewarded for their efforts develop skills as well as pride in accomplishment and become productive and achievement oriented. Lack of opportunity and support, as well as criticism, lead to feelings of inferiority.

Ego Strength: Competence

Identity versus Role Confusion (adolescence: the teenage years)

Adolescents must use newly developed cognitive abilities to develop a coherent sense of self that integrates past experiences with direction for further adult roles.

Ego Strength: Fidelity

Intimacy versus Isolation (young adulthood: 20s and 30s)

Young adults must develop the capacity to share with and care about others, without fear of losing their own identities. The alternative is to be alone.

Ego Strength: Love

Generativity versus Self-absorption (middle adulthood: 40 to 65 years)

Concern about future generations and the legacy one will leave behind us ushered in by a growing awareness of mortality at midlife. Those who fail at this task remain focused on their own needs and wants.

Ego Strength: Care

Integrity versus Despair (late adulthood to death)

Integrity refers to the ability to look back over one's life and see it as satisfying and meaningful. It also implies an acceptance of death. Those who despair see their lives as unsatisfying, have great regrets, feel that time precludes any attempts at change, and fear of death.

Ego Strength: Wisdom

Source: adapted from Lemme, 1995, p.46

Erikson's theory is an important one. For a long time it was one of the few which explicitly recognized that psychological development continued throughout life. It is also important because of its emphasis on the relationship between the individual and society in affecting personal development – something that is now a central idea in modern lifespan psychology. Note in particular the critical role that parents are seen to play during the early years. You will recall from Chapter 9 of the first course book that parents are seen as important early influences by psychoanalytic psychologists. This is also a central idea in attachment theory, which you will recall is the product of a variety of psychological perspectives, including psychoanalysis.

Activity 1.10

Look critically at Box 1.6 above. What difficulties do you see in the way Erikson has characterized later life?

Comment

Erikson characterizes later life in very narrow terms. Most developmental change is seen as occurring in early life with later life seen as a period of relative stability, where the primary concern is coming to terms with death and dying. As Peck argues, 'Ego-Integrity vs. Despair seems to be intended to represent in a global, non-specific way all of the psychological crises and crises solutions of the last forty or fifty years of life' (Peck, 1968, p.88). In an attempt to address this difficulty with Erikson's last two stages, Peck divided middle age and old age into additional sub-stages that attempt to characterize the crises in more detail. In doing this, Peck also characterized later life positively, as a time for growth (see Box 1.7).

1.7 Peck's characterization of later life

Middle age

The first crisis is *valuing wisdom versus valuing physical powers*. This describes the need to come to terms with a loss of physical strength and stamina, and in some cultures a loss of attractiveness. However, at the same time we experience gains in making informed judgements or 'wisdom'. Peck suggests that it is wrong for people to cling to physical ability as the main tool for coping with life's problems. This is followed by a crisis in personal relationships: *socialising versus sexualising*. Peck suggests that it is necessary in middle age to redefine individuals in terms of their personality and potential for companionship rather than viewing them as potential sexual partners. Another relationship crisis is *cathectic flexibility* (the ability to shift emotional attachments) *versus cathectic impoverishment*. This is seen as especially important in late middle age when children may be leaving home and the parent-child relationship is redefined. Individuals are often coping with the loss of their parents and friendships may also be affected by death. The ability to form new emotional bonds is therefore important. More positively, people at this stage have the opportunity for diversity in their personal relationships that may include friendship with both young and old. The fourth and final crisis of middle age is *mental flexibility versus mental rigidity*. Peck observed that a common criticism of middle age is that people become 'set in their ways' and closed to new ideas. Consequently, the ability to take stock of past experience while maintaining a flexible and open attitude to life is valued over rigid adherence to rules.

Old age

Ego differentiation versus work-role preoccupation relates to the crisis experienced on retirement from work. That is, some people may value their ability to do paid work (e.g. 'being the breadwinner'), but are unable to characterize themselves in other ways. Consequently there is a need for older people to engage in a range of valued activities to help redefine themselves.

The second crisis of old age relates to the increased vulnerability to illness and pain. *Body transcendence versus body preoccupation* refers to the need to cope psychologically with increased physical vulnerability and to learn to enjoy life through social relationships and mental activity, rather than becoming increasingly preoccupied with physical deterioration. The last crisis, *ego transcendence versus ego preoccupation*, relates to coming to terms with one's own death. The idea is that this crisis can be resolved by unselfishly contributing to one's own legacy through children, friendships and cultural contributions, so that one can die knowing that one's contribution to society will continue.

Activity 1.11

Think about Peck's characterization of later life. Does it seem valid based on your experience of and knowledge about growing old?

Comment

Culturally specific
Something that is relevant to one specific culture.

Peck's characterization seems appealing and accounts for many of the issues of later life and it emphasizes the role of social relationships in ageing. However, you may have noticed that it is **culturally specific** (as is Erikson's). For example, the need for cathectic (emotional) flexibility is based on assumptions about the age at which people typically have children and the age at which those children will leave home and gain independence. Both these factors will vary across cultures, and even across generations, and as a result this crisis may actually be encountered much earlier in life than Peck assumes. Work role differentiation is similarly based on the Western concept of paid employment and enforced retirement. While Peck acknowledges that some variation will occur as a result of gender differences and emphasizes the possibility that individual lives may influence the timing of these stages, little thought is paid to whether Peck's own cultural experience of ageing is 'universal'. He also assumes that people need to compensate for a decline in sexual activity. While there is evidence that sexual activity can decline with age, there is also evidence which suggests that sex continues to be fulfilling and plays an important role for people well into their 70s and beyond.

The issue of stereotypes of old age is not a trivial one as it has implications for the way society views the needs of older people. One example of this is the way that disability is seen as a 'natural' aspect of ageing. As a result of this, the opportunities for activity and independence that are presented to younger people with disabilities in residential care are not made available to many older people in sheltered accommodation (Walker and Walker, 1998). Such practices limit the opportunities available to older people to demonstrate that these stereotypes are misleading.

Losses and gains

Both Erikson's and Peck's models of later life are *person-centred* (see Chapter 9 in the first course book). Other psychologists have taken a *function-centred* approach that looks at just one type of behaviour (e.g. memory) and measures variation in it across the lifespan. This approach focuses on changes in ability with age.

'Successful' ageing is defined by Baltes *et al.* (1999) as maximizing gains while minimizing losses. It is suggested that we achieve this balance between loss and gain as we age by *selection, optimisation and compensation (SOC)*. They give the example of an 80-year-old concert pianist who was asked how he maintained such high levels of performance. He said that he played fewer pieces (selection), which he practised more often (optimization), and when he needed to play fast sections of music he would play the preceding section more slowly to make the next appear quicker (compensation). As we look at research into changes during adulthood, consider whether there is evidence of SOC taking place.

Memory

It has been suggested that episodic memory for older people obeys **Ribot's law** – that the past is remembered better than the present (Ribot, 1882).

Ribot's Law
The idea that older people remember past events better than recent ones.

Activity 1.12

Holland and Rabbitt (1991) asked two groups of people to generate as many memories as they could in ten minutes from each third of their life. Their results are shown in Figure 1.1. Which group do you think is older?

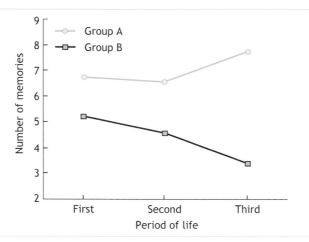

Figure 1.1   Results of Holland and Rabbitt (Source: adapted from Maylor, 1996, p.457)

Comment

Group B shows the recall of older people who were in residential care in the UK at the time of taking part. As you can see, their scores are consistent with Ribot's law. However, Group A also shows the recall from a group of older people of the same intellectual ability as the first group, but living in the community at the time of taking part. The results suggest that the need to rely on memory for day-to-day activities prevents the loss of recent episodic memories. Alternatively, the conversational activities and need to retain one's own identity that is especially important for people in residential care may lead to the rehearsal of older memories to do with family and friends. What this example illustrates is the effect of context and situation on cognitive development in later life. These differences in memory may reflect the effects of the different social contexts on SOC.

As the example from Activity 1.12 suggests, memory change in later life is not necessarily about decline, but about *qualitative changes* taking place. For example, Maylor (1994) contacted contestants from Mastermind (a formerly long-running quiz show on British television) and looked at their age and performance. She found that performance on the general knowledge questions (semantic memory) correlated with age – the older the contestant, the better they performed. In short, it appears that semantic memory improves with age.

These studies do not deny the biological fact that as we age, activity in our cerebral cortex, frontal lobe and hippocampus reduces: all areas that are involved in memory function. However, biological changes are affected by external influences. Kramer *et al.* (1999) have found that performance on cognitive measures such as speed of switching between two tasks can be improved by simple aerobic activity such as walking.

Twin studies show some genetic basis to memory functioning in later life, with short-term memory function showing the highest degree of *heritability* (Johansson *et al.*, 1999). However, the degree of heritability (see Chapter 5 in the first course book) is less for other types of memory and there is evidence from intervention studies that poor memory performance in later life can be improved by the tuition of specific memory strategies. For example, Noice *et al.* (1999) found that 65 to 82-year-olds who were taught to learn scripts by enacting the emotional states of characters in a study showed higher recall and recognition. Practising memory tasks also appears to result in improvement, regardless of age. Luszcz and Hinton (1993) asked two groups of participants (18 to 32 years old and 65 to 86 years old) to study a list of words. The list changed in each of four trials. They found that the repeated practice at the memory task particularly improved the performance of, and the strategies used by, the older group.

But while recall can increase after repeated exposure, studies of false memory suggest that this is not the whole story. McDermott (1996) found that, in general, adults remember twice as much correct information and half the number of false memories if they are tested on the same material five times, compared to just once. Kensinger and Schacter (1999) wanted to see whether older adults, who are more prone to false memories, also benefit from repeated exposure to stimuli (see Box 1.8).

1.8 Kensinger and Schacter's (1999) experiment

Kensinger and Schachter sampled two age groups: adults between 17 and 25 years, and between 60 and 75 years. The participants listened to a list of 45 words, which was constructed from three sets of 15 words. Each set of 15 words was semantically associated with a 'false' target word. After the list had been read out, the participants were invited to recall as many words from the list as possible. The same word list was then played a further four times and the participants were asked to recall the words from the list after each reading. The younger adults recalled more correct items than the older participants on the first trial and overall, and both groups correctly recalled more items in each successive trial. However, the younger group also recalled fewer false items in each successive trial. The performance of the older participants did not show this improvement.

You might conclude from this that older people have poorer memories than younger people. However, in this experiment it may be that older people were relying on using the gist of the information they were exposed to. This contrasts with younger adults who also learn details relating to the actual items as much as possible, rather than just relying on their overall impression of the stimuli. This successfully allows them to reduce false recall and recognition in experimental tasks of this kind. In other words, older people are simply relying on one strategy that is normally effective for day-to-day tasks – suggesting the operation of SOC once again.

Experimental studies of the kind described in this section are often problematic in their sampling of older participants. Many studies use a single group that covers a broad age range. The evidence presented in Section 4 so far shows that older people cannot be treated as a homogenous group (i.e. having similar characteristics):

> *... it is surprising that normative values for 'the elderly' are often based on mean performance data derived from populations with an age range from 60–100 years; no competent researcher would refer to 'the young', combining data from 10–50 years.*
>
> *(Richie, 1998, p.97)*

Intelligence

While it is a cliché that wisdom comes with age, it has been suggested that intelligence deteriorates with age. David Wechsler (1972) who devised the Wechsler Adult Intelligence Scale (WAIS) believed that just as we experience physical decline in later life, we also experience cognitive losses. However, this 'decline' depends upon the way intelligence is characterized and who is assessed.

Activity 1.13

Write down a definition of intelligence and ask some other people to do the same. How would you measure intelligence?

Comment

If you compare your definition to those of your friends, you may find some variation in what is believed to be the most important feature of intelligence. This high degree of variation suggests that there are a number of components that underlie intelligent behaviour.

Sternberg (1985) has suggested that we demonstrate intelligence in the way we adapt to our environment. This suggests that the nature of intelligence varies across cultures and ages. However, he also argues that there is a set of cognitive components that underlie intelligent behaviour, such as how we allocate attention or acquire knowledge. He argues that intelligence is best assessed by giving someone a novel task or by observing the automatization of new skills, as being able to do a task 'automatically' frees up cognitive resources (see Chapter 6 in the first course book). Traditional IQ tests measure a variety of cognitive behaviours, including memory, cognitive speed, vocabulary and problem solving, but do not attempt to address cultural or context specific aspects of intelligence.

Older people are not required to do as well as a younger person in order to be given an IQ score of 100 (which indicates 'average' or typical performance for a given age group), because of an apparent decline in cognitive performance with age. However, some tasks show more of a decline with age than others. For example, verbal sub-tests such as general knowledge, comprehension, verbal memory and vocabulary show relatively little decline. However non-verbal tasks do show a marked decline in ability with age. Horn and Cattell (1967) found that older people do better than younger people on tasks that require experience, such as general knowledge, vocabulary and so on. This type of intelligence is referred to as **crystallized intelligence**. Younger people do better than older people on tasks that measure efficiency of brain functioning and processing speed, known collectively as measures of **fluid intelligence**. As fluid intelligence is associated with brain function it is more vulnerable to loss and damage with age than crystallized intelligence is. For example after a stroke many crystallized abilities can be regained with time and training. This division between (crystallized) intelligence as acquired 'cultural' knowledge and (fluid) intelligence as information processing has been reflected in many theories of intellectual development but is most closely mirrored by Baltes' *two-component model* (see Figure 1.2).

Crystallized intelligence Abilities that are the product of experience (e.g. vocabulary, general knowledge).

Fluid intelligence Abilities that reflect efficient information processing (e.g. speed of processing).

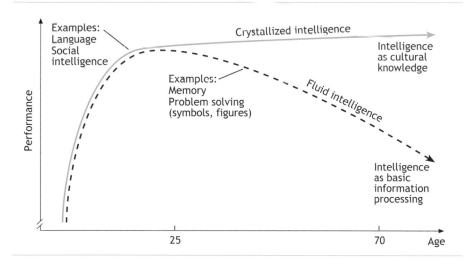

Figure 1.2   The lifespan trajectories of fluid and crystallized intelligence (Source: adapted from Baltes, 1987, p.615)

Cross-sectional versus longitudinal designs

Cross-sectional design
A research design that
compares the
performance of different
age groups.

The data supporting the distinction between crystallized and fluid intelligence were taken from studies using a **cross-sectional design**, where different age groups are compared to each other. This approach can be problematic when the range of age groups is large. In 1953 Schaie (1988) tested people aged from 22 to 70 years. The scores were grouped into age categories according to the year of birth and the average score for each age group was calculated (a cross-sectional approach). These averages showed a clear decline in performance with age. However, he then re-tested as many participants as possible in 1963, 1970, 1977 and 1984. When these data were analysed longitudinally, (i.e. when the scores of individuals were charted across their life), no decline in performance was observed (see Figure 1.3).

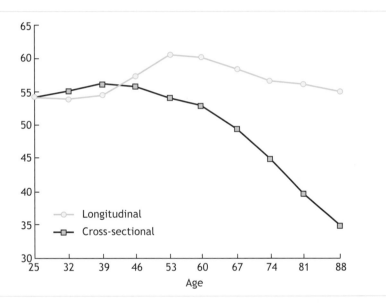

Figure 1.3   Lifespan trajectories for verbal meaning test scores analysed cross-sectionally and longitudinally (Source: adapted from Schaie and Willis, 1991, p.405)

Why would the data on the same people produce such different results? This is due to differences in ability across generations. That is, in many countries, each generation tends to differ from the one that preceded it, due to improvements in education, nutrition, healthcare and other historical factors known as **cohort differences**. Therefore, when a cross-sectional study presents data from participants aged 30, 40, 50 and so on, there will appear to be a decline because the younger people are slightly more advantaged than those in the older groups. However, if we look at the same person throughout their life, their mental abilities remain stable.

Cohort differences
Differences that occur
between different groups
because of changes in
external factors across
time (e.g. improvements
in state education).

Longitudinal data on people over the age of 70 years suggests that it is not simply the case that IQ will decline with age, but that other factors may differentiate between those whose IQ will drop and those for whom it will remain stable. Deary, MacLennan and Starr (1999) found that those with high verbal ability, high social class and better education are less likely to experience decline in verbal ability with age. Moreover, verbal intelligence is a good indicator of successful ageing as defined by living in the community without disability, with a good self-rating of health and a high score on a cognitive functioning test (Jorm *et al.*, 1998).

Instead of there being a decline in intelligence in later life, it appears that older people's reasoning is both socially and contextually orientated. For example, one study presented older people with a model meadow with a number of houses on it (Newman-Hornblum, Attig and Kramer, 1980, reported in Schaie and Willis 1991). The participants were asked if the arrangement of the houses would affect the amount of grass left to mow. Older participants did not get the answer right (the arrangement would make no difference), but their reasoning was perfectly logical. They explained that if there were a lot of narrow spaces it would affect the ease with which the grass could be mowed in some areas. In everyday settings older people are found to be especially efficient in their ability to handle complex social information and conflicting evidence. This sort of evidence supports theorists who have suggested that adult thought is characterized by *dialectical maturity* – the ability to live with and accept contradictory evidence.

Summary Section 4

- 'Age' can be defined in a number of ways, some of which are more objective then others.
- Holistic psychologists such as Erikson characterized later life in very narrow, undifferentiated ways. Peck elaborated on this period but presented a culturally-biased view of ageing.
- Function centred approaches focus on losses and gains in specific abilities during life. A balance can be achieved between loss and gain by selection, optimization and compensation of skills.
- Research suggests that there are qualitative changes in memory and intelligence with age (rather than loss). Overall, functioning in later life is affected by social contexts and adult thought is characterized by dialectical maturity.

5   Approaches to lifespan development

At the beginning of the chapter we talked about the contribution of multiple perspectives in psychology. Lifespan psychology reflects a wide variety of psychological perspectives that have each contributed to theories about how we develop with age. Attachment theory (see Section 3) is a good example of a developmental theory that has been influenced by the ideas of several perspectives. This final section is concerned with the historical development of lifespan psychology. The purpose is not just to explain the sources of contemporary lifespan psychology, but also to show that by drawing on multiple perspectives we can often achieve a more comprehensive account of a given topic area.

5.1   Darwin's influence on the study of development

Functionalism
The idea that changes occur in people and their behaviour because they serve a new and adaptive function.

One of the first major influences on developmental psychology was Charles Darwin. His theory of evolution (see Chapter 2 in *Mapping Psychology*) prompted a re-examination of the way people thought about human development. The first idea that developmental psychology inherited from Darwin's theory was a functionalist perspective. **Functionalism** means that explanations about why behaviours change are based on the idea that the change will serve a new and adaptive purpose (i.e. the behaviour has a function to serve). This idea directly derives from Darwin's theory, which argues that behaviours which increase the organism's chances for survival are selectively retained through evolutionary processes.

Prior to Darwin, the study of human development focused on describing the differences between adults and children. However, Darwin's work highlighted that there is considerable continuity and similarity between adults and children within any one species, as well as degrees of difference. This is reflected in his diary account of his son's first year of life. In it, Darwin observes that some of the behaviours his new-born son was exhibiting, such as sneezing, were as 'perfect' as those of an older child, while others were clumsy and still in the process of being learned. From this he suggested that some actions must be innate reflexes rather than learned behaviours. At any one moment in time an individual is the result of a gradual sequence of prior changes, both in a broad evolutionary sense and within that individual's own lifetime and further development and change lies ahead. This emphasis on gradual and continual change forms the basis of modern lifespan psychology.

The theories presented to you in this chapter reflect the influence of Darwin's ideas. For example, the account offered in Section 2 implies that social relationships are functional, as they promote both social and cognitive development in various ways. There is an implicit idea in attachment theory that attachment is functional because, it is argued, the bond between parent and child needs to be strong if the child is to become socially confident. The work presented in Section 4 proposes that change during later life is also adaptive in many respects.

5.2 Organismic approaches

At the beginning of the twentieth century, developmental psychologists were particularly concerned with charting the ages at which certain changes in behaviour 'normally' occur (e.g. when does a child talk for the first time). This developed into an approach to studying human development that is known as the *organismic* approach. That is, the individual (or 'organism') is its main focus.

The organismic approach assumes that human development has an end point or goal that is predetermined. Changes in behaviour throughout life are typically presented as a natural sequence of changes that occur one at a time, in a fixed order to bring the organism closer to the goal of development (referred to as a **stage theory**). For example, in the first stage of learning to walk the child is unable to support itself. As its muscles develop it becomes able to sit up unaided, perhaps crawl and finally take its first steps. As this example implies, one of the assumptions of an organismic stage theory is that environmental influences, while important, can only affect the speed of development. They may slow development down, or accelerate it, or even stop it, but they cannot alter the nature of the stages themselves, the sequence in which they occur or the end point they are designed to reach.

Stage theory
A theory that proposes that development occurs in a sequence of fixed order stages.

An early influential example of an organismic approach to human development was that proposed by Sigmund Freud (see Chapter 9 in the first course book) who claimed that children pass through a sequence of psychosexual stages. If a crisis occurred during any developmental stage, then it would be reflected in that person's personality. Consequently, Freud is credited with introducing the idea that the experiences we have as children will affect our personalities as adults. This theory, like many other organismic theories, assumes that adulthood is the 'product' of childhood – an end point rather than a time for change in its own right.

A more recent figure who adopted an organismic approach was Jean Piaget (1896–1980). Originally a biologist, Piaget became interested in children's intellectual development after working on the development of what became the Stanford-Binet intelligence test. Piaget noticed that when children made mistakes on the test, their errors often appeared to be systematic in nature. Piaget suggested that these systematic errors might hold the key to understanding how children's reasoning abilities develop with age. The idea that errors can be used to study mental processes is now commonly used in cognitive psychology. Cognitive processes are not directly observable, and have to be inferred from the way people respond to stimuli.

Still drawing heavily on the influence of Darwin's theory and influenced by his own biological training, Piaget began to study the development of intelligence as a form of adaptation to the environment. Piaget coined the term **genetic epistemology** to describe this area of study. Epistemology means 'the study of knowledge' and the term *genetic*, derived from 'genesis', refers to the origins of that knowledge. Like Darwin, Piaget observed his own children to formulate his ideas about cognitive development in childhood. From these observations, supported by work with larger samples of children Piaget suggested four main stages of cognitive development (see Box 1.10).

Genetic epistemology
Coined by Piaget, this phrase refers to the study of intelligence as a form of adaptation to one's environment.

1.10 An introduction to Piaget's theory of cognitive development

Sensory motor stage (approximately 0 to two years)

Children are born with innate behavioural patterns such as sucking and gripping, which are their first means of making sense of their world. They are able to take in new knowledge and experiences as far as they are consistent with their existing behaviours. Eventually children begin to generate new behaviours in response to their environment. As contact with the environment increases, they develop more elaborate routines or patterns of behaviour. This stage ends when children are able to represent their behaviours internally, through mental imagery or language.

Pre-operational stage (approximately two to six years)

Piaget saw the ability to build an internal representation of the world (a kind of mental model of how the world 'works') as a fundamental feature of cognitive development. At this stage children begin to use combinations or sequences of actions that can be carried out symbolically. For example, putting two objects together can be represented symbolically as an abstract mathematical principle (addition). However, at this stage children are only able to perform them as actions in the real world rather than representing them symbolically.

Concrete operations (approximately six to twelve years)

During this stage children are mastering the ability to act appropriately on their environment by using the sequences of actions they acquired in the pre-operational stage. They develop the ability to generate 'rules' based on their own experiences (e.g. noticing that adding something to a group of objects always 'makes more'). The children can now manipulate their environment symbolically too. They are still only able to understand the rules that they have had direct experience of, but they can begin some mental manipulation of these concepts. What they are unable to do at this stage is use rules to anticipate something that could happen, but that they have not yet experienced.

Formal operations (approximately over twelve years)

This is the stage at which children are able to reason in a purely abstract way, without reference to concrete experience. They can tackle problems in a systematic and scientific manner and become able to generate hypotheses about the world based on their accumulated knowledge of general rules of how it works. Piaget suggested that by the age of 14 or 15 years children achieve a stage where, having tried and rejected a number of personal theories about the way the world works, they finally devise a model of the world that is able to account for nearly all their experiences.

Although Freud and Piaget both adopted an organismic approach, their research methods and psychological traditions are very different. Freud, you will recall, was a proponent of psychoanalysis, whereas Piaget had a varied background that was informed by biological, evolutionary and psychometric perspectives.

Piaget's theory implies that adults demonstrate intellectual maturity as characterized by formal operational thought, and that there are no changes in the way we reason once we reach adolescence. As an adult student, your own experience of learning may tell you something rather different. We have already encountered evidence in Section 4 that intellectual development does continue into adulthood and context or personal experience are important influences on what we are able to achieve.

Piaget has also been criticized for the unproblematic way that he constructs intelligence. That is, 'formal' thought (rational, logical and deductive) is presented as the intellectual ideal. Kincheloe and Steinberg (1993) have argued that this is based on white, middle-class standards of 'intelligence' and as a result it devalues different forms of understanding that might be the product of other cultural experiences. They refer to other types of subjective reasoning which they call *post-formal thought.* They suggest that these are equally valid and characterized by an awareness of:

- what constitutes knowledge and how it is produced, including personal reflection on, and understanding of, one's own thought processes

- the hidden patterns and relationships that affect our experience of the world
- new ways of reading the world and attempting to make sense of oneself and society
- an appreciation that knowledge can never 'stand alone' from the context which it occurs within.

> *Cognitive development, then, is not a static, innate dimension of human beings, it is always interactive with the environment, always in the process of being reshaped and reformed. We are not simply victims of genetically determined, cognitive predispositions.*
>
> *(Kincheloe and Steinberg, 1993, p.300)*

Organismic stage theories continue to be appealing in their simplicity, but it is this same simplicity that is so often misleading and problematic. This chapter has presented you with two important ideas in developmental psychology: that development is influenced by interpersonal contexts and that development is lifelong. Organismic accounts underestimate the potential of the first idea and fail to acknowledge the second. The organismic accounts also assume the existence of an idealized end point to development, be it 'formal operations' in the case of Piaget, or an 'appropriate' mature personality resulting from successful negotiation of psychosexual development in the case of Freud. Attachment theory, having its roots in the psychodynamic perspective, also suggests an idealized outcome in the form of 'secure attachment', although there is awareness that this is culturally specific.

Contemporary approaches to developmental psychology attempt to acknowledge the full context of the individual and thereby offer a more fully informed account of influences on development. This approach is referred to as **developmental contextualism**.

Developmental contextualism
An approach to studying development by examining the interactions between the person and their environmental and historical contexts.

5.3 Development in context - developmental contextualism

Despite its name, the idea behind developmental contextualism is simple: *development does not occur in isolation, it is affected by the context of a person's life*. It is suggested that internal influences on development like an individual's biology and psychology interact with external influences such as their cultural context and interpersonal relationships. It is this interaction between influences that results in human development.

Activity 1.14

Think of something that you are good at, perhaps a sport or hobby. Try to think of all the things that influenced your development in this area. Think about them in terms of internal influences (biological or psychological tendencies) and external influences (friends, culture, prior life experiences).

Comment

Take the example of a woman who is good at tennis. She may be good because of repeated practice at tennis, because she is tall and physically fit (physical characteristics), because she received good tuition or because she is determined (personality). Practice, physiology, tuition and personality will all vary across individuals – in other words they can be thought of as *variables*. Come up with names that summarize the variables you identified as an influence on the development of your own 'skill'. Group your variables together into broad categories (e.g. interpersonal influences, cultural influences, cognitive factors). Each of these broad categories is referred to by psychologists as a *level of explanation* for why you are good at your chosen activity. Can you say that only one of your variables fully explains why you are so good? This is unlikely to be the case. This is the argument behind developmental contextualism: that even within just *one level of explanation* there are likely to be a number of variables that, in combination with each other, can explain development.

Another feature of this approach is that if just one of the variables influencing development changes, this can cause changes in other variables at the same or a different level of explanation. These changes will cause further changes of their own, and so on. This relationship between different variables and levels is referred to as **dynamic interactionism**. Some approaches might study human development at just one level of explanation, while acknowledging that other levels exist. Some theorists more dramatically suggest that just one level of explanation (e.g. biology) can account for changes that occur in all the other levels. However the idea of dynamic interactionism suggests that it is not possible to separate biology from the context of a person, an argument you may recall from the first course book, *Mapping Psychology*.

Dynamic interactionism
Used to describe the multiple interactions that can occur between different variables and different levels of explanation.

Physical environment

Figure 1.4 (overleaf) illustrates how internal influences are 'fused' into broader environmental contexts in a multidirectional way. The way human development is intertwined with a variety of contexts is referred to as **embeddedness**.

One person whose work illustrates such an approach is Urie Bronfenbrenner, who has proposed an 'ecological' theory of development, which attempts to acknowledge the full environmental and interpersonal context of development, and cognitive development in particular (see Box 1.11).

Embeddedness
Refers to the way development is 'rooted' in multiple contexts.

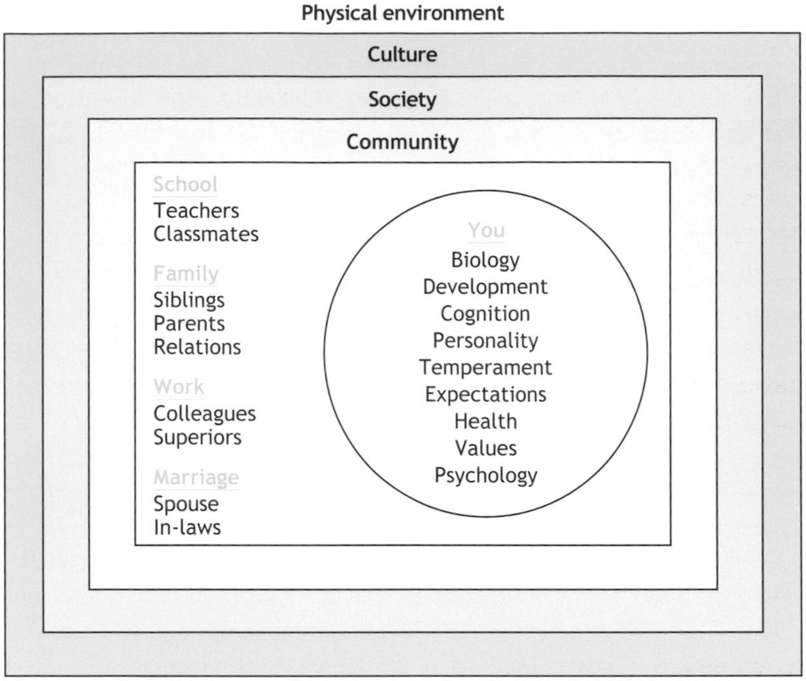

Figure 1.4   An illustration of contextual influences on the individual
(Source: adapted from Ford and Lerner, 1992)

1.11 An 'ecological' theory of development

Microsystem
The social, symbolic and physical characteristics of a person's immediate environment.

Mesosystem
Two or more environmental microsystems inhabited by the same person.

Exosystem
The links that occur between two or more environmental settings, where at least one of these settings is inhabited by the developing individual in question.

Macrosystem
The patterns of environmental systems that characterize any given culture or society.

According to Bronfenbrenner (1993), development is proposed to be the result of a person interacting with his or her environment. The term **microsystem** is used to refer to the social, symbolic and physical nature of an immediate environment: the social relationships present, the language used, and the physical resources available. But of course, environmental influences are much broader than any immediate setting. The term **mesosystem** is used to refer to two or more microsystems that are inhabited by the same person (e.g. a family setting and an OU tutor group) and how this combination of settings can jointly influence development. Perhaps you can think of ways that the combination of your home life and your activities in your tutor group have interacted to jointly promote your understanding of something. **Exosystem** is used to describe the links that take place between two or more settings, where at least one setting is inhabited by the developing person. This acknowledges the indirect, local influences on development such as the effect of a partner's job on a person's social development. Finally, the term **macrosystem** is used to refer to the patterns of microsystem, mesosystem and exosystem that characterize any given culture or social structure. All these levels of the environment are proposed to impact on the development of a given person in some way. Bronfenbrenner (1993) therefore urges developmental psychologists to build into their research an appraisal of the impact of culture on individual development.

This way of characterizing the nature of cognitive development contrasts with that of Piaget, although you will notice that it is consistent with the socio-cultural approaches to learning presented in Chapter 3 of the first course book. Piaget primarily explains development by reference to a child's microsystem, but does not include reference to broader environmental influences on development.

Box 1.12 summarizes the main assumptions of contextual approaches. As you can see, this approach suggests that people are able to act to promote their own development, rather than simply being subject to (and the product of) a variety of external and internal influences. If you re-read Section 2 you will notice that a contextual approach is reflected in much of the contemporary research presented there. Notice too how this approach contrasts with the ideas presented in attachment theory.

1.12 The guiding assumptions of developmental contextualism

(1) Variables from many distinct levels of explanation are involved in human life and development. The person and his/her internal psychology and biology must therefore be understood as embedded in the context of different levels of explanation.

(2) Individuals' development results from dynamic interaction within and between variables at different levels.

(3) Humans differ from one another in their genetic endowment and every human differs in the environments in which he or she is embedded during life. The dynamic interactions that occur between these two factors will also be unique for each person.

(4) Human development shows relative plasticity, so there is no single or ideal developmental pathway for any person.

(5) Individuals influence their own development through the decisions they make, their social networks, their effect on their environment, their environment's effect on them and their unique experience of the world.

(6) Individuals try to establish and maintain a correspondence between their personal characteristics and the contexts they are in, as well as trying to establish and maintain their own effective internal organization.

Source: adapted from Ford and Lerner, 1992, pp.88–90

What do the approaches covered in Section 5 have to say about development during adulthood? Organismic approaches like those adopted by Freud and Piaget seem to assume that there is little development after adolescence and adult cognition is portrayed as the product of psychological development rather than providing opportunities for continued development. Developmental contextualism explicitly acknowledges adulthood as a time for development and recognizes that the environment and biological factors and the interactions between them will result in a unique pattern of development for each of us. Psychologists are increasingly recognizing adulthood as a period of significant psychological change.

Summary Section 5

- The psychological development of an individual is subject to a number of influences.
- Organismic approaches to development emphasize the genetically and biologically predetermined outcomes of 'normal' development.
- Developmental contextualism emphasizes the multiple levels of influence on human development, including biological and environmental factors, and suggests that development is a lifelong process characterized by both losses and increases in ability.
- Psychological development is increasingly recognized as occurring during adulthood as well as childhood and adolescence.

6 Concluding remarks: factors affecting development

So what can we conclude about the development of the individual throughout life? Baltes (1987) provides a good summary of what we have learned from this chapter (see Box 1.3).

1.13 A characterization of lifespan development

- Development continues throughout life.
- Development is varied and complex: it occurs at different rates and is affected by a variety of internal and external factors.
- Development is characterized by both growth and decline in abilities at all stages of life.
- Development is characterized by the plasticity of individuals, whose developmental course is influenced by personal environment and experience
- Development is embedded within societies, cultures and histories.

- Development can be seen as the outcome of interactions between age-related factors (e.g. biological maturation, social events such as attending school), historical factors (e.g. evolution, the occurrence of war), and 'random' biological and environmental occurrences that only relate to one individual. This approach to lifespan development is known as 'contextualism'.
- Development is integrated, not just in the psychological perspectives it encompasses, but also the academic disciplines it draws upon, such as neuroscience, sociology and anthropology.

Source: adapted from Baltes, 1987, p.613

It is also worth reflecting on the breadth of methodological techniques that you have encountered in this introduction to developmental psychology. The reason why there are so many methods used to study human development is because of the way that lifespan psychology has sought to integrate ideas from a variety of psychological perspectives.

Revisit your answers to Activity 1.1 in the light of all you have read in this chapter. Would you change or expand your answers to this activity given the ideas that have been presented to you? Think about whether your answers 'fit' with the theories and research that we have presented to you in Sections 2 to 5.

Hopefully you now have a flavour of the complexity of human development, the need to consider multiple sources of influence that contribute to who we are today and the need to integrate multiple psychological perspectives to gain insight into them. The message of lifespan psychology is primarily a positive one:

> *Life is full of a smooth flow of events as well as unpredictable, fortuitous occurrences. Some people see and seize the opportunities that come to them and some do not. Some suffer from many more constraints on their possibilities than do others. Some suffer major life disruptions and create a reorganised life that is fulfilling in new ways, whereas others go through transformations that restrict rather than elaborate their lives. But the basic process is the same for all of us. The initial conditions of life do not determine one's life course.*

(Ford and Lerner, 1992, p.205)

Further reading

Crain, W. (2000) *Theories of Development: Concepts and Applications*, (4th edn), New Jersey, Prentice Hall.

This text is very readable and expands on the work of Ainsworth, Bowlby, Darwin, Erikson, Freud and Piaget. It also gives an account of the developmental significance of other psychologists that you will cover in the course, as well other figures whose work is of interest to lifespan psychologists.

 # References

Abramovitch, R., Corter, C., Pepler, D.J. and Stanthorpe, I. (1986) 'Sibling and peer interaction: a final follow up and a comparison', *Child Development*, vol.57, pp.217–29.

Ainsworth, M.S., Blehar, M.C., Waters, E. and Wall, S. (1978) *Patterns of Attachment: A Psychological Study of the Strange Situation*, Hillsdale, NJ, Erlbaum.

Azmitia, M. and Montgomery, R. (1993) 'Friendship, transactive dialogues and the development of scientific reasoning', *Social Development*, vol.2, pp.202–21.

Azmitia, M. (1996) 'Peer interactive minds', in Baltes, P. and Staudinger, U. (eds) *Interactive Minds: Lifespan Perspectives on the Social Foundation of Cognition*, Cambridge, Cambridge University Press.

Baltes, P.B. (1987) 'Theoretical propositions on lifespan developmental psychology: on the dynamics between growth and decline', *Developmental Psychology*, no.23, pp.611–26.

Baltes, P.B., Staudinger, U.M. and Lindenberger, U. (1999) 'Lifespan psychology: theory and application to intellectual function', *Annual Review of Psychology*, no.50, pp.471–507.

Bartholomew, K. (1990) 'Avoidance of intimacy: an attachment perspective', *Journal of Social and Personal Relationships*, vol.7, no.2, pp.147–78.

Bateson, G. (1955) 'A theory of play and fantasy', *Psychiatric Research Reports*, no.2, pp.39–51.

Berndt, T., Perry, T. and Miller, K. (1988) 'Friends' and classmates' interactions on academic tasks', *Journal of Educational Psychology*, vol.80, pp.506–13.

Bronfenbrenner, U. (1993) 'The ecology of cognitive development', in Wozniak, R.H. and Fischer, K.W. (eds) *Development in Context: Acting and Thinking in Specific Environments*, Hinsdale, NJ, Erlbaum.

Brown, J.R. and Dunn, J. (1992) 'Talk with your mother or your sibling? Developmental change in early family conversations about feelings', *Child Development*, vol.63, pp.336–49.

Crook, C. (1999) 'The uses and significance of electronic media during development', in Messer, D. and Miller, S. (eds) *Exploring Developmental Psychology from Infancy to Adolescence*, London, Arnold.

Crook, C. (2000) 'Motivation and the ecology of collaborative learning', in Joiner, R., Littleton, K., Faulkner, D. and Miell, D. (eds).

Damon, W. (1983) *Social and Personality Development*, New York, W.W.Norton.

Deary, I.J., MacLennan, W.J. and Starr, J.M. (1999) 'Is age kinder to the initially more able? Differential ageing of a verbal ability in the healthy old people in Edinburgh study', *Intelligence*, vol.26, pp.357–75.

Doise, W. and Mugny, G. (1984) *The Social Development of the Intellect*, Oxford, Pergamon Press.

Dunn, J. (1988) *The Beginnings of Social Understanding*, Oxford, Blackwell.

Dunn, J. (1993) *Young Children's Close Relationships*, Newbury Park, CA, Sage.

Faulkner, D., Ding, S., Woodhead, M., Littleton, K., Pretzlik, U. and Rowbotham, I. (2001) *ED840 Child Development in Families, Schools and Society, Project Guide, Audiovisual Notes and Video Transcript*, Milton Keynes, The Open University.

Fein, G. (1991) 'The self-building potential of pretend play or 'I got a fish, all by myself'', in Woodhead, M., Carr, R. and Light, P. (eds) *Becoming a Person*, London, Routledge.

Ford, D.H. and Lerner, R.M. (1992) *Developmental Systems Theory: An Integrative Approach*, Newbury Park, CA, Sage.

Freud, A. and Dann, S. (1951) 'An experiment in group upbringing', *Psychoanalytic Study of the Child*, vol.6, pp.127–68.

Göncü, A. (1999) 'Development of intersubjectivity in social pretend play', in Woodhead, M., Faulkner, D. and Littleton, K. (eds) *Cultural Worlds of Early Childhood*, London, Routledge.

Hamilton, C.E. (1994) 'Continuity and discontinuity of attachment from infancy through adolescence', *Dissertation Abstracts International Section A: Humanities and Social Sciences*, vol. 55, (2–A), p.217.

Harris, J.R. (1999) *The Nurture Assumption*, London, Bloomsbury.

Hayslip, B. and Panek, P.E. (1993) *Adult Development and Ageing* (2nd edn), New York, HarperCollins.

Hazan, C. and Shaver, P. (1987) 'Romantic love conceptualized as an attachment process', *Journal of Personality and Social Psychology*, vol.52, no.3, pp.511–24.

Holland, C.A. and Rabbitt, P.M.A. (1991) 'Ageing memory: use versus impairment', *British Journal of Psychology*, vol.82, pp.29–38.

Horn, J.L. and Cattell, R.B. (1967) 'Age differences in fluid and crystallized intelligence, *Acta Psychologica*, vol.26, pp.107–29.

James, W. (1892/1961) *Psychology: The Briefer Course*, New York, Harper Torch Books.

Johansson, B., Whitfield, K., Pedersen, N.L., Hofer, S.M., Ahern, F. and McClearn, G.E. (1999) 'Origins of individual differences in episodic memory in the oldest-old: a population-based study of identical and same-sex fraternal twins aged 80 and older', *Journals of Gerontology: Series B: Psychological Sciences and Social Sciences,* vol.54B, pp.173–9.

Joiner, R., Littleton, K., Faulkner, D. and Miell, D. (eds) (2000) *Rethinking Collaborative Learning*, London, Free Association Books.

Jorm, A.F., Christensen, H., Henderson, A.S., Jacomb, P.A., Korten, A.E. and Mackinnon, A. (1998) 'Factors associated with successful ageing', *Australasian Journal of Ageing*, vol.17, no.1, pp.33–7.

Kensinger, E.A. and Schacter, D.L. (1999) 'When true memories suppress false memories: effects of ageing', *Cognitive Neuropsychology*, vol.16, pp.399–415.

Kincheloe, J.L. and Steinberg, S.R. (1993) 'A tentative description of post-formal thinking: the critical confrontation with cognitive theory', *Harvard Educational Review,* vol.63, pp.296–320.

Kramer, A.F., Hahn, S., Cohen, N.J., Banich, M.T., McAuley, E., Harrison, C.R., Chason, J., Vakil, E., Bardell, L., Boileau, R.A. and Colcombe, A. (1999) 'Ageing, fitness and neurocognitive function', *Nature,* vol.400, pp.418–9.

Lemme, B.H. (1995) *Development in Adulthood*, Boston, Allyn and Bacon.

Luszcz, M. and Hinton, M. (1993) 'Try, try again: improving older adults' memory through practice', *Australian Journal on Ageing*, vol.12, pp.6–10.

McDermott, K.B. (1996) 'The persistence of false memories in list recall', *Journal of Memory and Language,* vol.35, pp.212–30.

Main, M. and Goldwyn, R. (1984) 'Predicting rejection of her infant from mother's representation of her own experience: implications for the abused-abusing intergenerational cycle', *Child Abuse and Neglect*, vol.8, no.2, pp.203–17.

Main, M., Kaplan, N. and Cassidy, J. (1985) 'Security in infancy, childhood, and adulthood: a move to the level of representation', *Monographs of the Society for Research in Child Development,* vol.50, pp.66–104.

Maylor, E.A. (1996) 'Ageing and the retrieval of specialized and general knowledge: performance of Masterminds', *British Journal of Psychology,* vol.85, pp.105–14.

Mead, G.H. (1934) *Mind, Self and Society*, Chicago, University of Chicago Press.

Noice, H., Noice, T., Perrig-Chiello, P. and Perrig, W. (1999) 'Improving memory in older adults by instructing them in professional actors' learning strategies', *Applied Cognitive Psychology,* vol.13, pp.315–28.

Peck, R. (1968) 'Psychological developments in the second half of life', in Neugarten, B. (ed.) *Middle Age and Ageing*, Chicago, University of Chicago Press.

Pennington, H. (1999) 'Cognitive aspects of ageing as portrayed in introductory texts', *New Zealand Journal of Psychology,* vol.28, pp.48–50.

Perret-Clermont, A.N. (1980) *Social Interaction and Cognitive Development in Children*, London, Academic Press.

Piaget, J. (1932) *The Moral Judgement of the Child*, London, Routledge.

Ribot, T. (1882) *Diseases of Memory*, New York, Appleton.

Richie, K. (1998) 'Establishing the limits of normal cerebral ageing and senile dementias', *British Journal of Psychiatry,* vol.173, pp.97–101.

Rutter, M., Quinton, D. and Hill, J. (1990) 'Adult outcome of institution-reared children: males and females compared', in Robins, L.N. and Rutter, M. (eds) *Straight and Devious Pathways from Childhood to Adulthood*, Cambridge, Cambridge University Press.

Schaffer, R. (1996) *Social Development*, Oxford, Blackwells.

Schaie, K.W. (1988) 'Variability in cognitive function in the elderly: implications for societal participation', in Woodhead, A., Bender, M. and Leonard, R. (eds) *Phenotypic Variation in Populations: Relevance to Risk Management*, New York, Plenum.

Schaie, K.W. and Wills, S.L. (1991) *Adult Development and Ageing*, New York, Harper Collins.

Selman, R. (1980) *The Growth of Interpersonal Understandings*, New York, Academic Press.

Shotter, J. (1974) 'The development of personal powers', in Richards, M.P.M. (ed.) *The Integration of a Child into a Social World*, Cambridge, Cambridge University Press.

Sternberg, R.J. (1985) 'Cognitive approaches to intelligence', in Wolman, B.B. (ed.) *Handbook of Human Intelligence: Theories, Measurements and Applications*, New York, Wiley Interscience.

van Ijzendoorn, M. (1995) 'Adult attachment representations, parental responsiveness, and infant attachment: a meta-analysis on the predictive validity of the Adult Attachment Interview', *Psychological Bulletin,* vol.117, no.3, pp.387–403.

Vygotsky, L.S. (1978) *Mind in Society: The Development of Higher Psychological Processes*, Cambridge, MA, Harvard University Press.

Walker, A. and Walker, C. (1998) 'Normalisation and 'normal' ageing: the social construction of dependency among older people with learning difficulties', *Disability and Society,* vol.13, pp.125–42.

Wechsler, D. (1972) '"Hold" and "don't hold" tests', in Chown, S.M. (ed.) *Human Ageing*, New York, Penguin.

Zimmerman, P., Becker-Stoll, F., Grossman, K., Grossman, K.E., Scheuerer-Englisch, H. and Wartner, U. (2000) 'Longitudinal attachment development from infancy through adolescence', *Psychologie in Erziehung und Unterricht*, vol.47, no.2, pp.99–117.

Acknowledgement

The authors would like to acknowledge the use and adaptation of the following material in the preparation of Sections 2.3 and 2.4 of this chapter:
Dorothy Faulkner and Martin Woodhead for material from ED840, *Child Development in Families, Schools and Society*, Study Guide.

Dorothy Faulkner, Sharon Ding, Martin Woodhead, Karen Littleton, Ursula Pretzlik and Iris Rowbotham for material from ED840, *Child Development in Families, Schools and Society*, Project Guide, Audiovisual Notes and Video Transcript.

Dorothy Miell for material from DSE202, *Introduction to Psychology, Volume 1*, Chapter 2, 'The self and the social world'.

Commentary 1: Lifespan development

This chapter has introduced a wide range of theoretical perspectives in lifespan psychology. It is apparent that some psychologists tend to believe that most of what an adult is has been very strongly influenced or even fixed by childhood. This includes Piaget and Vygotsky who focused on examining stages of development in childhood. Others, like Bronfenbrenner, tend to focus on change in terms of both influences in childhood and throughout adult life, and on the effects of agents of change like social context on behaviour, thought and experience.

Theory

1   Historically, where developmental psychologists have focused on describing stages of development, either in childhood or throughout life, there has been an assumption of a loss of function and capability as adulthood proceeded. This 'stage' loss of ability with age underlay many function-centred approaches which found decreases in functioning of memory, intelligence and problem solving as age increased. It has only been recently that researchers like Schaie have drawn results from longitudinal cohorts followed through the years which show how much historical factors and individual differences caused by different environmental conditions influence ability outcomes.

2   Many of the theories presented in the chapter are now viewed as culturally specific (e.g. those of Erikson and Peck), and it is important to be aware of culturally-biased judgements, such as reference to good or poor parenting styles or views on aging, when evaluating this research.

Methods

3   As lifespan psychologists are concerned with change and continuity to a varying degree, they use a range of research methods which have been designed to examine the ways in which individuals and groups develop through time. These include the use of cross-sectional and longitudinal designs.

4   Lifespan research tends to examine the development of children and elderly people. As such, psychologists have had to design methods which are sensitive to, and appropriate for, these populations.

Themes

5   There has been a historical movement within developmental psychology from an organismic approach focusing on the individual in isolation to one which sees development in context. Lifespan

psychology has looked at the dynamic interaction of different variables operating at different levels, and the embeddedness of development in particular contexts.

6   Whilst certain maturational changes are seen as principally determined by our biology, the question at debate is the degree to which psychological development is fixed or open to change through the influence of internal and external factors. Certain fixed global changes are experienced by the majority, such as adolescent stress and growth in particular aspects of intelligence and performance, yet there is clear evidence also of the complex interplay of a reciprocal relationship between the individual and their environment. This also parallels a key theme from Book 1: the nature or nurture issue. Fixity is most often assumed to be related to internal factors and change to external factors, and these positions are set in opposition. The developmental contextualism approach suggests, however, that this is a false dichotomy, and that the two can never meaningfully be separated. (This is also one of the more productive resolutions that has been offered to the nature–nurture debate.)

■ Thinking about theory

As you will recall from Book 1, psychologists within one discipline may explain certain phenomena using very different theoretical perspectives, and these perspectives may be viewed as complementary, conflicting or coexisting. Within lifespan psychology it can be a complex task to decide how the theories relate to each other, as the core aim in this field is to understand the multiple internal and external influences that shape individual development. Generally, theories are seen as complementary, as quite often theories are proposed to explain different aspects of the same phenomena. For example, Piaget focused more upon the internal biological aspects of cognitive development whereas Brofenbrenner examined the interactions between the individual and external influences, or contexts, which facilitated cognitive growth and learning. Whilst these theories offer different accounts of early cognitive change, the ideas can be seen as complementary rather than conflicting since the perspectives are focusing on different developmental influences.

Attachment theory is a good example of how varying perspectives can coexist and complement each other in an explanation of one phenomenon. Bowlby viewed early attachment primarily as a biological drive to achieve security with a primary caregiver, whilst subsequent theorists have focused more on the broader emotional and social benefits of attachment such as comfort and reciprocal care. Thus, early and later explanations of attachment motivations can be seen to coexist as they address different aspects of the same phenomena. In recent years, theorists have viewed early attachment styles and ongoing primary relationships and experiences as possible predictors of future attachment styles, and have focused heavily on the way our relationships can shape elements of our growth such as our cognitive and social learning. Here internal factors, such as personality and biological drives, and external factors, such as early and later experiences of attachment, can be posited in combination to explain in a complementary way attachment patterns and social learning throughout our lifespan.

Each of the perspectives covered in the chapter accounts for the influence of the interplay between the individual and their environment to a greater or lesser extent. This becomes clear when considering the historical development of theorizing about lifespan psychology. First, Darwin emphasized that the function of new behaviours was to adapt to our environment. Then, Piaget favoured the organismic approach which characterized developmental change in terms of the biological age at which change occurs in typical developmental pathways. Current thinking and developmental contextualism acknowledges the complex interplay between the individual and the contexts in which their growth is embedded.

Traditionally, psychologists have viewed the periods of infancy and childhood as the focus of study in developmental psychology, typically examining cognitive and social development through the use of evolutionary, organismic and contextual perspectives. However, the advent of the idea that many aspects of development or decline do not necessarily stop or start at a certain age, when adulthood is reached, has encouraged a reconceptualization of the field of developmental psychology, whereby development is considered across the entire lifespan. Accordingly, additional perspectives on the study of human development have been drawn upon to describe and explain growth and decline throughout the entire lifespan. For example, the holistic and humanistic approaches of Erikson and Peck offer a framework for understanding phases which may characterize cognitive, personal and emotional change in later life.

■ Thinking about methods

Lifespan psychologists draw on a wide range of methods to explore questions of developmental continuity and change. This chapter has presented examples of the cross-sectional design which examines development by sampling children from different age groups and comparing their responses on a range of observations and/or measures. For example, when assessing how peers interact and learn from each other during episodes of play, children are grouped into age bands and their cognitive development and social interaction are observed and compared on various measures, such as language ability and conversational turn taking, and between the age groups.

A key limitation of this approach is that the responses of groups of people are recorded at one point in time and this tells us nothing about how a particular individual may change over time. To gather an individual perspective on lifespan development, psychologists tend to prefer a longitudinal design whereby the same individuals can be traced through different points in their life. By comparing individuals of different chronological ages throughout constant periods of their lives, lifespan psychologists can then start to make claims about both age-related and individual pathways over time in various aspects of development. For example, we may be able to see that most children develop the ability to perform formal operations in late childhood by comparing children's thought between age groups. Yet, by also assessing an individual's cognitive development over time, we can understand how cognitive abilities develop differently between individuals between certain time points.

Lifespan psychologists employ a range of qualitative and quantitative approaches. Classic studies tended to employ an experimental and quantitative approach to infant development; for example, Ainsworth's Strange Situation which was designed to isolate and observe human infant-attachment behaviour. Yet increasingly, children and adults are observed and interviewed in different contexts to glean a fuller understanding of how the interplay of the individual and the environment operates to influence psychological development. The diverse and complementary perspectives that lifespan psychologists draw upon can therefore be seen to be reflected in the range of experimental, observational, interview and survey methods that are employed.

It is important to note how ethical considerations have influenced the ways in which psychologists have studied individual development, especially when children or elderly people are the focus of study. Care is taken to avoid, for example, the distress that infant separation may bring to the participants, and such considerations fundamentally inform psychologists' decisions about which approach to adopt and which measures to use.

■ Thinking about themes

Ourselves as human

Current lifespan perspectives see a close relationship between individual development and the role that our experiences with our immediate social and cultural contexts exert on our social, emotional and cognitive growth. Lifespan psychologists, such as Vygotsky and Bronfenbrenner, often concentrate on the theme of ourselves as human beings who are deeply embedded in the immediate and broader cultural contexts of our development. The influence of our relationships with others on our cognitive growth and on the social skills we acquire is emphasized in this chapter, with particular attention to the learning and emotional benefits that our relationships can bring.

From an evolutionary perspective we can be viewed as organisms that adapt to our environment to fulfil certain functions. From an organismic perspective, we are viewed as having innate predispositions to develop in relatively predetermined ways. From a holistic perspective, being human requires a progression though phases which require resolution before progression can be reached. From a dynamic interactionist or contextualist perspective, we are both an agent and a product operating in a context and being influenced by a continual interplay between ourselves and the host of people and contexts which we encounter. Accordingly, the evolution of ideas in the study of lifespan psychology has resulted in current thought viewing us as human beings who both individually shape, and are fundamentally shaped by, the people and events in our lives in different ways throughout our lifespan.

Fixity and change

Ideas of fixity and change are central to the field of lifespan psychology. Different aspects of psychological development have been regarded as more or less fixed depending on the theoretical perspective involved and the phenomena under investigation. When examining cognitive growth, for example, early theorists such as Piaget considered development to proceed through a fixed sequence of stages, largely constrained by broad maturational changes and largely unaffected by a fixed or changing environment. On the other hand, contextual theorists, such as Vygotsky and more recently Bronfenbrenner, who adhere to the idea of dynamic interactionism, see development as a more complex issue with a multitude of internal and external factors dynamically interacting to shape an individual's development. In this perspective, the particular developmental pathway that an individual experiences is flexibly determined by the interplay between the characteristics and responses of the individual and the social and cultural environment that the individual is embedded within.

   Recent discoveries in neuroscience have also contributed to a reconceptualization about fixity and change in relation to chronological age. Evidence of brain plasticity has led to studies which have shown that, whilst global cognitive changes, especially in early and later life, tend to follow a trend of growth and decline respectively, there is evidence to suggest variability of growth and decline between individuals. The concept of plasticity provides a useful way of understanding how the same experience or context may affect individuals differently, and how subsequent cognitive and emotional development may vary considerably between people in a way that is less fixed than early developmental theories would suggest.

CHAPTER **2**

Language and meaning

Troy Cooper and Helen Kaye

Contents

 ## Aims

This chapter aims to:

- evaluate debates about whether language is a distinctively human characteristic that distinguishes us from other animals
- consider evidence concerning how listeners and readers use the context of language to understand its meaning
- outline how computers can be used to model language understanding
- outline how the usage of language in everyday talk has been studied
- evaluate the differences between perspectives in terms of the relationship between language and thought, and language and the world
- consider the differences between perspectives in terms of what they take 'meaning' to be, and where the meaning is made

1 Introduction

Language is the main medium for communication between human beings and where we express, explore and pursue those goals that mean most to us: love and sex, friendship, intellectual thought and problem-solving, planning... the list is endless. This importance is reflected in the number of academic disciplines devoted to studying language, for example, how to use its current forms (modern language studies), its use for self-expression (literary theory), how different modern languages are related structurally and historically (linguistics), how the same language is used differently by various social and cultural groupings (sociolinguistics), and how language is used to communicate and create meaning (psychology).

As social beings, constantly interacting with others, we all spend a lot of time thinking about how to use language well to serve our needs. This is because language is one of the most important aspects of being human, arguably our most distinctive and interesting characteristic as a species. But why is that? What is so distinctive about human language in comparison to animal communication? As we shall discuss in more detail in the first part of Section 2, it is clear that animals can communicate, from bees doing their 'waggle' dance in order to give the directions to nectar, to higher primates who have learned a system of signs to communicate with humans. However, do these forms of communication have enough in common with human language to indicate an essential similarity, with only a difference in degree of sophistication? Or is there a *qualitative* difference? If there is evidence of a qualitative difference, then we shall need to explore how that difference came about and why.

Activity 2.1

Most people who have had a pet like a cat or dog, believe that their pet comes to understand what they say to some extent. Do you think this could be true and, if it is, what do you think pets might understand when their owners talk to them?

While language undoubtedly does convey information, that is not all it does. The owner who speaks to their pet like a child or a companion is being affectionate and playful, and the animal can respond to this by recognizing the purpose and value of the communication, without necessarily understanding any of the word–meaning content of speech. This prompts the thought that if most animal communication functions to convey information of set kinds, perhaps the qualitative difference between language and other animal communication is that language conveys the specific meanings of the separate noises generated.

Later on in Section 2, we will see how language can be used creatively, to say things that have never been said before, to build relationships and convey affection, to enable us to think about and try to represent the world to ourselves.

Having considered the defining characteristics of language and how it may have evolved, we shall spend the rest of the chapter considering how language is actually used. Sections 3 and 4 describe the development of two different psychological perspectives on language: cognitive and social approaches. These approaches take their evidence from very different bodies of research each with a different focus.

Section 3 explores the cognitive focus on how human beings understand language: how they process what they hear or read in order to extract meaning. People are very efficient at understanding language and this has led cognitive psychologists to use experiments in which the processes involved can be manipulated and measured. Computer models are also used to investigate how the various processes can fit together. The cognitive approach proposes that incoming linguistic information is combined with stored knowledge to construct a mental representation of the meaning of a piece of text or speech. In order to do this we need to look at the meanings of individual words and sentences as well as aspects of social and contextual knowledge about the communication. Have you ever come in half way through a conversation and made a contribution that you subsequently realise is foolish or mistaken once the speakers have told you what the topic actually is? Communication is often ambiguous and we will look at how people make sense of what they hear and read.

There is a distinction to be made between 'knowing' a language and 'using' or doing things with it. Using the distinction very broadly, cognitive approaches to language are concerned with what an individual must know about a language, and the context in which it is used, in order to be able to understand it. By contrast, in Section 4, the social psychological perspective proposes that our human world is created through language, and that this is one of its most powerful and important characteristics. This approach to language emphasises that individuals use language to take action and accomplish goals, and that understanding language and creating meaning in it is about using language to do things. This has produced a particular social psychological approach to language called discursive psychology, which has its own particular methods grounded in analysing talk and text from everyday activities. Discursive psychology proposes a model of how meaning is created in language that would, if accepted, entail a radical revision to how psychological theories are made and research is done.

From this brief outline you may appreciate that there are many points of debate about how to characterise the psychology of language. As you work through the chapter, keep thinking about whether the different approaches you are introduced to conflict, co-exist or complement each other. This is one of the main topics of debate currently within the psychology of language, and we shall discuss it in more detail in Section 5 at the end of the chapter.

The issues discussed in this chapter are very important questions that psychologists, together with those in other academic disciplines, are currently grappling with. We do not expect you to be able to provide answers to them by the end of the chapter, but we do hope that you will have a grasp on some of the evidence and terms of the debates that rage around them.

2   Origins of language

This section will consider the claim that language is a uniquely human ability. We will look at whether naturally occurring animal communication is similar to human language, and review one of many attempts to teach a human-like language to an ape. We will then look at differences between animals and humans and finally consider two ways in which human language may have evolved.

2.1 Communication and non-human animals

Animals can undoubtedly communicate in quite complex ways and we will briefly illustrate this fact using two very different species: honeybees and vervet monkeys.

Honeybees are social insects that live in hives. Individual bees have specialized roles, for example, worker bees are sterile females responsible for finding food for the community. Every day a number of worker bees leave the hive and forage for pollen and nectar. On finding food they return to the hive and 'tell' the other workers, who then go to collect more of it. Karl Von-Frisch (1950) carried out extensive investigation into just how this 'telling' is accomplished. If the source of food that has been located is within 50 meters of the hive, then the finder will perform a *round* dance. The bees near the dancer crowd around her, apparently observing her movement, and then fly off to the food location. If the food is more remote then a *waggle* dance is performed, which transmits information about the distance and direction to be flown. In a set of ingenious experiments Kirschner and Towne (1994) used miniature robot bees to discover that the sound of the finder bee's wings flapping was necessary for these dances to be effective. The finder also needed to distribute samples of the food that she had brought back with her. So it seems honeybees use various modalities – visual, auditory and chemical – to transmit and receive quite complex messages.

Vervet monkeys also live in social groups and communicate with their group members. Vervet monkeys give alarm calls when they spot a predator, and the kind of call varies depending on the predator. Seyfarth *et al.* (1980) report that if an adult monkey spots an eagle, then its call causes the other members of the group to look to the sky. A monkey call upon sighting a leopard in contrast elicits immediate fleeing to the safety of the trees, while the call upon sighting a snake causes the group members to look downwards.

Activity 2.1

What do you think are the differences between these examples of communication and the language that people use? Compare the range of events that the communication can refer to and how much flexibility there is in how the message is conveyed.

There are many other examples of natural communication systems used by a variety of species: birds use song to attract mates and warn off rivals, and the postures adopted by domestic cats and dogs signal aggression or submissiveness. So, animals communicate with each other in varied ways.

2.2 Criteria for language

The next questions we will ask are: can we say that these are instances of the same kind of communicative ability that humans have? Can we compare human language with animal communication? To answer these questions we need to decide what defines a language. Harley describes human language as involving 'associating a finite number of words with particular meanings or concepts, and using a finite number of rules to combine those words into a potentially infinite number of sentences' (Harley, 1995, p.11). Many researchers have proposed a set of **language design features** or general properties that characterise human language and could act as criteria for deciding how far animal communication qualifies as language. Hockett (1960) identified 13 such design features, Aitchison (1983) later refined these to 10 and proposed that four were unique to humans. Let's briefly consider these four criteria and the evidence that some animal communication might satisfy them.

The first two criteria Aitchison considered definitive of human language, **semanticity** and **displacement**, can be considered with evidence of the animal communication systems already described in this section.

Language design features
Properties that characterise language.

- *Semanticity*: in a human language each word has at least one specific meaning. Animals learn to respond to particular signs, for example, a vervet monkey will flee when one of their group gives a call indicating that a leopard is approaching. However, it is not clear that the monkey knows what the call means (a semantic representation), it could just be that it simply knows how to respond to the call, i.e. stimulus-response learning. The call could act as a signal for 'run away' rather than convey the meaningful message 'there is a leopard close by'. However, if you review Chapter 3, Section 2 of Book 1, you will see that there is evidence that animals do not simply *learn* stimulus-response relationships, but form internal representations. This means they are capable of representing and using knowledge about the world and that some kind of representation of meaning *may* be used in some animal communication.

Semanticity
A design feature of language relating to how a word reflects aspects of the world.

Displacement
The ability to refer to events and items that are not currently perceived.

- *Displacement*: people can talk about anything regardless of its displacement in time or space, whether it is true or not. People talk about the past and the future, about hypothetical situations, 'what would happen if ...', about ideas and even, as we are asking you to do in the activities of this book, use language to reflect on the use of language. However, no clear evidence has been found that animals do these things: as Harley puts it, 'Bees will never dance a book on the psychology of the bee dance' (1995, p.10). The strongest argument for such a possibility comes from the studies of communication in higher primates, which we shall review in Section 2.3.

The evidence concerning whether animal communication can satisfy the remaining two criteria has come largely from studies of higher primates who have been reared in captivity by researchers who have attempted to teach them a human-like language. The criteria are:

- Structure dependence. Language is characterized by a series of symbols that are abstract – they do not resemble in any way the object to which they refer. This means that the word 'dog' is a sound with no inherent 'dogginess', it is just a sound that happens to be attached to the concept of dog. In

English, words can be put together into units of meaning in which their place in a sentence or a clause is important to the meaning generated. 'Dog bites man' has a very different meaning to 'Man bites dog', and these different meanings are related to the structural placing of the two words 'dog' and 'man'. The set of rules that governs how words can be combined and modified to make sense is called *grammar* or **syntax**.

Syntax
The analysis of sentence structure.

- Creativity. Language can be used to produce utterances that have never been expressed before. It allows a great deal of flexibility in communication, people can produce an almost infinite number of sentences each conveying a different meaning.

The studies described so far in this section have adopted the methods of **ethology** pioneered by Konrad Lorenz (1952). These involve observing naturally occurring behaviour within the environment in which it normally occurs. Where there is experimental manipulation, such as the introduction of 'robot bees' great care is taken in ensuring that the situation remains as 'natural' as possible. We will now look at studies where the environment is considerably more controlled and artificial.

Ethology
The study of behaviour in its natural setting.

2.3 Teaching human languages to apes

There have been many attempts to teach apes using sign languages and artificial languages that involve manipulating plastic tokens (classic accounts are by Gardner and Gardner, 1969; Premack, 1971; Terrace, 1979). Most of the studies have shown some degree of success in enabling communication between the trainer and the ape, but there are a number of problems in interpreting the results. We will consider the nature of these problems of interpretation in relation to one of the most successful cases of communication development, the training of Kanzi, a Bonobo or Pygmy Chimpanzee, to use a sign language by Sue Savage-Rumbaugh, a comparative psychologist at Georgia State University in America. Kanzi's achievements have been detailed and analysed by Savage-Rumbaugh and colleagues (Savage-Rumbaugh and Lewin, 1994; Savage-Rumbaugh *et al.*, 1998).

2.1 **Case-study: Bonobo use of sign language (Savage-Rumbaugh and Lewin, 1994; Savage-Rumbaugh et al., 1998)**

Kanzi's adoptive mother, Matata was trained to use a computer keyboard with symbols on the keys, and was rewarded for pressing the correct symbols in response to her trainer's questions. In common with the other studies, Matata received intensive training from an individual trainer. When Kanzi was small, Matata would not be parted from him and so he accompanied her to those 'lessons'. The trainers noticed that Kanzi spontaneously began using the keyboard. Subsequently Kanzi was encouraged to interact with people in everyday activities. At age 9 years, Kanzi's keyboard contained 256 symbols and he had also adopted gestures, which were interpreted as having specific meanings. Kanzi used these symbols in strings of 2 or 3 to make requests, to which the trainers responded appropriately. On one occasion Kanzi had played with a garden hose and later apparently requested another game by pressing the symbols for 'water' and 'chase', there being no symbol for 'hose'. Kanzi's ability to understand spoken language was tested by giving him a set of instructions, such as 'Hide the toy gorilla'; 'Pour the Coke in the lemonade' (Savage-Rumbaugh *et al.*, 1998, p.69). Kanzi responded correctly to about 72 per cent of such instructions.

A bonobo using a computer keyboard to communicate

Although Kanzi has undoubtedly learned a good deal, there are difficulties in determining exactly the nature of his learning. Kanzi's ability to respond appropriately to verbal commands is impressive and is consistent with Savage-Rumbaugh's assertion that he understands what is said. However, it is equally possible that Kanzi had learned to respond appropriately to the sounds of speech (i.e. in a stimulus-response way), a similar argument to that made when considering whether the calls of the Vervet monkeys demonstrate semanticity.

This is an appropriate time to consider what exactly is meant by meaning or semanticity. According to Pearce (1987) 'a signal has meaning if it excites a representation of the event to which it relates' (p.266).

Meaning, as Pearce defines it, is equivalent to an individual's own representation. If we can infer that an animal, or indeed a person, forms a specific representation corresponding to a particular word, then we can say that they understand the meaning *of that word (note, however, that this is only one particular definition of the term meaning). As we signalled in the introduction we will consider different conceptions of 'meaning' as we progress through the chapter.*

Kanzi's behaviour does suggest that he forms specific representations in response to the words he hears. For example, if Kanzi is asked to fetch an object, such as 'an apple from upstairs', he will ignore other apples that are visible to him and go upstairs to retrieve the requested apple. Similarly, Premack (1971) reports that one of his chimpanzees, Sarah, was able to select a brown object when her only training with the word 'brown' was being told that it was the colour of chocolate. It seems reasonable to explain her behaviour by assuming that for Sarah the word 'chocolate' excited a specific representation. In other words she had coded specific information about chocolate and linked it to the word 'chocolate', including the colour of it. However, not all approaches to language would accept this is a full description of 'meaning' as humans deal with meaning, and we shall return to the issue of meaning later in the chapter. However, there does remain the possibility that the apparent 'understanding' by animals of language is actually a set of conditioned responses.

Activity 2.2

Can you think of a way in which Sarah could select the brown object by using generalisation of a conditioned response she had already acquired? You might find it helpful to reread the first part of Chapter 3 of Book 1 to remind yourself of these terms.

It is conceivable that the association Sarah had learned between the symbols for 'chocolate' and 'brown' led to a generalisation between 'brown' and the object most perceptually similar to chocolate. This possibility is the main reason why those investigating this area have turned to an animal's *production* of language as a more important test of its linguistic abilities than its *reaction* to language from someone else. Very early on it was noted that apes, unlike children, do not naturally mimic the speech sounds they hear. This, coupled with a vocal tract anatomy that would make production of some speech sounds impossible, meant that most studies have used non-vocal languages. Kanzi could have been taught sign language, as apes in other trials have been, but the muscles in a chimp's hand do not allow the same degree of flexibility as our own and so signing has been shown to be quite difficult for them. So Kanzi was given a keyboard with pictorial symbols that corresponded to particular events and objects with which he became familiar during his upbringing. Kanzi rapidly learned to press these symbols to communicate with his trainers. The drawback to this system is that his vocabulary was limited to 256 words, the number of keys that could be fitted on to a portable keyboard. That limitation is a considerable constraint for him to operate under if he is to show he is capable of using language.

As Kanzi produces communications that are quite restricted in length – arguably because of the constraints of the choice and type available on the keyboard – this means we do not have clear evidence either for or against his ability to understand structural dependence, or his ability to be creative with language. So the evidence for Kanzi's ability to produce language is not 'cut and dried' but has to be assessed within the context of these possible constraints.

Within this context then it seems that Kanzi can order the symbols consistently, but as with animals' 'understanding' of language spoken to them, we simply cannot determine whether this ordering reflects actions he has been rewarded for previously or a knowledge of syntax. Savage-Rumbaugh has argued strongly that Kanzi's utterances are very like those of a 2½ year old human being, and the simplest conclusion we can draw is that this reflects similar levels of linguistic competence and understanding. Therefore, Kanzi's achievements show that non-human animals have the capability for language, and rather than being qualitatively distinct from other animals, we are on one end of a continuum with them.

There are, however, psychologists who disagree with Savage-Rumbaugh's conclusion, arguing that a 2½ year old child is still developing linguistic competence, and that the inevitability of progression makes a great difference. Within a few years a child's vocabulary expands to adult size, and sentence length and complexity increase steadily to resemble adult speech. There is no clear evidence from any of the now long-standing and continuing research programmes in this area that any ape trained to use symbols to communicate undergoes a similar process of progress, despite increasing age and training. This has led some researchers, such as Pinker (1994), to conclude that language is a uniquely human ability.

There are many similarities between animal communication and human language. Both use symbols to represent events in the world and both rely on the sender and receiver of the message sharing a similar representation. Studies with captive primates suggest that they can learn the meanings of arbitrary symbols for communication. However, there are important differences too. Studies of animal communication have not provided evidence that animals can communicate about events other than the 'here and now'. Intensive attempts to teach human-like languages to primates have at best produced individuals with the linguistic abilities of a small child. These studies are continuing, but the evidence at present suggests that while there are many similarities between animal communication and human language, there may be important qualitative differences separating the two.

2.4 Natural selection of language

In Chapter 2 of Book 1, you were introduced to evolutionary theory and the concept of natural selection. Other species have very different lifestyles to our own and have been subjected to very different selection pressures in comparison to humans within their evolutionary history. We will turn to this theory now to develop an account of the historical emergence of communication systems in animal species. We will then consider whether we can identify particular factors or pressures within evolutionary history that suggest the possibility of *divergence* between human and other species modes and uses of communication. Finally, we will look at the idea that language may have arisen as a by-product of other aspects of human evolutionary development.

Within any species there is a certain amount of variation among individuals with regard to what form a characteristic (that is a behaviour or bodily feature) takes. Sometimes a characteristic helps the members of the species who have it to gain food, or mates, or to survive predation within their particular environment. This means that those individuals who possess that characteristic may live longer and may be more likely to produce greater numbers of offspring that survive to breed than those who do not possess it. Any characteristic that confers this advantage is called adaptive, because it adapts the individual to fare better (and reproduce successfully) in a particular environment than other members of the species that do not have the characteristic. These adaptive characteristics may have a genetic basis and be passed on to the offspring who will also tend to be more successful. This is, in essence, a consequence of natural selection: individuals with advantageous characteristics that enable them to survive and breed more effectively in their environment will leave more descendants than individuals without those advantageous characteristics. Subsequently, over time the proportion of individuals with advantageous characteristics will increase in a population, as individuals without that characteristic become less common. The population as a whole will have changed, and evolutionary change can be said to have occurred.

If you are having difficulty remembering what is meant by natural selection, go back now and review Chapter 2 of Book 1, Evolutionary Psychology.

Let's examine natural selection in the two examples of animal communication we began the section with. Within a beehive all of the individual bees are closely related and hence tend to share characteristics. Imagine the situation where the bees in only some hives are able to communicate the whereabouts of food to each other. Suppose that the workers from these hives have an advantage in producing food over worker bees from other hives that do not have this ability. The hive may well expand faster because more food is available and more larvae are produced and reared. Queen larvae eventually leave the hive to go and find other hives. If more queen larvae are produced and reared, then the 'communicative' bees may establish more new hives that in turn will repeat the cycle of success. In time the total bee population will gradually consist of more hives where the individuals can communicate with each other. Communication will have evolved by natural selection.

However, most adaptive characteristics have costs as well as benefits – for example, the dance that bees use to communicate about the location of food uses energy. The environment is crucial in determining the balance between costs and benefits, which constitutes adaptive value. If, for example, pollen and nectar were invariably found directly south of a hive, there would be no advantage to hives of bees with the abilities to communicate with each other about direction. Hence there would be no impetus for this ability to spread through the bee population, and the cost associated with it would make it likely not to spread.

Similarly, for vervet monkeys living in an area where there was only one type of predator, or where the optimal response was the same for all of the predators that were present, there would be no advantage to producing different calls. Conversely, if the environment changed so that there was an advantage in communicating more information rather than less, then a group containing individuals who were able to do this would be more successful. So a particular characteristic is adaptive for an individual if, in the current environment (called the environmental niche), it increases the individual's chances of successful breeding.

Perhaps then it is not so peculiar that human beings have developed language where Chimpanzees have not. As Pinker (1994) explains, we share DNA with modern apes, but the evolutionary lines leading to humans and to non-human primates split some 5–8 million years ago. However, other hominid species, for example, *Homo habilis* and *Homo erectus*, with whom archaeological evidence suggests we shared the evolved capacity for more highly developed language, have all become extinct. This has left us with our nearest DNA related species as apes, who did not evolve language because of their quite different evolutionary history after the split in primate lines. So perhaps the difference in communication abilities between humans and other species is an indication that the evolution of language conferred greater adaptational benefit only upon hominids in their particular environmental niche. Note that an environmental niche relates not only to the physical environment, but also to the interaction of individuals in their social groupings.

2.5 The adaptational costs and benefits of human language

If the theory of language as an evolved characteristic is to have validity we need evidence for it. In particular we should be able to find physical differences between humans and other animals that would have been produced by natural selection, and that can be directly linked to our propensity for using language. We also need some idea of what language does, or what we can do with it, that makes it adaptive. Briefly, this involves looking at a characteristic that exists now and deducing the conditions that led to its evolution.

Humans have a throat anatomy that is unique among mammals. The larynx (which houses the vocal cords) is positioned low down in the throat allowing a large amount of freedom of movement for the tongue. This allows us to articulate vowel sounds. However, it also means that, when we eat, food passes across the trachea (windpipe) bringing a risk of choking. This arrangement also compromises our breathing and chewing. Other mammals have a larynx positioned so that air can pass directly from nose to lungs avoiding these hazards. (Incidentally, newborn human babies have the typical mammalian throat anatomy and the larynx descends to the lower position only during infancy.) So, the physical ability to speak involves a cost, but to have evolved it must have conferred a greater benefit. We explore the nature of this benefit in the next section.

Planum temporale
Area of cortex involved in language.

The structure of the brain is also different in humans in comparison to other primates. A particular area of the cortex (the **planum temporale**) is larger, in most people, in the left cerebral hemisphere than in the right. (This area is implicated in dyslexia.) There is archaeological evidence of similar asymmetry in extinct hominids. This is not found in other primates and if parts of this area are damaged, by brain injury or stroke, a high proportion of patients exhibit language disorders. A neurologist named Carl Wernicke, working at the end of the 18th century, noted that damage to a particular area of cortex (**Wernicke's area**, situated within the planum temporale) often results in the inability to understand language, combined with the ability to produce fluent speech, which has normal intonation but which is meaningless. This has been termed **fluent aphasia**. A few years previously Paul Broca (another neurologist) had identified a more anterior cortical region that appears to play a role in language. This is known as **Broca's area** and when it is damaged a patient typically has difficulty in producing coherent

Wernicke's and Broca's area
Areas of cortex involved in language.

Fluent aphasia
An inability to produce meaningful speech despite being coherent.

speech, but instead generates disconnected words, a condition termed **non-fluent aphasia**.

The area corresponding to Broca's in non-human primates has similar anatomical features but is involved in the control of non-linguistic arm and mouth movements. Broca's area has retained this function in humans but has added to it a role in language (Preuss, 2000). There are difficulties, however, in distinguishing between Broca's and Wernicke's aphasia and their anatomical correlates, and brain imaging techniques suggest a good deal of individual variability exists in terms of the areas of the cortex that are involved in language. Strong evidence that parts of our anatomy, which continue in structure and function to be similar to those of other primates, have also changed specifically to support the additional needs of language.

We now need to consider what is it about language that could make it such an adaptive characteristic.

Activity 2.3

Look back at the beginning of this section on the differences between animal communication and human language, try to list activities that those differences of semanticity, displacement, structural dependence and creativity can be specifically used for.

Language and the evolution of social ability

It seems plausible that the ability to use a language may have given those individuals who possessed it some advantage in procuring food, perhaps via some enhanced representation of likely places to forage, or by enabling cooperative hunting behaviour. Human languages allow flexible communication about features of specific situations rather than the stereotypic signals used by vervet monkeys, for example. This advantage alone might lead to greater reproductive success, thus allowing language to spread. But human behaviour is more complex than this, and in Activity 2.3 above you may have identified social activities, like competition between individuals, forming alliances or social manipulation, that are greatly enhanced by language. Language allows knowledge and values to be transmitted so that, as well as working with others, individuals can benefit from others' experiences and perspectives. Language allows people to agree on plans and goals, and to work collaboratively, thereby enabling achievements beyond the grasp of individuals. So features that we have identified as distinguishing language from animal communication systems (whether qualitatively or quantitatively) can also support a very powerful (and possibly unique) set of abilities and activities that could confer distinctive adaptational advantage.

To summarise then: language may have evolved because it conferred an advantage that allowed humans to prosper within their physical environment and indeed, as we'll discuss in Section 4, enabled them to create and manage their own social environment. The ability to use language was accompanied by anatomical changes in the throat and brain, and the costs incurred by this were outweighed by the benefits of the ability. Pinker (2000) provides an interesting review of work that has produced computer models of how aspects of language may have evolved by natural selection.

However, there are alternative accounts of how language may have arisen. Some researchers have proposed that language began evolving once humans had developed specific mental abilities. In other words rather than language *making* humans different from animals, language is seen as a *consequence* of humans being different from animals. The next section will introduce one such account.

Language and the evolution of thought

Metarepresentation
An individuals representation of another person's representation, or of their own process of reflection.

According to the philosopher and anthropologist Dan Sperber (2000) there are aspects of the ability to model what others are thinking that confer a very special adaptational advantage. In Chapter 2 of Book 1, you were introduced to the concept of theory of mind and Premack's evidence that Sarah (the chimpanzee) could understand the *intentions* of a human actor. Theory of mind is part of a set of abilities that Sperber refers to as **metarepresentations**, which essentially allow us to reflect on our own and others' mental processes. A teacher can say 'I think that some students may believe that their dog understands English'. This is a representation of a student's representation of their dog's representation – a metarepresentation. This ability doesn't necessarily require language – a footballer may use his body to try to fool the goalkeeper when taking a penalty kick, and the goalkeeper may likewise interpret the other's body movements as bluffs for his real intentions! The ability to reflect on the mental processes of other people could confer a large advantage: if we can predict what someone else is likely to do in a situation, then social interaction of all kinds will be greatly facilitated.

Activity 2.4

Can you think of a situation where you respond to what you perceive as other people's intentions rather than their actions?

Sperber suggests that the ability to use metarepresentation conferred a huge evolutionary advantage so that this, as a characteristic in its own right, was selected for and this then *led* to the development of language. The reason that this led to language development according to Sperber is because language allowed human beings to formulate the difference between the meanings of 'I think', 'I think she thinks', and 'I think she thinks he thinks' and communicate these differences to others. It also allows us to lie to others. When we use language we seek to communicate something about our mental representations and understand those of other people. This ability lies outside of the 'concrete' nature of animal communication and requires the qualities of semanticity, displacement and structural dependence that seem to be the hallmarks of language. Thus 'metarepresentation ... . creates a favourable environment for the evolution of a new adaptation, a linguistic ability' (Sperber, 2000, p.127). The fact that apes that show limited metarepresentational abilities acquire only a limited linguistic ability is consistent with this.

So here are two possible accounts of how language could have developed through evolution, and each has very different implications for how we view its importance and the role it plays in the social and intellectual functioning that seem to distinguish humans from other species. One account claims that the facility for language development and use appeared at some point in history and delivered an adaptational advantage to those who had it. The mechanism of natural selection led to this facility for language becoming widespread in our species. What's more this suggests that greater and greater language capability would have been selected for as it conferred even greater fitness, and so language formed the foundation of development of our other cognitive capacities. A second account suggests a rather different process: that it was the development of abilities for metarepresentation, reasoning and information processing that were selected for. In this view language arose as a by-product of other cognitive capacities. So far we have presented this as an alternative to natural selection acting directly on language, but perhaps the two processes feed off each other. So while the ability to metarepresent might enable language to begin to develop, language development might in turn facilitate metarepresentational and other cognitive skills. In effect a 'ratchet' mechanism could operate, making language and other cognitive abilities interdependent.

Summary Section 2

- Animal communication is widespread, but is qualitatively different from human language.
- Attempts to teach language to apes have resulted in a few individuals achieving levels of competence arguably similar to a two to three year-old human child.
- Humans appear to have special anatomical features related to language.
- Language may have evolved through natural selection, perhaps in conjunction with other cognitive abilities.

3   Understanding language

In this section, we will explore from a cognitive perspective how people understand language. If you have ever tried to learn a new language as an adult, you will probably agree that the first and most obvious difficulty is the lack of a large vocabulary, simply not knowing what words mean. In fact, when you listen to people conversing in a foreign language, it is not always easy even to identify individual words. Speech seems to be continuous. However, as you learn the language, the words stand out as discrete items and we can begin to understand their meanings. The starting point of this section will be to look at how we recognise words. However in addition, to make sense of the conversation, we need to know something of how words relate to each other. In everyday speech sentences rarely exist in isolation and the context they are set in is important to meaning too. The way we say a particular sentence can alter its meaning. The piece of text a sentence is set in influences its meaning and frequently in conversation the speaker will rely on the knowledge that they assume the listener already has. So to use and understand language effectively in communication we need access to several different sorts of knowledge. This section will look at how these three different levels of context – the word, the sentence or clause, and the larger textual context – have been theorized and investigated in terms of their contribution to understanding language.

A major concern of psychologists working from a cognitive perspective has been to investigate how this knowledge is represented and what processes are used to enable meaning to be communicated between people. As Pinker (1999) puts it 'the speaker has a thought, makes a sound and counts on the listener to hear the sound and recover that thought' (p.3). Cognitive psychologists are interested in the properties of the sound and the processes of recovery. Of course not all language is spoken and we will also look at a recent modeling of the processes involved in identifying written words, called computational modeling.

If you want to remind yourself about the characteristics of the cognitive perspective, look back at the commentary sections of Book 1, Chapters 3, 6 and 8.

3.1   Recognizing words

If you have ever looked at a piece of text written in an unfamiliar alphabet, it most likely looked like nothing more than squiggles. When you look at something written in your own language though, words jump out of the page at you. The Stroop effect, on which you worked in your experimental project, (a test in which, for instance, participants try to respond 'blue' to the word 'red' written in blue ink) is a good example of how over-ridingly important semantic meaning can be when you see a word you can read. Similarly, if you hear someone speaking an unfamiliar language it can sound like a continuous stream of noise. Contrast this with your ability to pick out words in your own language even when heard on a badly tuned radio or noisy telephone line. How is it that we are able to pick out familiar words so readily? One factor that has been identified is context. Mayer and Schvaneveldt (1971) investigated the effects of semantic **priming** on a task in which participants had to decide whether or not a letter string that was flashed briefly on the screen formed a word. This task, termed a lexical decision task, was found to be much quicker when the target letter string was preceded by a word that was semantically related, that is of similar meaning. So people were quicker to judge that the letter string 'nurse' was a word if it was preceded by the word 'doctor' than if it was preceded by an unrelated word such as 'bread'. The finding that one word facilitates the recognition of another does not necessarily mean they are semantically related. Moss and Gaskell (1998) report evidence that words that frequently occur together can also facilitate the recognition of each other, for example, the word 'pillar' primes 'society', and 'elbow' primes 'grease'. This is termed *associative priming*.

> **Priming**
> A method of investigating the effect on recognition of a target word by preceding it with a different word: the priming stimulus. In semantic priming the two words are related in meaning. In associative priming they are typically words that occur close together in text or speech.

The effects of context can also be demonstrated for individual letters and sounds. Warren (1970) played tapes of sentences to participants in which a letter sound in some words was replaced with a meaningless noise. Several such sentences were used and two examples were: 1) The *eel was on the axle and 2) The *eel was on the shoe, where * represents the meaningless noise. Participants presented with the first sentence reported hearing the word 'wheel', whereas those who were presented with the second sentence heard 'heel'. Again a similar phenomenon has been reported with written text. Reicher (1969) performed an experiment in which a string of letters was very briefly shown to participants who had to identify, say, the middle letter. He found that if the letter string formed a meaningful word then the target letter was more easily identified. This is termed the **word superiority effect**. Interestingly there is also a pseudo-word superiority effect in which a letter is recognized more easily when it is presented in a letter string that could be a word but is not. For example, 'tife' could conceivably be an English word, whereas 'tfei' could not.

> **Word superiority effect**
> The finding that a letter is detected more readily when it is embedded in a word then when it is not.

Activity 2.5

Look at the two pairs of letter strings below. If you were asked to name the third letter from the left in each, which of each pair would be easiest to recognise if there was a word superiority effect and a pseudo-word superiority effect?

Pair 1) Fold or Fdlo.

Pair 2) Flod or Dfol.

Note: in an experiment the letter strings would be presented for a very brief period (20ms) and then you would be asked to identify the letter in a particular position.

McClelland and Rumelhart (1981) proposed what has proved to be an extremely influential model of visual word recognition. The model was designed to account for the word superiority effect, and uses general principles of information processing that have subsequently been the basis of a particular kind of model used widely in cognitive psychology to simulate other aspects of cognition. This type of model is often referred to as a **connectionist model**, although you may come across the terms 'parallel distributed processing' (PDP) and 'neural networks', which are sometimes used as near synonyms in some textbooks.

Connectionist model
A type of computer model that contains simple units that are connected to each other in a network structure.

We will look quite closely at the way this model works to give you a basic understanding of what is involved in this kind of approach within the cognitive perspective on language (and indeed other aspects of cognition). We will then briefly outline how connectionist models of language are currently developing.

The connectionist model of language processes proposes that processing of a word occurs at three levels, and that all these levels can interact with each other. So if we take the process of recognising the word 'TIME', when we first see it, processing will occur at the level of features, letters and words. At the level of features, it is proposed that there are detector units in our information processing system that respond to the features of letters like curves to the left or right, circles, vertical and horizontal lines and so on. On seeing the first letter T of 'TIME' the feature detectors for a horizontal and a vertical line will respond strongly. This in turn will send a charge of energy to all the letters at the letter level of processing that incorporate, as part of their features, horizontal and vertical bars – letters like L, Z and T. But the amount of energy will be proportional to how much the letter exactly matches only the features that have been charged up by the stimulus letter, so most energy will go to the letter T.

The letter T will in turn pass on energy to the word level, to all those words that have the letter T in first place in the word, and so among the many words energised will be the word TIME. The energisation of the word TIME feeds back to the letter level, sending energy to letters I, M and E, so that when the second letter, I, is seen as the word is read, those letters already possess some energy and this is increased by actually seeing the features of the letter I. So the I is more easily recognised as the next letter of the word, and this feeds even more energy to the word level for the word TIME, and this in turn feeds back to energise the letter detectors for M and E. This makes M and E even more easy to recognise and so on. Many different types of this model have been developed, but the core principles remain those we have described. One of the earliest formal models was the Interactive Activation with Competition Model, shown in Box 2.2 below.

2.2 The Interactive Activation with Competition (IAC) model (McClelland and Rumelhart, 1981)

This model is designed to show how two sorts of information can interact to allow a word with four letters to be recognized. The two sorts of information are first that coming in from the sense organs (bottom-up processing), and second a stored representation of the word (top-down processing). The main features of the model are set out below:

- The basic framework or architecture involves a large set of units arranged in three levels, a feature level comprising 14 units, a letter level of 26 units and a word level of 1179 units. Figure 2.1 shows a simplified illustration of this with considerably fewer units.
- The model analyses each letter separately so four copies of the letter and feature units are needed, one for each letter position.
- When a feature is detected the matching feature unit becomes excited.
- Each feature unit can pass excitation to the units for each letter that contains that feature. This is an example of bottom-up processing.
- Each letter unit can pass excitation to the units for each word that contains that letter in the appropriate position. This too is an example of bottom-up processing.
- Each word unit can also send excitation down to its constituent letter units. This is top-down processing.
- When a letter or word unit reaches a critical level of excitation it is recognized.

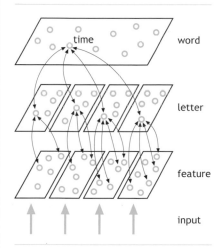

Figure 2.1   A simplified sketch of the IAC network (McClelland, 1985)

The input is T I M E. Each of the four boards at feature and letter level refers to a particular letter position.

As well as these excitatory links the model incorporates *inhibitory connections*. These are shown in Figure 2.2, which is a more detailed picture of what happens during the detection of a letter in the initial position of the word. Inhibition is represented by lines ending in small circles rather than arrows.

The rules governing inhibition are as follows (McClelland and Rumelhart, 1981):

- For a particular letter position when a unit at the letter level is excited it passes inhibition to every other letter unit.
- When a unit at the word level is excited it passes inhibition to every other word unit.
- Between levels excitation in a letter unit sends inhibition to words that do not have that letter in the appropriate position.
- A feature unit likewise sends inhibition to every letter unit corresponding to a letter that does not posses that feature.

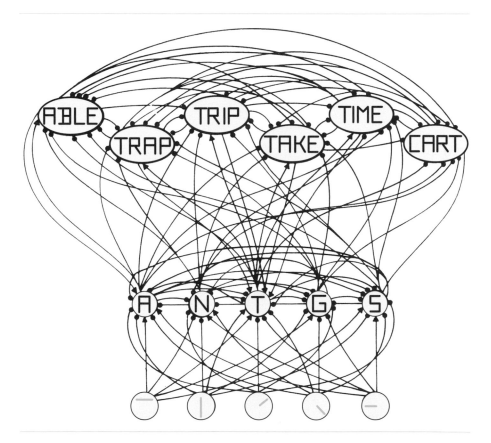

Figure 2.2   The microstructure of the IAC network showing inhibitory (●) and excitatory (▲) connections for the first letter position only (after McClelland and Rumelhart, 1981)

So, looking now at Figure 2.2, when the letter 'T' unit is excited it sends inhibition to all other letter units, this means that it becomes more difficult for those letters to be perceived in first letter position. Similarly, when the 'TIME' unit is excited it sends inhibition to all other word units. 'TRIP' and 'TRAP', which receive <u>excitation</u> from 'T', will also receive <u>inhibition</u> from 'TIME'. When the second letter 'I' is detected more excitation will be sent to 'TIME' but inhibition will be sent to 'TRIP' and 'TRAP'. 'TIME' will thus receive most excitation. The model is interactive in the sense that perception is occurring at all three levels: when a word is activated it excites the units corresponding to its constituent letters, which as we have noted are also excited by the feature units. The 'competition' in the name of the model refers to units receiving excitation and inhibition from different sources, and those that receive the highest net 'energy' determine what is perceived. One very important feature of this model is that the different processes occur in parallel with each other, so letter and word identification occur at the same time as feature detection. This enables very rapid word identification, corresponding to human abilities.

Activity 2.6

Looking at Figure 2.2 if 'A' is detected in position two which word units would be energised? (Answer at the end of Section 3.)

This model can account for what are termed the word superiority and pseudo-word superiority effects. Look at the example in Activity 2.5. When the word 'FOLD' is presented excitation from the letter units F, O & D will excite the unit that represents 'FOLD' and this in turn will transmit excitation to 'L' thus reducing the amount of energy it needs from the visual input. With FDLO very little excitation will occur at the word unit level and hence the 'L' letter unit will need to gain more excitation from the visual input in order to be recognized. The pseudo-word effect reflects the overlap with actual English word patterns. So the stimulus 'FLOD' (which is a pseudo-word) will produce some excitation in, for example, 'FLOW' and this will raise the excitation of the 'O' unit, so it will require less 'bottom-up' excitation to be recognized.

The original model does have a number of limitations (perhaps the most obvious of which is that it can only recognise a limited number of words and these must all be composed of four capital letters!). However, since 1981 computational models using these basic principles of a continuous interaction between stored and sensory information have been successfully applied to explain some of the range of linguistic processing phenomena discovered experimentally. For example, Moss and Gaskell (1998) discuss how semantic and associative priming effects can be modelled using this approach.

3.2 Understanding sentences

When we have recognized a word how do we know what it means? Most current models of language postulate a **lexicon** or 'mental dictionary'. The lexical entry for a word contains everything we know about that word, how to pronounce it (phonology), spell it (orthography), its definition (semantics) and

Lexicon
A mental dictionary that contains information about individual words.

what role it can play in a sentence (syntactic information). With this information we can start to build a representation of the meaning of a sentence. The issues involved in understanding sentences are somewhat different from those involved in recognizing words. Pickering (1999) has identified three differences. First, we *recognise* words, but the sentences we typically encounter are novel. For example, you are presumably familiar with each individual word in the sentence you have just read but have probably never heard or read that particular sentence before. Therefore, a representation has to be *formed* rather than *retrieved*. A second point is that sentences are sequential, the words are encountered in a particular order and this raises the question of when we begin building the representation. Do we wait until the sentence is complete or begin building as the words are being perceived? Finally, a sentence contains two types of information – the meanings of the individual words and the syntactical structure. To illustrate these consider the two possible utterances below:

1   Colourless green ideas sleep furiously.

2   Skid crash hospital

The first sentence is perhaps the most famous sentence that the linguist Noam Chomsky ever wrote. He used it to demonstrate a grammatically correct though totally meaningless sentence. The second (from Scott and Spencer, 1998) is agrammatical and yet we know what it might mean, it conveys semantic information. How then do we combine these two sorts of information?

One problem with experimentally investigating how we understand sentences is that we are extremely quick and accurate in doing so. This makes measurement of the time it takes to read and to understand quite difficult. So psychologists have used sentences that are unusual and take longer to understand in order to investigate the processes we use to form representations of these and, by extrapolation, more usual sentences. For example, **garden-path sentences** are often used, so called because they initially trick the reader into a wrong conceptualisation – taking the reader (as the saying goes) up the garden path.

Garden path sentences
Ambiguous sentences in which the structure that is usually selected first is incorrect.

Activity 2.7

Read the following sentences.

1   As Jay always jogs a mile seems a short distance.

2   The old man the boats.

3   As the women edited the magazine amused all the reporters.

Did the sentences seem odd? And were you aware of having to puzzle over any particular word or words? See below for a discussion of why these sentences are difficult to understand.

In an experiment similar to Activity 2.7 above, Frazier and Rayner (1982) found that readers presented with the first sentence took longer to read the sentence than did those who received an identical version but with the word 'this' placed between the words 'mile' and 'seems'. They also looked at eye movements and found that, in reading the sentence, readers looked back at the first part of the sentence immediately after reading 'seems'. Reading the sentence with 'this' in did not produce this backtracking. This suggests that people do begin to process a sentence before it is completed. The next question to consider then is how we process an entire sentence. At the beginning of the section it was mentioned that the entry in the lexicon or 'mental dictionary' for a word includes information about the syntactical role or roles they can take in a sentence. So, for the second sentence (taken from Greene and Coulson, 1995, p.75) the word 'old' can be either an adjective (as in 'old man') or a noun (as in 'a home for the old'). Similarly, 'man' can be a noun or a verb. In processing the sentence then, we have the option to choose one of two syntactic structures and follow it through. So in the second sentence we might assign 'old' to an adjective and 'man' to a noun, which works fine until we encounter 'the boats' and realise that the words don't make sense. We would then need to backtrack and reassign words: this fits with other evidence that we move our eyes back to the words that need to be reanalysed.

Of course there is another source of evidence that will help us to make sense of the syntax of a sentence: semantic knowledge. Pickering and Traxler (1998) investigated another version of the third sentence, above. In that other version, the word 'sailed' was substituted for 'edited'. Both verbs can either take an object, so it makes sense to say 'edited a book' or 'sailed a boat', or not take an object, with just 'Jane sailed' or 'Jane edited' as acceptable. In their experimental study, Pickering and Traxler found that the 'sailed' version of the third sentence did not lead participants up the garden path, although the 'edited' version did. One interpretation of this finding is that the semantic information stored in the lexical representation of a word helps determine the syntactic role it is assigned.

An alternative way to consider how semantic knowledge could be used to make sense of 'The old man the boats' is to look at the context in which it occurs. If this sentence was encountered immediately after the phrase 'when the young leave the fishing village', then 'old' would be more likely to be identified as a noun.

This idea that semantic and syntactic knowledge are used in an integrated way to understand a sentence is still a topic of debate. The philosopher Jerry Fodor claims that sentence understanding happens too quickly for us to be able to bring all of our semantic knowledge to bear on every word. He suggests instead that syntactic knowledge is encapsulated in a module that analyses sentence structure, and it is only once this is done that semantic knowledge is used to understand the meaning of the sentence (Fodor, 1983). Steven Pinker suggests that the reason why some sentences lead us 'up the garden path' could be because certain words are associated in a non-semantic way with each other (Pinker 1994). So the reason why the word 'edited' induces a garden path effect, whereas 'sailed' does not in Activity 2.7, is because when the words 'edited' and 'magazine' have previously been encountered close together, then 'edited' has taken an object. If the syntax module can use statistical information such as this, then it is more likely that a correct syntactical category will be selected for an ambiguous word. The statistically most probable category is usually the correct one, so garden path sentences are deliberately chosen to trick the reader. This debate over whether linguistic analysis is accomplished by independent modules or by the integration of different knowledge sources has yet to be concluded.

3.3 Understanding stories

We now move to the level of how people understand written text and speech, or pieces of **discourse**. So far we have implied that people listen to individual words then put them together to try to decode the meaning of each sentence. But, unless they are carrying out a grammatical exercise, people are usually trying to grasp the meaning of the whole story. We continually make assumptions about events in the real world in a process referred to as **effort after meaning** (see Chapter 8 of Book 1).

Discourse
In cognitive psychology, a piece of text or speech consisting of related sentences.

Effort after meaning
The attempt by listeners and readers to understand the meaning of discourse.

Activity 2.8

Read the following passage and judge how easy it is to understand:

> *If the balloons popped the sound wouldn't be able to carry since everything would be too far away from the correct floor. A closed window would also prevent the sound from carrying, since most buildings tend to be well insulated. Since the whole operation depends upon a steady flow of electricity, a break in the middle of the wire would also cause problems. Of course, the fellow could shout, but the human voice is not loud enough to carry that far.*
>
> *Taken from Bransford and Johnson, 1973, p.289–90*

Bransford and Johnson found that participants rated the story in Activity 2.8 as incomprehensible unless they were shown the picture in Figure 2.3 (shown at the end of Section 3.3) before reading it. Now look at the figure and re-read the text in Activity 2.8. Another way that allowed participants to make sense of similar pieces of discourse was to provide a meaningful title before it was read. Bransford and Johnson concluded that, in order to make sense of a discourse, we must know the context in which it is set. In other words, we need a framework for organizing information.

One good example of such a framework is Schank and Abelson's representation of every day knowledge that is needed for understanding stories. The authors use the term **script** to describe events in normal situations. (A script is a kind of schema – see Chapter 6 of Book 1). According to this model, people build a representation of what has typically happened in the past, and use this to build an expectation of what will happen when that situation is encountered again. If we have this kind of information, then we can supply the knowledge to make sense of a piece of text in which all of the details are not spelled out. For example, to understand an utterance such as *'If you try that new restaurant, make sure you have plenty of time, and money'* you need to draw heavily on stored knowledge about restaurants, such as that you have to wait to be served and pay money for the meal. Scripts could be said to contain encyclopaedic information about particular situations that we have encountered in the past, and we can use that information to make inferences such as the money will be needed to pay for the meal. As we already noted, language also contains a good deal of bottom-up information and a number of models of understanding discourse have been proposed that take some of the principles of schema-based knowledge (i.e. top-down knowledge) and incorporate them with bottom-up processes.

Gernsbacher and Foertsh (1999) have presented three models with this kind of integration, but we will take one of these as an example: that of Kintsch (1988, 1994). This model takes the **proposition** as the basic unit. Propositions are the smallest unit of meaning that can be taken from a sentence or clause. For example, the sentence 'The black bat is in the barn' contains two propositions, the bat is black and the bat is in the barn. Propositions can be thought of as the simplest string of words that can be either true or false.

As you read the text, 'The black bat is in the barn', word meanings in the text are accessed and these produce propositions. Kintsch proposes that each proposition is represented by a unit that is similar to the units in the IAC model you encountered in Section 3.1. When a proposition is encountered the unit that represents it becomes energised. The unit passes energy at the same time to any other units that represent propositions about the barn that have previously been encountered. For example, the proposition 'the bat is in the barn' may energise propositions such as 'the ball is in the barn' and 'the barn is very dark'. The next proposition is then analysed and energises other stored units. In this way a huge number of units are activated and these form a propositional network or web composed of those in the text and those retrieved from long-term memory. This network is *constructed* of propositional units with varying levels of energy, as some of the stored units

Script
A schema that represents a typical event.

Proposition
A statement consisting of a single idea or unit of meaning.

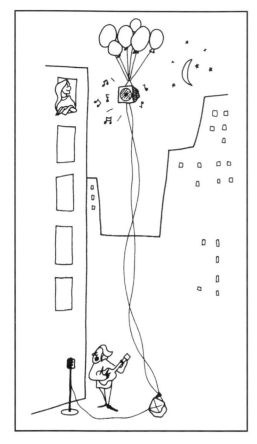

Figure 2.3   Picture for Activity 2.8

will receive energy from other incoming propositions. So, for example, if another proposition, 'bats roost', was read then 'bats roost' will excite propositions that relate to roosting places and bats as animals, so it will also energise 'the barn is very dark'. It is the most highly excited units that will be *integrated* to form a stable representation of the text as a whole, a *mental model* of the meaning of the communication. Those units that are only weakly excited will not be part of the network that, because it has become strongly linked together, represents what the meaning is.

Kintsch has also incorporated a learning mechanism into his model that allows the excitatory links between units to be strengthened whenever they are activated in quick succession. So when two propositions are read sequentially the energy link between the units representing them is strengthened. Then, whenever one of them is subsequently activated again, excitation will be transmitted to the other related unit. This kind of system can be used to explain the ways in which past experience or knowledge is used. Kintsch called this a *construction-integration* model and in contrast to Schank and Abelson's scripts it is *driven* by information taken from the text. So, for example, the propositions formed from 'the bat is in the barn' may activate propositions in long-term memory that involve cricket and flying mammals. As subsequent clarifying propositions are read, they in turn will activate either units concerning 'cricket' propositions or different units concerning 'mammal' propositions so that, by the system of strengthening energy links described above, the correct sense of the proposition will gradually become apparent and the incorrect sense will be ignored.

3.4 Conversation and pragmatics

So far then we have looked at how cognitive psychologists suggest people understand well-constructed monologues. Experiments typically present participants with a written piece of prose to read, or a recording of an individual reading, often in a monotone, from a scripted piece of text. But our everyday language is more often *dialogue* – we hold conversations with each other. We may use rhythm and stress in our voice to clarify a sentence. For example, the utterance 'It was you' can be a statement or a question depending on the way we utter it. This intonation is termed **prosody**.

Prosody
Aspects of the sound of speech, such as stress and rhythm, that function to clarify or reinforce the meaning of a sentence.

Activity 2.9

Try saying 'The waiter gave Jim a drink then he gave him some money' in different ways, so that 'he' refers first to the waiter and then to Jim.

Prosody is another source of information that enables us to build a representation of meaning. It can be thought of as analogous to punctuation in written language. To indicate that 'It was you' is a question in written text we add a question mark. In speech we raise the pitch of our voice on the final word. Similarly, we could use a comma to clarify the written sentence in Activity 2.9, but we vary the stress on the words when we say them.

Conversations by their nature are social ventures so, as well as using linguistic information and our own knowledge, we also need to consider the knowledge of our conversational partner. Grice (1975) proposed that, in order to converse successfully, both parties need to cooperate and obey a number of maxims or principles on which to base their interaction. According to Sperber and Wilson (1986), the most important of these maxims or principles is the maxim of relevance. The sender and receiver of information enter into a kind of contract, such that the recipient of any information expects it to relate to the representation he or she already has. So the person sending or making the communication tailors it to fit the expectations and knowledge of the receiver. The proposal is that this kind of contract for communication allows ambiguities in conversation to be resolved, so individuals take turns to be speakers and to work on making their communication effective within the context of the knowledge and expectations of their listener. This fits with Sperber's later ideas, discussed in Section 2, of the importance of metarepresentation to the evolution of language in *humans*.

This use of metarepresentation in making communication means that our utterances are not simply composed to convey information. They are designed to carry meanings that are not contained within the syntactic and semantic content of the words alone. The statement 'It is nine o'clock' is a literal statement of the time, but the actual purpose of the statement may be to suggest that it is getting too late for something or that a particular event has occurred that was scheduled for nine o'clock. The statement 'you are standing on my foot' is generally intended and understood as a request for action rather than a simple communication of fact. These other factors contributing to the meaning of a particular communication, are called **pragmatics** – the knowledge of the contingent particulars of circumstances in which a communication is made, and of the knowledge, desires and intentions of the people involved in the communication.

Pragmatics
The way that the intended rather than the literal meaning of language is inferred.

So, in order to 'recover the thought' that someone is trying to communicate, cognitive psychologists working on language argue that we need to take account of many different types of information. We need to recognise words, we need to know how these words fit together, we need to select relevant information we already possess to interpret the new material, and we need to know about our expectations and those of the communicator. Cognitive psychologists characterise meaning in different ways. In the context of the connectionist models we have mentioned, meaning refers to the patterns of connections between units. In Kintsch's model outlined above, the meaning of a proposition in a piece of text depends on which other propositions are related to it. Cognitive psychologists have also investigated how the meaning of any particular word or string of words depends upon the context in which they are perceived. Finally, in conversation, meaning depends on perceptions of what a communicator meant to communicate, and on the hearer's metarepresentation as well as the speakers representation. In Section 4, we shall see how social psychologists studying language have taken up the issues of pragmatics; namely that meaning does not reside simply in the words and sentences of language, and that the purpose of communication may encompass more than recovering the thoughts of others.

Summary Section 3

- In order to understand a piece of text or an utterance people use a number of different kinds of information.
- Lexical, semantic and syntactic information, and also knowledge of what typically happens in our world, are all important for understanding. In order to engage successfully in a conversation, participants need knowledge of each other's representations and intentions.
- Cognitive psychologists are interested in how people integrate these different kinds of information to build representations of text meaning.
- Connectionist models have been developed that can explain how top-down and bottom-up processing might interact to produce various language phenomena.

Answer to Activity 2.6

The answer to the question posed in Activity 2.6 is: 'TAKE' and 'CART'.

4   Using language, creating meaning

In the previous section, you were introduced to the cognitive psychological perspective on language that focuses on how an individual understands language. Section 3 described how the recipient of a communication might successfully reconstruct the communicator's application of syntactic rules and semantics, and use their knowledge of the working of scripts and script events, and the social context of the communication.

4.1 Introduction

In this section, we turn our attention to social psychological approaches to language, which focus on understanding language and its meanings as first and foremost a social process. In this approach, it is crucial that language always takes place between at least two people. Language is seen as inherently social because it involves something taking place *among* a number of people, and it is in this social interaction that the meaning of language is made.

Activity 2.10

Below is a piece of dialogue that illustrates the importance of the social nature of language production. Read the dialogue and try to answer the questions that follow it.

Man: Right you can go back a little further, maybe a foot, then you'll have room to straighten up as you go forward.

Woman: Could you just let me do it on my own – I'll only learn by doing it myself.

Man: You could just go back and I can tell you when to stop – I'm taller than you are so I can see the car behind better

Woman: I wouldn't need you to tell me if I learnt to do it myself.

Man: I'm only trying to help, don't go off the deep end!

Woman: You're always trying to help me; I feel like I can't do anything without you offering advice.

Man: You trot out this kind of rubbish whenever I try to help you, no matter how gentle I am about it. If that's the way you feel, fine; I won't offer any help at all in future.

- Look at the first utterance to 'go back a little further' – how many different contexts can you think of where that instruction might be given?

- At what point did you realise that the context concerned parking a car – was it before the car itself was mentioned in the third communication - how did you infer this?

- What do you think the relationship is between the man and woman: are they friends, family members, driving instructor and pupil?

- How do you know? What kinds of knowledge are you drawing on?

- What is the argument about that is taking place in this dialogue – is there one topic of argument or several, and do the speakers agree about what they are arguing about?

A social psychologist would propose that there is much more to understanding the meaning of the conversation in Activity 2.10 than the knowledge of syntax, semantics, pragmatics and script sequences – no matter how much these are modelled as interactive within a cognitive language processing system. Consideration of this piece of 'real-life' dialogue presents us with an example of how meaning *emerges* during a whole episode of communication. It demonstrates that the argument taking place is not so much about informational content (i.e. how to park the car), as about what each proposes the other accomplishes by their contribution. The meaning that the man intends for his first utterance – giving advice – is interpreted by the woman as being domineering or exercising control. As the conversation continues the argument develops not about who can see better to park, but about the intentions of the speakers involved and what they seek to achieve. In other words the argument does not occur because the woman has failed to understand the words that the man says about his intention when giving advice. She is arguing with him instead about whether these really 'were' his intentions, since the effect of what he said seems to fit with another intention (to make her feel dependent).

Contested
The process by which an individual challenges the meanings being constructed, or actions accomplished, by another speaker.

Meanings here are constructed and **contested** between speakers as the interaction proceeds. It is clear in this context that there are meanings, and disagreements over meanings, that relate to an entire history of the relationship between the man and the woman. Most western readers of this exchange will have used their cultural knowledge of intimate, personal relationships between men and women to infer that these two people are probably husband and wife or living in some close relationship to each other. They will know that control and autonomy is currently a common area of contention in this kind of relationship. This knowledge is a crucial part of how meanings are dynamically constructed here; it is not simply additional context that is necessary to successfully reconstruct the meanings that each speaker intended to give their utterances.

There is a second further point to be made about the exchange above that reflects a contrast between the focus of social psychological and cognitive approaches to language. In social psychological approaches the purpose of language is not to reflect individuals' internal perceptions, cognitions or feelings and convey them neutrally to another. Instead it is proposed that when we communicate it is always because we want to <u>do</u> something: there is an action to be accomplished. In the conversation above, giving information about how to park is not a neutral act of describing the world. Would the man have given his advice if he thought the woman was capable of parking on her own, and could judge the distance and space adequately? Almost certainly not, so that is the apparent purpose in giving advice. The argument that then ensued was about whether the apparent purpose was the real one, or whether there were other intentions underlying the giving of advice and its results. The woman felt positioned by the man as 'inadequate' and 'dependent', while the man positioned himself as 'helpful' and 'caring'. It is a central theme of social psychological approaches to language then, that the meaning of any actual communication episode does not lie in the rules of syntax and semantics, or the application of pragmatic knowledge about scripts and schemas. Meaning lies in the goals, purposes and use of any communication, and in the interpretation of particular meaning by those (with their own goals and purposes) for whom the communication is intended. In the social psychological approach, this process of construction of meaning applies equally to solitary thinking or reading, where the use of language is in a dialogue with the self.

In this section, we shall explore the idea of meaning making as a dynamic social activity. We shall look at how individuals use language not only to interpret and understand their world but to become active agents within it, and use language to achieve their goals and purposes. We shall also examine the more general thesis of the social constructionist perspective on language, namely that language is the medium though which our selves, our actions and our knowledge of the world are constructed. In particular, this approach proposes that all knowledge about what people think, experience or do – all psychological knowledge – should be grounded in the study of how language creates that thought, experience and behaviour, not only at the level of the individual but at the level of groups and society.

4.2 Language and the social world

The focus on language as an arena of social activity, where people use language to pursue the goals and purposes of everyday life, came initially from a group of sociologists who began to study language in qualitative ways. They wished to move away from the assumptions of quantitative analysis, which they saw as excessively dominating work on language and social interaction. One sociologist, Harold Garfinkel (1967), developed a method called **ethnomethodology** – literally the study of how people(s) do things. The method in ethnomethodology meant that the researcher lived with the particular people or social group they were interested in, as one of them. By living their life, doing things the way they did them and listening above all to what was said (as this constitutes the most important medium for action), researchers were to analyse how things were done. They were to formulate

Ethnomethodology
A study of the socially shared knowledge of rules, roles and conduct, that individuals draw upon to analyse, understand and act in everyday life.

descriptions of frameworks, procedures and rules that represented a complete description of how things were done in everyday life.

A classic study by Wieder (1974, cited in Potter and Wetherell, 1987) is a good example of this method. Weider was a sociologist who went to stay in a half-way hostel for newly released prisoners that aimed to help them find their feet once out of prison and keep them away from drugs. He took part in all the routines, observed the running and business of the hostel, slept and ate and talked with the residents. It is part of accepted sociological knowledge that in most institutions there is an informal set of rules that guide the behaviour of those who live there, quite separate from the formal rules of the institution. Wieder identified such a set of rules for the hostel that he called 'The Code'. He claimed that 'The Code' gave the rules of conduct by which the residents lived.

The Code (taken from Potter and Wetherell, 1987, p.20)

There are eight basic maxims to 'The Code'

1   Above all, do not snitch.
2   Do not cop out.
3   Do not take advantage of other residents.
4   Share what you have.
5   Help other residents.
6   Do not mess with other residents' interests.
7   Do not trust staff – staff is heat.
8   Show your loyalty to other residents.

But The Code itself was not seen by Wieder as the *explanation* for behaviour, as the set of rules that caused residents to behave the way they did. Instead, it was the *resource* that residents used to actively interpret their world and construct what they and others did. For example, Wieder noticed that quite often when he was chatting amicably to a resident he (the resident) would close the conversation with a comment that he did not wish to talk any further because he was not a 'snitch' (which is one of the very strong rules of The Code). Weider thought about the regularity with which this occurred and concluded that talking to him could be constructed as a risky thing to do – making the community vulnerable by giving information about them to an outsider. Wieder concludes that, by finishing the conversation in this way, the resident was not passively 'acting out' The Code, but using it to actively define the boundaries of his action – talking but not 'snitching' – and to use the rule that they don't snitch to control the extent of talk and risk being taken.

This sociological approach to language as a resource, actively used by speakers to construct their social world and take action within it, led some social psychologists to begin rethinking psychological approaches to language. They began to develop an approach that proposed that the personal and apparently individual world of experience, cognition and emotion was also constructed and enacted through language.

Discursive psychology: how meaning is constructed.

In Chapter 1 of Book 1 the notion of discourse, in terms of the construction of identity, was explained as 'ways of thinking and talking about issues currently available to our culture ... the processes by which people construct meaning' (see Section 5.2 of Chapter 1, Book 1). Discursive psychology focuses on the proposal that the meaning created through discourses conditions our thinking about and understanding of the external world and of ourselves within it.

Parker (1992) describes a **discourse** as 'a system of statements which defines an object' (p.5). By this he means that discourses are sets of symbolic meanings created through the use of language (in talk, story-telling, novels, magazines, advertising, television, radio and so on) to construct a particular version of events or represent a particular thing in a particular way (note that discursive psychology uses 'discourse' in a different way to that of cognitive psychology). For example, in Chapter 1 of Book 1, you were given the example of the difference between calling Nelson Mandela a terrorist (as he was called by the apartheid supporting government of pre-1989) or a freedom fighter (by the apartheid opposed African National Congress movement of the same era).

Discourse (Social Psychology)
In discursive psychology discourse is the spoken or written matter by which a particular object is constructed.

Activity 2.11

Think about the description 'terrorist'. What thoughts come to mind? Think wide-rangingly and freely. How does a terrorist view their country, the value of human life, the issues of democracy and of morality? Think a bit more widely. Is a terrorist a socially integrated person, likely to give priority to friends and family in their lives? Are their interests going to be wide-ranging or narrow; will they be liberal minded or authoritarian? Now answer exactly the same for 'freedom-fighter'. Where do you think you have got this kind of awareness of what these two types of people are like?

You will probably have read books, films, newspapers, heard radio and TV news and so on, and so have a whole history of exposure to a wide variety of representations about these words, apparently descriptive of only one aspect of behaviour, but actually about a whole person and what they are like. This 'system of statements' defines the object under discussion – terrorist or freedom fighter – in quite complex and broad ways. They do much more than simply relate to the reason why an individual is engaged in acts of aggression against the powers of the state. These two words represent two different discourses that can then be used for the same person and construct him or her in two entirely different and complex ways, giving two different accounts of 'reality'.

Discursive psychology is not proposing that the representations and descriptions developed through discourse create an account that is imposed upon reality. After all, how can we establish whether Nelson Mandela was *really* a terrorist or a freedom fighter? Rather, discursive psychology proposes that discourses create what we think of as the reality of the world, and that is why Parker said that discourses *define* objects. The descriptions of Nelson Mandela as either terrorist or freedom fighter were not simply a difference of opinion about the nature of his activities, but constructions of reality that constituted or defined Mandela as a particular type of person (or 'object'). This in turn constructs or defines how all that he did and said is understood and given meaning.

Discursive psychology proposes that discourses are 'designed' to accomplish particular constructions of reality, in that discourses are chosen or created by individuals or groups to construct a reality that best serves their interests or needs. An important feature of language then, as hinted at in the Nelson Mandela example above, is that in any one situation there will often be a number of *competing* discourses being used by different people or groups with different interests. This competition is about which construction of reality will prevail; that is which will be accepted and acted upon by the larger community or those with power. Discourse psychologists propose, therefore, that an understanding of the interests and investments involved in the use of discourse, the goal or purpose of gaining or maintaining power at any level large or small, is an important part of understanding language use.

Given this view of language, discourse psychologists have found two areas of research important to pursue. One is to look at the actual content of particular discourses: how are people who use a given discourse constructing the world? You were given a flavour of this kind of research when we looked at the words 'terrorist' and 'freedom-fighter' in Activity 2.11. Discourse analysis of the content of the discourses of 'terrorist' and 'freedom-fighter' would look systematically at instances of talk or text that used these terms in order to establish how they are constructed in relation to each other and other objects of social, political, cultural and personal life. The second area focuses on one obvious consequence of the notion of many competing discourses being available to individuals or groups. This is that individuals are continually involved in choosing which discourses to use in order to construct and act within their world, and quite often they will need to be creative in finding a discourse that does what they want. They may even choose two or more discourses to construct parts of their world that are in conflict with each other. In that case, they will need to find some way of reconciling that conflict.

At the time of writing this chapter, one of the authors (Cooper) is a mother of two young children, and working full-time for The Open University: if I want to construct myself as a good mother I will have to draw on the dominant cultural discourse of traditional motherhood, which positions good mothers as loving, nurturing and self-sacrificing to their children. However as a woman working full-time, I am not constantly available to my children, and I have not sacrificed my career or economic independence to be with my children full-time. In constructing my identity as a good mother, I can resist seeing my involvement in paid work as selfish by drawing on a more recent discourse of motherhood, which includes in the notion of good mothering ensuring that one's children are provided for materially. Paid work is positioned as selfish in one discourse but not so in another.

There are many other discourses about being a good mother that I could bring in to use within my account of myself as a good mother. This act of creating an identity for myself as a good mother in relation to all these discourses is called the creation of a **subject position** (in that I have created my identity by positioning myself as the subject of particular discourses in particular ways). As we saw in Chapter 1 of Book 1, the construction of identity is an important and continuous part of an individual's life. Discursive psychology proposes that individuals are continually building and adjusting identities through the creation of subject positions in all kinds of discourse or set of discourses. Of course they are also positioning other people, by creating subject positions for them as well.

I have created my subject position as 'good mother' using a very active process. I was drawing on some elements of different discourses of motherhood and rejecting others. The knowledge that I had of available discourses about what constitutes being a good mother, and the strategies I used to reposition behaviour that the traditional discourse might construct as bad mothering, is called my **interpretative repertoire**. Discourse psychologists use a method called discourse analysis to explore and establish the types of discourse that are available for people to use, and the way these are employed in particular interpretative repertoires.

> **Subject position**
> The place or character an individual can construct for themselves using discourses and particular recognized positions like 'the good mother'.

> **Interpretative repertoire**
> The sum of different discourses, and the ways that they can be combined or mixed together, which the individual has at their disposal to construct subject positions.

2.4 FEATURED METHOD

Discourse Analysis

Because of their emphasis upon the active construction of accounts, discourse analysts interested in the identification of interpretative repertoires (they sometimes refer to themselves as 'discourse psychologists') very often use transcripts or interviews and 'natural' conversations as their material for analysis (e.g. McKinlay and Potter, 1987, pp.443–63; Potter and Wetherell, 1987, Marshall and Raabe, 1993; Gill 1993). However, other kinds of material are occasionally used, such as newspaper reports (Edwards and Potter, 1992), television programmes (Potter et al., 1991) and child-care manuals (Marshall, 1991).

Interpretative repertoires ... are seen as linguistic resources or tool-kits available to speakers in the construction of their accounts. They are seen as analogous to the moves of a ballet dancer: finite in number and available to all ballet dancers for the design of a variety of dances suitable to a variety of occasions. If you went to enough ballet performances, you would eventually begin to recognise the repertoire of moves that the dancers have available to them. The idea of a repertoire, therefore, involved the idea of flexibility of use; the moves can be put together in different ways to suit the occasion (a feature not present in the idea of discourses as coherent, organized sets of statements.)

Researchers in the 'interpretative repertoires' field look for the metaphors, grammatical constructions, figures of speech and so on that people use in constructing their accounts. By examining the talk of different people when they are, say, interviewed about a topic, it is possible to monitor the way that some figures of speech, metaphors and so on keep turning up in the talk of different people. By abstracting such usages across different interviews on the same topic, it is claimed that the researcher can identify such repetitions or 'moves' as a repertoire. Therefore, both variability and repetition are features which such analysts are looking for in their material. Variability can be expected within a single interview, because respondents can be expected to make use of different repertoires to suit their current purposes. Repetition across different interviews can be expected because the same repertoires will be used by different people.

Burr, 1999, p.176–7

4.3 The implications of discursive psychology for doing psychology

Because of their position that language constructs thought and action rather than reflecting it, discourse psychologists have challenged many of the assumptions made within other perspectives in psychology. One of these is that language is a process that reflects 'underlying' cognitive processes taking place in an individual's mind. To illustrate how this challenge can be supported let us take as an example attribution theory.

At the end of Section 3, Chapter 7 of Book 1, there was a critique of the findings of actor/observer difference, and the fundamental attribution error and the theory used to explain them. The critique was based on two key points. The first is that a model of the individual as scientist trying to find causal explanations of behaviour is not a very plausible one because it disregards the issue of when people might look for the causes of social behaviour. We do not do it for all episodes of social behaviour (that would probably be impossible to do since it would take up so much time and attention): we only tend to do it when we need an explanation for that behaviour. It seems most likely that we need to do it when things go wrong in a particular situation ('why was that shop assistant rude to me?'), and when we need to attribute responsibility or social accountability for a particular action ('why has that person pushed in front of me in the queue?'). The second point is that, in terms of looking for who is accountable or responsible for actions, we may be looking at our own actions, not just the actions of others. In that situation we will have interests to protect as well as goals and aims to pursue.

These two aspects of the rationale for causal attributions for behaviour show that they are required by particular needs – to accomplish certain ends. When things go wrong in a social situation, or when we attribute responsibility, we may well want to find out if there are actions we could take that would make the situations go better for us. The discursive psychology perspective argues further that attribution takes place in the kinds of circumstances outlined above because speakers need to be able to construct an account, to create a subject position within their interpretative repertoire, which enables them to manage the responsibility or accountability in ways that are best for them.

To show how this is done, Derek Edwards and Jonathan Potter (1992) re-examined some of the data from a published study (Burleson 1986) that had used traditional attribution theory from the cognitive perspective to investigate the discussion about a failing student between two junior teaching assistants in an American college. The student is in the class of one of the teaching assistants (Don), and has just failed a test. She has also failed other tests that she was given on this course. In Box 2.5 is part of the transcript of interview material that Burleson used to illustrate how attributional information would be sought, by applying principles like consistency and consensus. (See Section 3, Chapter 7 of Book 1.)

2.5 *Transcript of interview material (Burleson, 1986)*

Don: She has – I gave quizzes which, you know, cover the material. So she's got copies of the quizzes which led up to the midterm, and some of the questions on that midterm are just lifted off the quizzes. Just exactly the same as those quizzes.

Bob: And you did go over those quizzes, right?

Don: Oh yes, yes I did. And she was still missin' those that are exact copies of the ones on quizzes that she's got copies of.

Don: (Pause) I just don't see that I can do anything for her. I just have — I know the day has passed for dropping the course, but I gotta —

Bob: — Does she know she failed it?

Don: No.

Bob: Oh.... I don't envy you man. What are you gonna say to her?

Don: I'm just gonna say 'you failed it again. This is the last straw. I'm gonna get you out of this class'. I don't know how I'm gonna do it.

Traditional attribution theory would interpret the exchange in Box 2.5 as evidence that Bob and Don are weighing and considering information relating to the cause of the student's failure. Bob is looking for evidence of consistency and asks Don whether the student still fails the tests when she has been given quizzes that cover the material to be tested (quizzes with questions exactly the same as those in the test). Evidence of consensus is that this student has failed, but the others in the class have passed. But Edwards and Potter propose that in this exchange what seems to preoccupy these teaching assistants is not causal inference about the reasons for the student's failure, but their own accountability for it. As university teaching assistants they are held responsible for a variety of duties in teaching students and with providing adequate support for students to be able to pass their tests. Their work will be under scrutiny on these grounds, not only by their students but also by their university supervisors. This conversation takes place in the context of being in a teaching post in which students' pass results are important both to positive evaluation from colleagues and superiors, and to permission to continue in the post. The effect of this conversation is to create two subject positions through the use of particular interpretative repertoires concerning 'responsible teaching' and 'good studentship'.

Activity 2.12

Look at the transcript of the conversation between Bob and Don and make some notes about the following. What do Bob's questions tell you about his interpretative repertoire for 'responsible teacher'? What do Don's responses tell you about his interpretative repertoire for 'good student'? Finally make some notes about how the subject positions that are created justify the proposal for taking a particular course of action at the end of the exchange.

Don is located firmly within the discourse of responsible teacher, and the student within the discourse of 'inadequate student'. The entire exchange could be described as the creation of subject positions that will serve to justify Don in expelling her from his group. This working of the account by Don in creating these subject positions is where the play of power comes in. Specifically he achieves a representation of the world that best serves his interests by placing responsibility for the situation with the student.

4.4 Conclusion

Discourse psychologists regard much of the traditional research in cognitive psychology as mistaken in assuming that processes such as attribution and remembering can be transparently reported. They believe that language does not simply *represent* cognition, because the act of formulating thoughts into words *changes* them. Discourse psychologists also argue that, because words always have a particular function within the context in which they are spoken, it is necessary to rethink the basis of psychological methods that rely on language to produce evidence.

This challenge to established psychological methods can be illustrated in the work of discourse psychologists on memory. In the cognitive analysis of memory, as we saw in Chapter 8 of Book 1, concern is focused on how memories are represented, encoded and stored. This has been reflected, for example, in a long tradition of research involving memorizing of nonsense syllables within a laboratory. In this experimental paradigm, the issue has been how accurate an individual's recall of a list is. However, discourse psychologists would argue that, in ordinary life, recall is used for purposes other than simply an accurate representation of what was. They would argue that what people recall is always done to answer a purpose or need – for example, the need to attribute responsibility for a particular outcome (which is how Don was using his remembering in the example above). The meaning attached to Don's recall of his treatment of his student is not about accurately and objectively representing the details of his actions, but about presenting the evidence for a moral judgement as to his responsibility for a particular outcome. His recall is organized around interpreting his responsibility. In fact, in Chapter 8 of Book 1, the section on autobiographical memory shows how the meaning of memories, the reason why recall is occurring, may influence how people *go about* remembering past events in their lives. What is remembered will vary with factors like audience, with time of life and proximity to the event, relationship to other meaningful events, and so on.

Discourse psychologists contend that, just as there is no sense in looking for the 'truth' of whether Nelson Mandela is a terrorist or a freedom fighter, so, for most memories, there is equally little sense in asking how accurate or 'truthful' a representation is about what actually happened. There is certainly an individual cognitive process of representing, coding and storing a memory and there are questions about those processes and how they work. But access to memory in recall is through language, and is not a case of 'retrieving' a stored memory which is then reported transparently, but of re-presenting and reconstructing whatever is stored through the medium of language. Furthermore, if language is used to construct the world in line with the interests or purposes of the individual, so the language used within an act of remembering – the expression of memory – will be directly connected to the socially realized purpose of remembering (Edwards *et al.*, 1992).

For all these reasons discourse psychologists propose that their perspective represents a new way of understanding the place of language in psychological research and theory.

> It [language] exists as a domain of social action, of communication and culture, whose relations to the external world of event, and to the internal world of cognitions, are a function of the social and communicative actions talk is designed to do.
>
> *Edwards* et al., *1992, p.442*

Summary Section 4

- Meaning is not created by the individual who speaks, but is produced jointly by the speaker and by those who receive and respond to a communication.
- Meaning is often contested between those involved in communication and may change dynamically as communication proceeds.
- Language is a resource used by individuals to construct objects within the world, and take action within it.
- The constructive function of language means that it cannot be assumed that it transparently represents cognitive processes in psychological research that uses verbal report.

5   Conclusion

You have been introduced to several different perspectives on language, each of which has different theories and methods associated with it. A central question that must be addressed is how to compare these perspectives, and on what grounds they can be found to be complementary, contradictory or independently co-existing. The evolutionary perspective looks at the similarities and differences that exist between communication used by humans and other species of animal. This approach argues for the adaptational advantage that might have been conferred by the development of language. The cognitive perspective focuses on what happens in the mind when language is heard or read. Traditionally a computational metaphor has been employed that portrays humans as sophisticated information processors. The emphasis is on how representations are constructed by integrating information from the input, from stored knowledge and from the wider social context within which language is encountered. In order to specify exactly what information must be extracted and how different sorts of information might be combined, most cognitive study of language has been done in experimental settings. The social constructionist perspective on language is linked to traditions that began in the sociological study of language. These look at the actual use of language in particular social episodes to examine how speakers use language as a resource to interpret and construct the world. The social constructionist perspective is based on the analysis of everyday conversations within the social world, outside laboratories or formal settings of study, and in open-ended interviews.

These different perspectives offer different understandings of language based on their level of analysis. The evolutionary perspective sees language as an adaptive acquired characteristic at *species level*, characterized by the ability to create meanings quite different to those of other species' systems of communication. The social constructionist perspectives see language as the vehicle for the socially produced and sustained meaning that operates *between individuals, in groups and society*: here language is the means by which individuals construct their world, interact with others and act to achieve their goals. The cognitive perspective sees language as the part of the information processing system that resides in the *individual* brain. Meaning is generated by the individual as they hear others speak or need to speak to others. To this degree, all the perspectives might be seen as complementary to each other.

These different levels of analysis are reflected in the methods and analysis used by each perspective to investigate language. The evolutionary perspective uses evidence about other animals' systems of communication to create hypotheses regarding the kinds of adaptational pressures that could have produced the species-specific characteristics of human language. The social constructionist perspective looks at evidence from actual language use in day-to-day life. It uses discourse analysis to describe how language users organise their talk, using particular strategies like the creation of subject positions or constructions of the world, to achieve particular ends. The cognitive perspective collects evidence from the experimental setting about the kinds of response or output the cognitive language system would have to make to particular and controlled input. In addition it uses computational models to hypothesise the general parameters and operations of the language system.

These different understandings of what language is and how to investigate it entail different understandings of what meaning is and where it is made. According to the cognitive perspective, meaning precedes language and is transmitted by language. The social constructionist perspective proposes that the meaning of language arises out of negotiation and construction with others, and so language creates meaning. The evolutionary perspective presents a view of meaning as created by evolutionary forces acting to produce linguistic ability and its capacity for creating meaning. These perspectives' different understandings of meaning can be broadly differentiated in terms of where they locate the creation of meaning to take place. For example, in this context the evolutionary and social constructionist perspectives could be said to be co-existing in terms of locating the creation of meaning in processes outside the individual.

Table 1   Differences between where and how perspectives on meaning is made

Evolutionary view of meaning	Cognitive view of meaning	Discursive view of meaning
In section 2 on comparative models and the evolution of language, human language was distinguished from other forms of communication by the ability to use hypothetical constructs and abstractions, and to be originally creative. It was suggested that these characteristics allowed the creation of meaning that is distinctive to language, for example, through metarepresentation. Meaning is, therefore, a property of the development of particular characteristics of the language that humans use.	In section 3 meaning was defined in terms of the parameters of the individual's linguistic information processing system based in the brain. This system involves the parallel processing of a variety of types of syntactic, semantic, contextual and social information which creates meaning for what is to be said, or extracts it from what is heard. Meaning is, therefore, created by these information processing systems, and how they work to produce or understand language.	In section 4 meaning was suggested to be created not by individual cognition and understanding, but the inherently social process of language. Speakers use language in order to pursue particular goals, desires or needs, and adopt particular language strategies to help them. Meaning is continually negotiated, contested and actively constructed between speakers. Here meaning is created between individuals who use language to accomplish certain goals and purposes.

Finally, one of the interesting problems with research and development of theories of language is the problem of **methodological reflexivity**: we must use language itself as the medium by which we investigate language. This problem is at the heart of a dispute between cognitive and social perspectives on language: to what extent (if any) does the very necessity of responding in language predetermine what is said? From the cognitive perspective has come a tradition that assumes that there are separate cognitive processes that language can represent in communication to others, or in dialogue with the self. That representation will be more or less accurate depending on how closely language can map the cognition behind it. In studying what people say, cognitive psychologists believe that the thought processes underlying language can be studied more or less successfully. The critique produced by discursive psychology is that, when individuals use language, they always do so in a context, with an audience and for a purpose. Even in an experimental setting they are making assumptions about what their interlocutors know, understand and want, and what is relevant and what is not. Discourse psychologists propose that, in studying language, we can actually only study what language is used to do, and this forces us to revise the basic premises and methodologies of much other psychological research.

Recommended reading

Burr, V. (1995) *An Introduction to Social Constructionists*, London, Routledge.

Pinker, S. (1995) *The Language Instinct: The New Science of Language and Mind*, London, Penguin Books.

Aitchison J. (1997) The Language Web: The Power and Problem of Words, Cambridge, Cambridge University Press.

References

Aitchison, J. (1983) *The Articulate Mammal*, (2nd edn) Oxford, Blackwell.

Berry J.W., Poortinga Y.H., Segall M.H. and Dasen P.R. (1992) *Cross-Cultural Psychology: Research and Applications*, New York, Cambridge University Press.

Bransford, J.D. and Johnson, M.K. (1973) 'Consideration of some problems of comprehension', in Chase W.G. (ed.) *Visual Information Processing*, New York Academic Press.

Burleson, B.R. (1986) 'Attribution schemas and causal inference in natural conversation', in Ellis, D.G. and Donahue, W.A. (eds), *Contemporary Issues in Language and Discourse Processes*, Hillsdale, NJ, Lawrence Erlbaum.

Burman, E. and Parker, I. (1993) *Discourse Analytic Research: Repertoires and Readings of Texts in Action*, London, Routledge.

Burr, V. (1999) *An Introduction to Social Constructionism*, London, Routledge.

Edwards, D.E. and Potter, J. (1992) *Discursive Psychology*, London, Sage

Edwards, D.E., Potter, J. and Middleton, D. (1992) 'Towards a discursive psychology of remembering', in *The Psychologist*, vol.5, no.10, pp.439–46.

Fodor, J.A. (1983) *Modularity of Mind*, Cambridge, MA, MIT Press.

Forrester, M.A. (1996) *Psychology of Language: A Critical Introduction*, London, Sage.

Frazier, L. and Rayner, K. (1982) 'Making and correcting errors during sentence comprehension: eye movements in the analysis of structurally ambiguous sentences', *Cognitive Psychology*, vol.14, pp.178–210

Gardiner, R.A. and Gardiner, B.T. (1969) 'Teaching sign language to a Chimpanzee', *Science*, vol.165, pp.664–72.

Garfinkel, H. (1967) *Studies in Ethnomethodology*, Englewood Cliffs, NJ, Prentice-Hall.

Garrod, S. and Pickering, M.J. (1999) *Language Processing*, Hove, Psychology Press.

Gernsbacher, M.A. and Foertsh, J.A. (1999) 'Three models of discourse comprehension', in Garrod, S. and Pickering, M.J. (eds).

Gill, R. (1993) 'Justify injustice: broadcasters' accounts of inequality in radio', in Burman, E. and Parker, I (eds).

Goffman, E. (1976) 'Replies and Responses', *Language in Society*, vol.5, pp.257–313.

Greene, J. and Coulson, M. (1995) *Language Understanding, Current Issues* (2nd edn) Open University Press, Buckingham.

Grice, H.P. (1975) 'Logic and conversation', in Cole, P. and Morgan, J. (eds) *Syntax and Semantics: Vol 3 Speech Acts*, New York, Academic Press.

Kirschner, W.K. and Towne, W.F. (1994) 'The sensory basis of honeybee's dance language', *Scientific American*, vol.277, no.6, pp.52–9.

Harley, T.A. (1995) *The Psychology of Language: From Data to Theory*, Hove, Psychology Press.

Hockett, C.F. (1960) 'The origin of speech', *Scientific American*, vol. 203, pp.89–96.

Lorenz, K.Z. (1952) *King Solomon's Ring*, London, Methuin.

Kintsch, W. (1988) 'Role of knowledge in discourse representation: a construction integration model', *Psychological Review*, vol.95, pp.163–82.

Kintsch, W. (1994) 'The psychology of discourse processing', in Gernsbacher, M.A. (ed.) *Handbook of Psycholinguistics*, San Diego, Academic Press.

Marshall, H. (1991) 'The social construction of motherhood: an analysis of childcare and parenting manuals', in Lloyd, E., Phoenix, A. and Woolett, A. (eds) *Motherhood: Meanings, Practices and Ideologies*, London, Sage.

Marshall, H. and Raabe, B (1993) 'Political discourse: talking about nationalisation and privatisation', in Burman, E. and Parker, I. (eds).

Mayer, D.E. and Schvaneveldt, R.W (1971) 'Factors in recognizing pairs of words: evidence of a dependence between retrieval operations', *Journal of Experimental Psychology*, vol.90, pp.227–34.

McClelland, J.L. & Rumelhart, D.E (1981) 'An interactive activation model of context effects in letter processing. Part 1: an account of basic findings', *Psychological Review*, vol.88, pp.375–407.

McClelland, J.L. (1985) 'Putting knowledge in its place: a scheme for programming parallel processing structures on the fly', *Cognitive Science*, vol.9, no.115.

McKinlay, A. and Potter, J (1987) 'Model discourse: interpretative repertoires in scientists' conference talk', *Social Studies of Science*, vol.17.

Moss, H.E. and Gaskell, G.G. (1999) 'Lexical semantic processing during speech comprehension', in Garrod, S. and Pickering, M.J. (eds).

Parker, I. (1992) *Discourse Dynamics: Critical Analysis for Social and Individual Psychology*, London, Routledge.

Pearce, J.M. (1987) *An Introduction to Animal Cognition*, Hove, Lawrence Erlbaum Associates Ltd.

Pickering, M.J. (1999) 'Sentence comprehension', in Garrod, S. and Pickering, M.J. (eds).

Pickering, M.J. and Traxler, M.J. (1998) 'Plausibility and recovery from garden paths. An eye-tracking study', *Journal of Experimental Psychology, Learning, Memory and Cognition*, vol.24, pp.940–61.

Pinker S. (1994) *The Language Instinct*, London, Penguin.

Pinker, S. (1999) *Words and Rules*, Weidenfeld & Nicholson, London.

Pinker, S. (2000) 'Survival of the clearest', *Nature*, vol.404, pp.441–2.

Potter, J. and Wetherell, M. (1987) *Discourse and Social Psychology: Beyond Attitudes and Behaviour*, London, Sage.

Potter, J., Wetherell, M. and Chitty, A. (1991) 'Quantification rhetoric - cancer on television', *Discourse and Society*, vol.2, no.3, pp.333–65.

Premack D. (1971) 'Language in Chimpanzees?', *Science*, vol.172, pp.808–22.

Preuss T.M. (2000) 'The argument from animals to humans in cognitive neuroscience', in Gazzaniga, M.S. (ed.) *Cognitive Neuroscience*, Oxford, Blackwell.

Reicher, G.M. (1969) 'Perceptual representation as a function of meaningfulness of stimulus materials', *Journal of Experimental Psychology*, vol.81, pp.274–80.

Savage-Rumbaugh, E.S. and Lewin, R. (1994) *Kanzi: The Ape at the Brink of the Human Mind*, London, Doubleday.

Savage-Rumbaugh, E.S., Shanker, S.G and Taylor T.J. (1998) *Apes, Language and the Human Mind*, Oxford, Oxford University Press.

Scott, P. and Spencer, C. (1998) *Psychology: A Contemporary Introduction*, Oxford, Blackwell.

Schank, R.C. and Abelson, R.P. (1977*) Scripts, Plans, Goals and Understanding*, Hillsdale, NJ, Lawrence Erlbaum.

Seyfarth R.M., Cheyney D.L and Marler P. (1980) 'Vervet monkey alarm calls: Semantic communication in a free ranging primate', *Animal Behaviour*, vol.28, pp.1070–94.

Sperber, D. and Wilson, D. (1986) *Relevance: Communication and Cognition*, Oxford, Blackwell.

Sperber, D. (2000) 'Metarepresentations in an evolutionary perspective', in Sperber D. (ed.) *Metarepresentations: A Multidisciplinary Perspective*, Oxford, Oxford University Press.

Terrace H.S. (1979) *Nim*, New York, Knopf.

Von-Frisch, K. (1950) *Bees: Their Vision, Chemical Senses and Language*, Ithaca, NY, Cornell University Press.

Warren, R.M. (1970) 'Perceptual restoration of missing speech sounds', *Science*, vol.167, pp.392–3.

Wieder L. (1974) *Language and Social Reality*, The Hague, Mouton.

■ Commentary 2: Language and meaning

This chapter uses three main perspectives to examine the complex area of language. These perspectives focus on different aspects of language including the evolutionary development of language, the processing of language and the construction of meaning through interaction.

Theory

1   The three perspectives in this chapter ask very different questions about language and conceptualize language in different ways, and hence can be seen as broadly complementary. However, this chapter should also have made you aware that we may need to break this down a little further to examine areas like the focus, methods and themes of the perspectives in terms of the three Cs. One clue to this is the difference between the perspectives in 'object of knowledge' where this means what is taken to be the focus of enquiry. The evolutionary perspective looks at the origins of language and the possible benefits it conveyed to earlier human beings. The cognitive perspective looks at the processes that enable meaning to be transmitted between communicating individuals as its object of knowledge; and the social constructionist perspective looks at the co-construction of meaning between communicating individuals which only occurs once the words have left a speaker's mouth. There is therefore conflict between the social constructionist and cognitive perspectives with regard to meaning and whether it is transmitted between individuals or constructed between them.

Methods

2   The cognitive and evolutionary perspectives use methods within a scientific framework which focus on both material and behavioural data. The cognitive perspective uses connectionist models within the information-processing framework, and constructs models which can be tested by the collection of data. The evolutionary perspective attempts to establish how language might have been produced by a particular set of characteristics and environmental conditions. The social constructionist perspective searches for meaning in the use of communication between individuals and makes use of hermeneutic methods to identify the nature of that usage.

Themes

3   This chapter has examined the central theme of the distinctiveness of language, debating whether it is a uniquely human capacity with qualitative rather than quantitative differences from communication in

other, non-human animals. One further interesting theme is whether language evolved because it conferred an adaptational advantage which became the basis of other cognitive abilities (which then underpins better a cognitive perspective on meaning), or whether it conferred an advantage more narrowly in terms of social interaction, communication and cooperation (which favours a social constructionist perspective on meaning).

■ Thinking about theory

It can be a complex issue to decide how perspectives relate to each other, as they can be compared using a variety of dimensions, such as the definition they adopt for the topic of language itself, or the level of analysis they use. The three perspectives presented in this chapter show that there is considerable debate within current psychological thinking about language. In this commentary, we are going to look further at this issue by considering three specific examples of how aspects of these perspectives can be seen as conflicting, coexisting and complementary.

Before considering this complex debate it is important to remind ourselves about the different objects of knowledge sought by each of the perspectives. The object of knowledge for the evolutionary perspective is the species-specific development of language and the process by which language may have evolved. The cognitive perspective is interested in the ways in which we understand and process language and this perspective produces theories which focus on how language is processed by the individual in terms of lexical, syntactic and semantic information. The object of knowledge of the social constructionist perspective is how meaning is co-created and negotiated between individuals through their choice of language and the effects it has. This perspective sees language as inherently social and underpins discursive theories of meaning emerging from context and interaction.

First, the perspectives can be seen as complementary in relation to the levels of analysis they take. The evolutionary perspective looks at language at the species level by comparing human abilities to create meanings with those of other, non-human animals. The cognitive perspective looks at language as an information-processing system which resides in the individual brain, and the social constructionist perspective looks at meaning operating between individuals, in groups and society. There is a good argument too that the cognitive and social constructionist perspectives are complementary because the former focuses on individual production and generation of meaning, and the latter on what happens in terms of meaning once an utterance is made.

Second, we can also see that there is conflict between the cognitive and social constructionist perspectives in relation to what meaning is and where it is made. According to the cognitive perspective, meaning to some extent precedes language, and communication includes the transmission of meanings between individual speakers. The social constructionist perspective disagrees with this view and argues that meaning comes out of negotiation and the acts performed by language. While the cognitive approach to understanding the meaning of a conversation includes consideration of syntax, semantics, and script sequences, the social constructionist approach emphasizes that meaning is created between people and lies in the goals and purposes of conversation, and may often be contested by those involved in communication. The constructive nature of language means that it cannot be assumed that language simply and unproblematically reflects cognitive processes.

Third, to complicate matters further, we can also see that there may be conflicting accounts presented within a single perspective. Two accounts are presented with different implications for how we view language and its importance in the evolutionary perspective. The first account provided by Pinker (2000) argues that the facility for language appeared at some point in our evolutionary history and offered an adaptational advantage. The capacity for language then spread by the mechanism of natural selection as it promoted evolutionary fitness. This view argues that language is the foundation for other cognitive abilities. An alternative explanation is provided by the philosopher and anthropologist Dan Sperber (2000). Sperber argues that our capacity for metarepresentation, the ability to reflect on our own and others mental processes including theory of mind, conveyed a large advantage in allowing humans to predict how others might behave within social interactions. The ability to use metarepresentation led to this being selected for, with language developing because it enabled people to formulate and communicate these ideas. Sperber therefore argues that reasoning and information processing developed and language arose as a by-product of these other cognitive abilities.

We have seen in this section that the topic of language is currently generating considerable debate for psychologists and that relationships between the perspectives are not always straightforward.

■ Thinking about methods

As you might have inferred from some of the previous discussion, the methods chosen by psychological perspectives relate directly to the questions they ask and their objects of knowledge. Those working within the cognitive perspective explore how people understand language and investigate how knowledge is represented and the processes used to communicate meaning internally. This perspective makes use of metaphor to help with theorizing, and model building to infer 'what goes on in the head' through the development of connectionist models which are based on the general principles of information processing. Connectionist models such as McClelland and Rumelhart's Interactive Activation with Competition (IAC) model attempt to explain how words are recognized, and other models look at how sentences and stories are understood. The cognitive perspective also uses scientific methods associated with the experimental tradition to investigate language at the word and sentence levels. Using these approaches, cognitive psychologists can explore the contribution of both bottom-up and top-down processing (see Book 1, Chapter 6) to our understanding of language.

We have noted before that evolutionary psychologists make use of a variety of methods to evaluate their theories and this is evident when they search for evidence that language is an evolved characteristic. In this chapter we have seen that evolutionary psychologists use scientific methods such as brain-imaging techniques to compare the structure of the brain in humans and other primates. They also use observations of communication in non-human animals and comparative studies of attempts to teach language to primates. Overall, we can see that the evolutionary perspective takes an inductive approach to data collection, looking for patterns in data which lead to the emergence of theories.

The social constructionist approach to language focuses on understanding language and meanings and uses hermeneutic methods to explore these. This approach notes that language takes place between at least two people and is essentially a social activity. For this reason, discourse psychologists choose to study language as it is used in daily life by looking at real communications from transcripts, interviews, conversations and TV programmes, to examine competing discourses and constructions of reality along with interpretative repertoires and subject positions.

■ Thinking about themes

Thinking about ourselves as human

The evolutionary and social constructionist perspectives both take the view that language is uniquely human in the ability it confers upon us for subtle and meaningful interactions. The evolutionary perspective is not concerned with the uniqueness of humanity, rather the process by which we came to be similar to and different from non-human animals. This chapter considers the question of distinctiveness with reference to human language and discusses whether language is a uniquely human ability, distinct from naturally occurring animal communication. The claim relating to the distinctiveness of human language is examined by considering the extent to which primates can be said to possess Aitchison's ten 'design features' of language, especially the four which are said to be unique to humans. We have seen from studies which attempt to teach human language to primates that they can indeed develop impressive linguistic abilities including semanticity and the ability to form representations. However, it is difficult to gain evidence that primates understand structure dependence or possess language which is truly creative due to the constraints of the keyboards used in such studies. We have also noted that there is argument as to whether the linguistic abilities seen in primates can be explained through principles of association and learning. Some researchers such as Pinker (1994) have argued that primates may lack other crucial features of language such as the ability to communicate about events other than the 'here and now' leading them to conclude that language has uniquely human features.

References

Pinker, S. (1994) *The Language Instinct*, London, Penguin.

Pinker, S. (2000) 'Survival of the clearest', *Nature*, vol. 404, pp. 441–2.

Sperber, D. (2000) 'Metarepresentations in an evolutionary perspective' in Sperber, D. (ed.) *Metarepresentations: A Multidisciplinary Perspective*, Oxford, Oxford University Press.

The psychology of sex and gender

Wendy Hollway, Troy Cooper, Amy Johnston and Richard Stevens

Contents

Aims

This chapter aims to:

- present four different psychological perspectives on sex and gender, and evaluate their respective strengths and weaknesses
- enable you to understand the different meaning of the terms sex and gender and to use them appropriately
- introduce you to some influential pieces of psychological research on sex and gender
- examine the ways in which the four perspectives complement, conflict or coexist with each other
- provide a theoretical example to illustrate how biological and social perspectives can complement one another within a psychological account of the experience of sex and gender.

1 Introduction

The psychology of sex and gender is one of the most topical, important and engaging subjects that psychology must address. It has been a controversial topic since the inception of psychology as a discipline, and it powerfully illustrates some of the diverse approaches within the field. It demonstrates the numerous levels of analysis that psychology must accommodate – from genes and neurons, to language and socially-structured power relations. To add to the interest, the topic of sex and gender highlights the political and ideological implications that arise from explanations of differences between the sexes. Or should that be 'genders'? Every choice of word has different theoretical connotations and political implications!

In this chapter we are going to present four psychological perspectives with which you will be familiar from Book 1:

- biological sex differences: the sexing of bodies, sex differences in the brain, and biological correlates of behaviour;
- an evolutionary psychology account of differences in the behaviour of human males and females;
- social constructionist theories of gender differences;
- psychoanalytic accounts of the development and meanings of sexual difference.

To give you a feel for each perspective, we shall first briefly summarize the question that each one poses in this area. Despite the fact that they are all asking 'how do we understand the differences between men and women in sex and gender characteristics?', our four perspectives are posing the question in such different ways that the focus of their enquiry and conclusions are different in each instance. In this sense we can say that each has different *objects of knowledge:*

Biological psychology asks what effect biological processes have on behavioural differences between men and women, and in turn what influence behaviour has on the biological processes. Its object of knowledge is biological (physiological, cellular, biochemical and molecular) processes. It investigates the effects of these processes through scientific procedures.

Evolutionary psychology asks how evolution might have shaped human thinking and behaviour. We focus on why particular forms of sexual behaviour might have been selected for in different animal species, including humans. Its object of knowledge is how evolution has shaped human thinking and behaviour. It derives hypotheses based on evolutionary reasoning and, where possible, aims to test them empirically.

Social constructionist psychology examines how knowledge about sex and gender has been constructed within particular historical and social contexts. Its object of knowledge is these social constructions and their influences. It uses evidence largely taken from what people say and write.

Psychoanalytic psychology asks how girls and boys acquire a sexed and gendered sense of themselves, given that, at birth, infants appear to have no psychological awareness of either themselves or others as sexed beings. Its object of knowledge is psychic development and the consequent meanings of sex differences. The evidence for psychoanalytic theory is largely based on clinical observation, experience and testing through the interpretative work between analyst and patient.

These are not the only psychological perspectives that can be applied to studies of sex and gender. In Chapter 3 of Book 1, for example, the behaviourist, cognitive and sociocultural perspectives were applied to learning, while the discussion of life span development in Chapter 1 of this volume was informed by Piaget's genetic epistemology, and by developmental contextualism. All of these perspectives have also made contributions to our understanding of sex and gender.

By keeping an eye on the different objects of knowledge here, we want to encourage you to ask, following a theme in the first book of the course, in what ways can these perspectives complement each other, in what ways do they conflict, and in what ways do they just coexist? In the concluding section, we shall return to this theme by looking comparatively at the strengths and weaknesses of each account, arguing that none of them offers the whole story.

1.1 'Sex' and 'gender': what do they mean?

It is necessary to clarify the two central terms, sex and gender, and their relationship to one another. Why does the chapter title need to include both concepts? Take a look at Activity 3.1 and try answering the questions, then read the comment before reading on.

Activity 3.1

When you use the term 'sex', what are you referring to? Try to list several things you mean by the term.

When you use the term 'gender', what are you referring to? Try to list several things you mean by the term.

In constructing your lists think about the terms 'male' and 'female' and 'masculine' and 'feminine'. Do these pairs of terms have different resonances?

Comment

One response to the first two questions in this activity might be:

'Sex' means:

- the act of sexual intercourse
- the fact of being biologically male or biologically female
- 'being a man', 'being a woman'.

'Gender' means:

- the differences between the sexes (as they are manifested in behaviours, relationships, practices)
- coming across as, or feeling, 'masculine' or 'feminine'
- 'being a man', 'being a woman'.

These comments touch on two main themes: the range of different meanings between 'male/female' and 'masculine/feminine' and the either/or of being a man or being a woman. These are discussed further in the following sections.

First consider the definition of sex as the act of sexual intercourse. At first glance, the inclusion of this definition appears to mean something different from the sex or gender of a person. Why is the same term used? Presumably the connection is in the idea of sexual reproduction and the necessity of two different sexes (of fertile age and status) to take part in the act. This assumes heterosexual sex, however. The understanding of homosexual or heterosexual partner choice is one that deserves a whole chapter to itself and we cannot focus on it here. Our focus is on the meanings that cohere around the feeling of 'being a woman' or 'being a man'. Often 'sexuality' is used to refer to this more psychological object of knowledge, whereas 'sex' refers to a biological or anatomical differentiation. To complicate matters, 'sexuality' also commonly refers to sexual orientation, that is: homo or heterosexuality.

1.2 From 'male/female' to 'masculine/feminine'

'Male' or 'female' is usually a simple assignment after the birth of a baby, based on visible genital differences. We use the terms to make a morphological distinction at the birth of a child and assume that other biological differences between the sexes (such as hormone levels, patterns of hair growth and loss, height, voice register and muscular strength) will fall into line in the course of sexual development.

However, these characteristics are not distributed in a strictly dichotomous way. It is only when averages are used that men and women come out looking so distinctly different. Many individual attributes that are characterised as 'typically' male or female, such as being tall or short and deep- or high-voiced, have *overlapping distributions*. Despite this, our perceptions, language and social practices place humans into one of two mutually exclusive categories – 'female' or 'male'.

The attribution of 'femininity' and 'masculinity' is also done on a dichotomous basis. The idea that these attributes are dichotomously opposed seems to be part of the straitjacket of gender difference, for are we not all a bit of a mixture? Carl Jung was probably the first psychological thinker to introduce the notion of *androgyny*: the coexistence of masculine and feminine characteristics in a single person. Later, Sandra Bem became well known for her measure of androgyny, published in 1974. She used a list of adjectives and asked people to decide if each word was referring to 'masculine' or 'feminine' characteristics (see Activity 3.2).

Activity 3.2

Which sex do you think each of the following adjectives from the Bem Sex Role Inventory (BSRI) refers to:

Affectionate, analytical, forceful, loyal, sympathetic, flatterable, individualistic, ambitious, compassionate, cheerful. (The answer is at the end of the chapter.)

Bem used *m* and *f* (masculinity and femininity) measures from scores on the BSRI and found high and low scorers on *m* and *f*, among both women and men (more specifically among Californian students of both sexes in a Hippie era). In other words, she found that masculinity and femininity did not necessarily tally with people being male and female. This is important because it makes clear that gendered characteristics do not follow biological sex differences. There is a world of difference between male/female and masculine/feminine: whereas the former are supposedly biologically prescribed, the latter are psychological characteristics, shaped by the experience of growing up within certain relationships, language possibilities, practices, role models, structures of expectation and opportunity. This has been the traditional distinction between 'sex' and 'gender': the distinction between the biological and the social (see Activity 3.1). There is a problem distinguishing between the two terms, however, because, as we shall see in this chapter, biological sex is expressed in behaviour that is influenced by social arrangements and psychological meanings. Therefore sex and gender can only be separated out for theoretical purposes.

As you read through this chapter, notice the use of the phrase 'the other sex' rather than 'the opposite sex'. Avoiding the use of the term 'opposite sex' unsettles the idea that men and women can be defined by their opposite characteristics.

In using 'the other sex', you should note the active effect that words have. They do not simply reflect meaning, they also create it. For example, the common usage of 'opposite sex' serves to encourage us to forget the many characteristics that women and men have in common and the way that both sexes combine so-called masculine and feminine attributes.

Notice that, in Activity 3.1, 'being a man' or 'being a woman' was listed under the categories of both sex and gender. This is where the overlap is between the categories 'sex' and 'gender': in the 'being'. The idea of 'being' itself needs quite a bit of unpacking. This refers to the *experience* of being a woman or a man, living one's life from within a gendered identity, however taken for granted, however fraught with conflict. Sexual difference is a rule of human culture (a rule that is occasionally broken) and it is impossible to develop a sense of who one is without reference, not only to one's sex, but to one's gender, which includes the social meanings and practices that surround that sex. A *psychology* of sex and gender should have something illuminating to say about the *experience* of being either a woman or a man.

1.3 The either/or of being a man and being a woman

In 1970, in the US, Broverman and her colleagues conducted a study that explored the use of sex-role stereotypes in clinical judgements of mental health.

3.1 Sex-role stereotypes and judgements of women's mental health (Broverman et al., 1970)

Broverman *et al.* (1970) asked many clinically-trained mental health professionals (including both men and women and ranging from 23 to 55 years old) to fill in a 122-item questionnaire containing behavioural adjectives such as aggressive, independent, hides emotions, competitive, acts as leader, talkative, gentle, expresses tender feelings. Each adjective had two poles, for example 'very aggressive' and 'not at all aggressive'. The participants were asked to indicate, on each item, which pole would be closer to a 'mature, healthy, socially competent' adult. One third of the clinicians filled out the questionnaire for an adult, sex unspecified, one third for a man and one third for a woman.

Both the women and men described the 'mature, healthy, socially competent adult' and the 'mature, healthy, socially competent man' in virtually identical terms. The 'mature, healthy, socially competent woman' differed 'by being more submissive, less independent, less adventurous, more easily influenced, less aggressive, less competitive, more excitable in minor crises, having their feelings more easily hurt, being more emotional...'(Broverman *et al.*, 1970, p.4).

There are four important points to draw from this study:

1 Mental health professionals drew on common categories about differences between the sexes.

2 They equated what it was to be a man with what it was to be an adult. Men were taken as the human norm and women were contrasted to this.

3 The values contained in the judgements put women in a very contradictory position, namely that to live up to being a mature, healthy socially competent woman, she had to be suitably 'feminine', even though the traits associated with femininity were very different and often the opposite of those desirable in a mature, healthy, socially competent adult.

4 It is important to locate this study both in time and place and not to universalize its findings. It is unlikely that all of these stereotypes are still in use now at the start of the twenty-first century.

Sex role stereotype
Based on beliefs about typical masculine or feminine behaviour. Using sex-role stereotypes (also known as gender stereotype) tends to exaggerate the differences between women and men and underestimate people's individuality.

What is the difference between a descriptor, such as 'gentle', and a **sex-role stereotype***? In the 1970s, with the growth of feminism both outside and inside psychology, the study of sex-roles and stereotyping became influential in social psychology. Sex roles were seen as a product of socialization influences that* *imposed differences on girls and boys. Stereotypes were thought of as distorting lenses used to accentuate behavioural differences between the genders. The biological origins of these behavioural differences were strongly contested, because they made them appear unchangeable. However, socialization could presumably influence girls to be more 'caring' than boys, irrespective of whether 'caring' is a stereotype about women's behaviour. In this case, to use the adjective 'caring' might reflect reality – albeit a social constructed reality. The clinicians participating in Broverman et al.'s study might have been basing their judgements on clinical experience, rather than, or as well as, using stereotypes, which by implication means imposing distortions.*

The tendency to treat men and women as having separate and opposite characteristics was particularly pronounced in psychological research that employed the psychometric approach to measure sex differences. By the 1970s, this type of research was regularly reported in scientific psychology journals. Such studies would test both women and men, for example on spatial ability, then a statistical test of significance would be done to discover whether the two sexes had performed differently. Maccoby and Jacklin (1974) evaluated hundreds of published articles concentrating upon performance differentials between men and women. They called into question the interpretations of studies that often dwelt on girls' poorer performance – for example on intelligence tests and in maths. Their book became a reference point for feminists who were suspicious of the way in which psychological research was reporting so many sex differences that found boys and men doing better. The guidelines set out in Box 3.2 are the result of feminist psychologists' criticism of poor scientific practice in writing and publishing reports.

3.2 FEATURED METHOD

Guidelines for non-sexist research on gender differences

Janet Hyde (1994) pointed out that many studies of sex differences did not follow basic procedures of good science. She recommended that:

- Researchers and journal editors should take care that research that found no significant gender differences was published. (This is often not the case because journals tend to be interested only in findings of significant differences.) Failure to publish research that finds no significant sex differences has meant that publicly available knowledge in psychology has been biased towards highlighting gender differences not gender similarities.

- Published papers should take care to specify the magnitude of any gender differences.

- Interpretations of sex differences should be careful not to start off with the assumption of the male standard as norm and women's difference as problematic.

- Researchers should not infer biological differences from performance tests based on behaviour. Biological differences should only be invoked if biological measures have been collected.

Extracted and modified from J. Hyde (1994).

Feminists were wary of biological arguments because they were so readily used to suggest that women's and men's characteristics were unchangeable, although as we shall see, this is not an accurate extrapolation from biological psychology.

Hyde's guidelines are one example of the results of feminist politics taking a critical look at scientific psychology and questioning whether it had been as objective as claimed when measuring sex differences. She and many others concluded that science *could* be objective if practices were improved along the above lines (e.g. Eagly, 1994; Halpern, 1994). Other feminist psychologists became so sceptical about the possibility of an objective scientific psychology that they started developing alternative methods of inquiry and other criteria of evidence. While these challenges have affected all branches of psychology, the debate has raged most fiercely, not surprisingly, where psychologists are studying sex and gender. As you read the following sections, bear in mind, therefore, that the perspectives you come across vary not only in their theoretical forms but also in their political and ideological implications. These political implications can often be discerned in the object of knowledge and even in the use of a word (sex or gender?). We hope that this introduction enables you to read the following sections with an increased capacity to notice how these terms are being used, what effects they have for the understanding of what it is to be a woman, or to be a man, and how these relate to what we share as human beings.

Summary Section 1

- The psychology of sex and gender illustrates many of the difficult issues that psychological explanations must address, including the political implications of different perspectives and the challenge of integrating explanations including biological, evolutionary, social and psychoanalytic.
- The four perspectives presented in this chapter pose somewhat different questions, have different objects of knowledge and use different notions of evidence. These perspectives may be complementary, conflicting or may simply coexist.

- Sex is commonly used to refer to the biological basis of differences between the sexes, whereas gender usually refers to socially constructed categories pertaining to these differences.
- The psychological question of what it is to be a woman or a man provides a bridge between definitions of sex and gender.
- Masculine and feminine are categories that do not necessarily follow from being male and female. This idea is the basis of the concept of androgyny.
- In the 1970s, political differences were expressed about the measurement of sex differences, with challenges by feminist psychologists to scientific practices. These challenges have broadened and contributed new approaches to psychological investigation.

2   A biological psychology of sex and gender

This section describes some of the various methods used to 'sex' humans, and will identify some of the problems with each of these methods. It evaluates some of the evidence for structural (anatomical) differences in male and female human brains. Finally it illustrates the complex implications of approaching the question 'what enables us to become a woman or a man?' from a biological perspective.

2.1 Male or female? Sexing human bodies

It is surprisingly difficult to come up with universal and infallible biologically-based rules to define what is a male or a female human being. A part of this difficulty arises because a number of different methods are used to classify male and female humans and the results from one method do not always agree with the results from another.

Physical characteristics

The most obvious method, and the one that is most commonly used to 'sex' children after birth, is observation of the external (visible) genitals. In most cases (more than 98 per cent) this is a simple and reliable method of sexing babies. However, this method is not always straightforward. Neonates (newborn infants) are exposed to hormones circulating in their mothers' blood prior to and during birth, and these, together with the mechanical pressure associated with vaginal birth, can cause swelling of various portions of the genitals so as to make it difficult to identify male or female genitals clearly. Moreover, one person in every 500 is born with genitals that do not match their sex chromosomes, although they may never know it. Even when the assessment of the external genitals looks correct, the sex organs that are visible on the outside of the body may not necessarily match those inside the child. There are several recorded cases of boys who, early in development, have much reduced levels of an enzyme that would enable boys to produce a version of the typical 'male' hormone, testosterone. As a result, these boys have visible sex organs that look most like those of a female. They begin producing normal levels of this testosterone-like substance from (internal) testes at puberty, the penis grows and the testes descend from the groin, so in terms of external genitals, the children appear to switch from female to male at puberty. These cases are the exception rather than the norm. Nevertheless they do rule out observation of the external genitals at birth as a totally foolproof mechanism of determining sex.

Hormones

Sex organs, or at least their early external appearance, depend on hormones. Moreover, some psychologists suggest that the action of hormones during development also determines some behaviour patterns and the structure of some regions of the brain. Adult hormone profiles, or the relative levels of the various 'sex' hormones such as testosterone ('male'), oestrogens and progesterone ('female'), can also be used to help define male or female humans. However, a simple hormone screening test cannot be conclusively used to differentiate males from females for the following reasons.

- Sex hormones are produced in different amounts in different individuals and at different stages of development. For example, young children usually have lower levels of the sex hormones and more balanced sex hormone profiles than adults.
- Both males and females mostly have both 'male' and 'female' hormones and so it is the *balance* (the relative levels) of these hormones, rather than their mere presence, that generally produces the secondary sexual characteristics commonly associated with men and women.
- The 'male' hormones can be chemically converted to 'female' hormones within both the body and the brain, so it is not only the level of a specific hormone produced, but also what happens chemically to that hormone that is important for understanding its actions, particularly on brain structure and behaviour.
- Even if the hormone profile, assessed from a standard blood sample, falls into the normal range for one sex, the hormones may not be able to send the normal messages to the body tissues because they lack receptors for that hormone. (If you need to remind yourself what a receptor is, look back at Chapter 4 of Book 1). This means that the hormonal message is sent, but the

body does not have the receivers to be able to action the message. The most commonly cited example of this is **androgen insensitivity syndrome** (AIS).

● It is possible to ingest synthetic hormones and so alter the 'natural' hormone balance. For example oestrogens are sometimes used as a part of treatment for some cancers. Does this make men having this treatment female? The common answer is 'of course not' because most people recognize that it is more than just your hormone profile at a particular stage of life that makes you male or female.

Genes

Can biologists come up with a universal rule for sex determination using genetic screening tests? Humans usually have 23 pairs of chromosomes, one of which is used to direct the sex of the person. Males typically have different chromosomes in this pair; an 'X' and a 'Y' (so called because they are said to resemble an 'X' and a 'Y' under the microscope). Women typically have two 'X' chromosomes. In the vast majority of cases this sort of genetic test can show the pattern of sex chromosomes people have – defining them as men or women. But even genetic testing is not quite as conclusive as was originally thought. Estimates suggest that around 1 in 500 men have **Klinefelter's syndrome** – which means that they have an XXY genotype. AIS (referred to above) is even more rare (around 1 in 20,000), but it is interesting as some of those with AIS may look like women and have lived their lives as women but have an XY (or sometimes XXY) genotype.

Androgen insensitivity syndrome
Medical syndrome affecting 1 in 20,000 of those born with an XY genetic make-up and affecting the typical male/female bodily appearance. Symptoms include infertility and external genitalia that can range from completely male to completely female. Those with the syndrome may be raised as either male or female.

Klinefelter's syndrome
Medical syndrome affecting 1 in 500 males, in which the typical male chromosomal complement – XY – is replaced by XXY. Accompanying features are unusually tall stature, enlarged breasts, infertility and problems such as diabetes.

3.3 Genetic sex testing

At the Sydney Olympics in 2000, officials abandoned genetic sex testing. This was sparked, at least in part, by several cases of ostensibly female athletes who were found to have a Y chromosome. As such they had previously been excluded from competition. The rationale for this exclusion was that, because they had high levels of testosterone being produced from internal testes (a kind of inbuilt steroid treatment), they had an unfair advantage. But as these women had AIS, the testosterone did not significantly alter their physiology and so the claim that they had an unfair advantage was unfounded. This internally produced testosterone did not 'make' these women men, just as an extra X chromosome in men with Klinefelter's syndrome (XXY) does not 'make' these men women (though in both syndromes, the profile of genetic, hormonal and bodily characteristics is extremely atypical for the assigned sex).

While these genetic abnormalities are, by definition, unusual, they do make the point that it is not just our genes that make us male or female. Hormones are produced from the actions of genes and, while they usually fall into 'female' and 'male' patterns they are also not invariably a reliable measure of sex. Sex organs and secondary sexual characteristics depend on hormones and, as such, are also not completely reliable indicators of 'sex'. Yet, as we saw in the introduction, all human cultures divide people into either men or women. Is there a clear biological basis for sex differences?

2.2 Male or female brains?

As is generally recognized, adult women and men often behave differently. Just as with height or weight, the two populations overlap, but there are some behaviours more common to one sex than the other. Why is this? Could it be because they have different brains? As with height and weight, men tend to have larger brains than women. However, most evidence suggests that brain size in mammals, including humans, is proportional to body size and so it seems unlikely that sex differences are due to brain size alone.

It seems more likely that there are differences in the *parts* of brain that are involved in the processing of different tasks in which men or women seem to excel. This hypothesis is based, in part, on some experiments using rats. Male and female rats have very different sexual behaviours and scientists have shown that these behaviours depend on the balance of hormones that is present during a critical period of early development. Males usually mount females whereas receptive females adopt a lordosis position (with arched back and head up). However, by providing male rats with 'female-type' hormones, or female rats with 'male' hormones, during their critical period of early development, it was possible to show reversed sexual behaviours, so that treated females mostly attempted to mount other rats, while treated males mostly adopted the lordosis position (Young, 1964; Beach, 1938). These differences were shown to match differences in a brain structure called the *sexually dimorphic nucleus* of the *preoptic area* (SDN–POA). This area of the brain demonstrates **sexual dimorphism**.

Sexual dimorphism
Where a part of the body (including the brain) shows visible differences between males and females.

Testosterone was shown to be converted into a female-type hormone in the brain (estradiol) and to induce the SDN-POA to become larger. Thus, there was a difference in brain structure that correlated with a difference in sexual behaviour (Fitch and Denenberg, 1998). Of course, experimental studies of this kind cannot be conducted on humans. Is there any evidence of differences between human males and females in comparable brain regions?

Human brain region differences?

Biologists have examined a brain area in humans that is comparable to the SDN–POA, and the initial studies suggested that it may be larger in men than in women (the INAH-1 region; Swaab and Fliers, 1985). Later studies suggested that, while *this* brain region was not sexually dimorphic, two other adjacent regions, (INAH-2 and INAH-3), were indeed larger in males than in females

(Allen and Gorski, 1990). Still further studies have shown sexual dimorphism in only one of these regions – INAH-3 (LeVay, 1991). It therefore seems that sexually dimorphic brain regions are much harder to describe consistently in humans than in other animals (Cooke *et al.*, 1998). Researchers generally do not find sex differences in these brain regions in children less than 6–10 years old (Hofman and Swaab, 1991). We have to be careful how to interpret this finding. Although it suggests that the influences of genes and early hormones have not affected this brain region during childhood, this does not necessarily rule out the effects of genes and early hormones on later sex differences. Many later aspects of development – for example changes at puberty or patterns of ageing – are shaped by genes and early appearing hormones in interaction with environmental factors. In other words, the effects of both genes and hormones can be set up around birth but triggered later.

Before discussing the mostly commonly reported brain sex difference, it is worth considering the measurement methods such studies use. These methods are considered in Featured Method Box 3.4.

3.4 FEATURED METHOD

Techniques for measuring brain differences

Brain regions in people are usually measured either manually in post-mortem tissue or by brain imaging techniques, such as MRI in living tissue. Neither method is completely reliable:

- Using post mortem tissue dissection: this method needs to take into account any effects of the accident or disease that brought the person to the morgue on the brain tissue to be measured. Furthermore, chemicals such as formalin used to preserve brain tissue are known to induce uneven shrinkage.

- Using MRI measurements: these involve many individual observations which are averaged by a computer. This could potentially lead to errors, although these would be unlikely to have systematic effects on the identification of sex differences. The number of such studies completed thus far is relatively small, so we need to consider how well these results generalize. (For example, MRI studies are almost always conducted in developed countries and use participants from those countries. Any potential findings might conceivably reflect plastic changes due to Western social arrangements.)

As mentioned in the introduction, studies that do not show sex differences are less likely to be published than those that show differences. This applies also to these medical methods, perhaps skewing the available data towards findings of sex differences.

Corpus callosum
A thick tract of neurons connecting the two hemispheres of the human brain, which enables the two sides of the brain to 'talk' to each other.

Using these methods researchers have investigated the possibility of sex differences in the area of the brain called the **corpus callosum**, which enables the two sides of the brain to 'talk' to each other (see figure 3.1 below). Like any piece of brain tissue, the corpus callosum is divided into various sub-regions. Some researchers suggest that sex differences might lie in the thickness of various sections of the corpus callosum, such as the splenium. There have been a number of studies, some of which show some larger splenium regions in women, and others that fail to replicate these findings but show women as having other larger callosal regions (all regions aside from the splenium, see Rogers, 1999). The effect of a larger splenium region in females is hard to explain, because the splenium seems to carry visual information from one hemisphere to the other and thus aid in visuo-spatial ability, yet behaviourally, visuo-spatial abilities seem to be more developed in men (Fausto-Sterling, 2000). In general there appear to be difficulties in interpreting such sex differences in the size of the corpus callosum (Bishop and Wahlsten, 1997).

While the evidence for sex differences in the size or shape of brain sub-regions in adult humans is ambiguous, recent fMRI studies have shown that adult men and women do tend to use some brain regions differently (Schneider *et al.*, 2000). Again, this does not necessarily mean that these differences are present from birth. As you saw in Chapter 4 of Book 1, the brain is not fixed throughout life but rather is 'plastic' and able to change. The human brain continues to grow and change substantially after birth, the total amount of brain tissue not peaking until between 12 and 18 years old (Giedd *et al.*, 1999). Some smaller changes are possible even after this time. Animal studies have shown that brain regions, neuronal cell numbers and even synapse numbers can rapidly increase and decrease in direct response to both activity (use) and hormonal conditions throughout life. This is important because the plasticity of brain structures is consistent with the claim that sex differences in brain and behaviour are not due solely to what is specified either at conception (genes + maternal environment) or at birth (genes + early hormones + early environment). Sex differences could be the result of interactions between biological, psychological and social processes. All of these clearly play a role in the anatomy and functioning of the brain. In simple terms, genes, hormones *and* environment all interact in influencing women's and men's brains to become differentiated according to uses and experiences that are themselves gender differentiated.

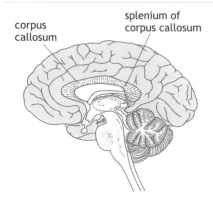

corpus callosum

splenium of corpus callosum

Figure 3.1　　The corpus callosum

Imagine you decide to become a cyclist. To be successful, you will need well-developed thigh muscles, so you start training to build these up. You become successful and someone says that this is because you have well-developed thigh muscles. BUT is this because you have exercised or because you were genetically 'pre-destined' for physical excellence? Most likely it reflects an ongoing interaction between environment (e.g. training opportunities), genetic endowments (e.g. bone structure and muscle fibre types) and motivation.

It's clearly very difficult to separate these different factors as they work so closely together. As we learn more about genetics, physiology and psychology it is becoming increasingly clear that a simple dichotomy between nature and nurture is not tenable.

2.3 Biological factors in behavioural and cognitive gender differences

Are biological influences involved in generating differences in behaviour and cognitive skills between girls and boys? One famous study that examined this question was by Money and Erhardt (1972). In this study they looked at the 'masculinization' of the behaviour of girls who had been exposed to 'male-type' hormones *in utero* due to the administration of an anti-miscarriage drug progestin. They compared the behaviour of these girls with their sisters, who had not been exposed to progestin and also with girls who had adrenal hyperplasia (a condition in which girls have higher than average levels of the male hormone testosterone, produced by the adrenal glands). In all cases they asked the mothers to report whether the girls liked playing with 'girls toys' or 'boys toys', what sort of clothes they liked and the style of their play. (It's worth noting the 'implicit' understanding in this study of what is girlish and what is boyish.) They found that both the girls affected by hyperplasia and the progestin-affected girls seemed to play in a more boisterous 'tomboy' manner, that they preferred boys clothes, that they had higher IQ scores and showed a non-traditional pattern of preference for career over marriage. (This was at a time when most women felt that they had to choose one or the other.) However, the study employed directed questions (such as 'is your affected girl more tomboyish than your other girl?') which might have tended to bias responses. Moreover, some of the sisters of the affected girls also showed 'tomboy-like' behaviour patterns – suggesting that this was not just an effect of the altered hormonal profiles. In a follow-up study, which addressed these methodological difficulties, the only remaining difference found was that the hormonally affected girls seemed to play more energetically (Baker and Erhardt, pp.53–84, 1974).

Brain lateralization
Structural or functional
asymmetry in the brain.

Other research has reported differences between girls and boys in cognitive abilities, and particularly in mathematical ability. All of these findings, and especially those relating to mathematics, have generated controversy. In the US, Hyde conducted a large-scale meta-analysis of one hundred studies, representing the test results from over three million people. She found a very small difference in male and female distributions for cognitive ability and argued that the uncritical acceptance of these studies has promoted the idea that sex-based cognitive differences are more significant than they in fact are (Hyde, pp.207–23, 1990). However, those who accept sex-based differences in ability point to different **brain lateralization** between girls and boys as a causal basis for this result. There is evidence that the right and left hemispheres specialize in different cognitive functions: the left in language and the right in visuo-spatial and mathematical functioning. Relatively enhanced development of the left or right hemisphere respectively was thought to correspond with girls' and boys' respective strengths as measured on cognitive tests.

In conclusion, the search for biological correlates of behavioural and cognitive differences between the sexes is a complex and confusing one. The main lesson seems to be that a single influence such as a sex hormone does not alone make the difference between becoming male or female. Indeed, only in non-human animals does it appear to have a clear-cut influence on particular behaviours, for example mounting or lordosis, and effects on specific brain regions. The effects of biological processes in human beings are likely to be more complex as a result of our unique capacity to reflect on our experiences, and modify our behaviour accordingly.

Summary Section 2

- Assigning a sex to humans is sometimes a complex process. Biological characteristics (genetic, hormonal or molecular), used to designate 'male' or 'female', are unreliable in a small proportion of cases.
- In humans, unlike in other animals such as rats, clear-cut differences in brain structures that correlate with differences in adult behaviour patterns have proved difficult to demonstrate.
- Nonetheless, imaging studies show some sex differences in brain functioning of Western adults. This is probably due, at least in part, to brain plasticity.
- While some sex differences are clearly established at birth for most individuals, bodies and brains may become *gendered* over a lifetime of use.

3 An evolutionary psychology perspective on differences between the sexes

What light can evolutionary psychology throw on the question – 'what is it to be a man or a woman'? Evolutionary psychologists would argue that there are few consistent differences between the sexes. However, one of the areas in which evolutionary psychologists do assert that there are some differences is in sexual behaviours and attitudes. This is because of the different reproductive strategies that have evolved in men and in women.

Activity 3.3

Before reading further, go back to Chapter 2 of Book 1 and remind yourself of the core concepts in evolutionary psychology. In particular, look at Section 2 on what evolution is and how it works.

3.1 Parental investment and its implications

To explain sex differences, evolutionary psychologists focus particularly on the processes involved in sexual selection. This, as you will remember, relates to the characteristics or patterns of behaviour that promote reproductive success (that is, **optimal reproductive style**). There are critical differences in the process of successful reproduction between males and females and hence in their optimal reproductive styles. Specifically, females have what evolutionary biologists (e.g. Trivers, 1972) call a greater **'parental investment'** in their offspring, in that considerable effort and energy is necessarily required for every infant they produce. For primate females, this involves a long period of gestation and most likely a long period of suckling and care. This means they can usually bear relatively few offspring during a limited period of their lives. For males on the other hand, only a few minutes of copulatory activity may be required. The only limit on the number of offspring they can have is the availability of potential mates. Evolutionary psychologists argue that this basic difference means that reproductive success for the two sexes in primate species would have been best achieved by different patterns of behaviour.

Evolutionary psychologists do not argue that animals or humans used conscious and deliberate strategies to achieve a particular type of behaviour in

Optimal reproductive style
Characteristics and behaviours that are most likely to result in producing children/ descendants.

Parental investment
The amount of energy and effort required to produce and rear offspring.

order to maximise reproductive success. Rather, they argue that the behaviour that just happened to result in reproductive success will have been selected for by evolutionary pressures precisely *because* of the reproductive advantage that it conferred. As modern primates are all the descendants of male and female ancestors who were successful reproducers, the sexual behaviours of males and females today are the result of reproductively successful behaviours that have been selected for over the history of the species.

Evolutionary psychologists infer that, given the relatively few offspring a female primate could produce (and thus her greater reproductive investment), being choosy would have been very important. For her, reproductive success depended on her selection of circumstances (including a mate) that were likely to ensure that her relatively few offspring would survive to sexual maturity and so in their turn pass on her genes.

By contrast, for a male, with his far more extensive potential capacity to reproduce, number of matings would have been the critical factor. For if these matings were sufficiently frequent, and particularly if they were with fertile and healthy mates, this would have been an effective reproductive strategy.

However, given that females would have been choosy about which males they mated with, male primates would have to compete with each other for females who, in terms of sexual availability, were in shorter supply. One result of this male competition would be much greater variability in reproductive success among males than among females. For while the majority of females would have had little difficulty in ensuring that they had offspring (as males would be competing to mate with them), some males would have succeeded in fathering many offspring but others may well not have produced any at all.

One consequence of this would be that characteristics promoting reproductive success in the face of competition, such as strength and size, would have been selected for in males. Thus ancestral human males evolved to have greater body weight and size in relation to females. In modern humans, men are on average 1.15 times bigger than women. The ratio in other species varies and (consistent with the reasoning above) appears to be related to the degree of sexual competitiveness. In the case of chimps, where there is considerable competition in selection of sexual partners, males are about 1.3 times as big as females. It is worth noting that there are a few species of birds and fish in which male investment in the caring and rearing of offspring is greater than that of females. In such species, there is female competition for males and females are often the larger and more aggressive sex. The kinds of difference we are discussing here are all average ones, of course. They derive from overlapping distributions and do not mean that all men are, for example, heavier and taller than all women.

Pursuing the same line of reasoning, if females evolved to maximize their own reproductive success, their choice of mate in particular would need to have been consistent with this. As well as selecting a fertile, healthy mate capable of producing healthy and reproductively successful children, a female would choose factors like status and resources, which would ensure a protective base for the long process of rearing her children. However, these would not be relevant unless the mate was prepared to commit such resources to the relationship and children. So male commitment would also have been a key criterion. In other words, those females who happened to choose males on the basis of such features would have been likely to produce most offspring and so the predilection to choose in this way would have been selected for in females. Note that, one of the difficult questions this raises is how female primates might have recognised characteristics such as commitment in potential mates.

3.2 Particular features of human evolution

So far, our discussion has concentrated upon primates generally, because, as with humans, their long gestation and suckling times suggest differences in parental investment between mother and father. But what about humans in particular? Are there any features specific to the evolution of our human ancestors that might have influenced their optimal reproductive styles and therefore, according to evolutionary psychologists, had some consequences for contemporary human sex differences?

One difference between humans and other primates is that, as a result of the evolution of an upright gait, the human pelvic girdle took on a size and shape that served to constrain the size of the neonate's brain at birth. So full development of the much larger brain, characteristic of the human primate, can only take place after birth. This, coupled with the need for sophisticated socialization that the development of language and culture made necessary, meant a longer period of dependency for human infants than for other primates. The upshot, evolutionary psychologists argue, is that behaviour that resulted in paternal investment (resources and support) would have taken on increased significance in ensuring survival of infants to sexual maturity.

The emergence of human sexual behaviour was also affected by the fact that human females have 'hidden oestrus': in contrast to other primates, there are no obvious signs of ovulation and human females may mate at any time during the menstrual cycle. A consequence of this is that pair bonding (which allows for consistent mating over time) and 'mate guarding' – ensuring that no other male has sexual access to his mate – also became important strategies for human males in ensuring their reproductive success. Whereas a female can be confident that a child is hers, for males paternity is never assured. Given this and human males' greater paternal investment, it is argued that human males have become particularly sensitive to female sexual infidelity.

The way that evolutionary psychologists seek to test their claims about the effects of genetic selection on contemporary human sexual behaviour is illustrated in a study on jealousy (Buss *et al.*, 1992). They found that, while both men and women reported experiencing jealousy at the thought of their partner being involved with another person, there were differences in the focus of their concerns. For men, it was the thought of sexual infidelity that triggered the most intense feelings of jealousy, whereas for women it was the possibility of their partner's emotional involvement with another. Similar studies have now confirmed this finding in a variety of cultures from China to Sweden (Geary *et al.*, 1995; Wiedermann and Kendall, 1999). Buss interprets this as in line with the evolutionary psychology prediction, namely that commitment would be valued by both sexes but for rather different reasons: for males it would be related to their particular concern for sexual fidelity, for females to the need to ensure continuation of support and resource.

3.3 Differences in sexual style

Evolutionary arguments have been further extended to explain observed differences between contemporary men and women in sexual attitudes and behaviours. Such differences are not only the regular diet of Western magazine discussions, media portrayal (e.g. Fielding, 1997; 2000) and popular psychology (e.g. Gray, 1993) but, as we shall see, have been documented in research studies involving both experiments and questionnaires with respondents from many cultures.

There is considerable evidence of difference between men and women, for example, in the *style of their sexual interest*, as exemplified in an experiment carried out on an American college campus by Clark and Hatfield (1989). An attractive stranger approached participants of the other sex, engaged them in conversation, and then made one of three invitations: to a) go out with them that night, or b) go back to their home, or c) have sex with them. Their results showed that while about 50 per cent of both men and women who were approached agreed to a date, only 6 per cent of the women who were approached compared with 69 per cent of the men were prepared to go to the stranger's college apartment. None of the women who were approached, compared with 75 per cent of the men, consented to sex. The investigators interpreted these results as being consistent with evolutionary psychology arguments about evolved optimal reproductive style. As it might be possible that women's greater physical vulnerability could better explain the difference found, the investigators analysed the reasons given by both women and men for refusing sex. They found these to be more or less identical (reasons such as they had a boy/girl friend or they did not know the person well enough) and the women's explanations placed no special emphasis on potential danger. Also, in a follow-up experiment (Clark, 1990), participants were given various assurances by friends about the integrity and trustworthiness of the stranger. These seemed to have the effect intended in that no woman participant expressed any concern about her safety, but the results remained essentially the same.

Could there be alternative explanations that make sense of this finding? One is that many men internalize social expectations that, in order to be successfully masculine, they should express constant interest in heterosexual sex. Most women, on the other hand, have internalized the idea that 'nice girls don't'. Some evolutionary psychologists (e.g. Dunbar et al., 1999) have proposed that evolved behavioural predispositions underlie many of the cultural patterns that we observe. So one possibility here is that evolution may have shaped cultural practices that in turn serve to reinforce patterns of evolved behaviour. Western morals that have regulated women's sexuality have been changing however. Consider recent British reports about 'ladettes' (young women who behave in laddish ways), who among other things have sex with many men who are strangers to them. Among a 'ladette' group of participants, the finding of Clark and Hatfield's study would perhaps not be replicated.

You may also like to consider the ethical issues raised by experiments designed along these lines. Guidelines drawn up by the British Psychological Society (BPS) can be found in the Introduction to Book 1.

Sex differences in number of sexual partners desired and readiness to have sex with strangers has been documented in confidential questionnaires and other research studies in different cultures and periods (e.g. Johnson, 1970; Buss, 1989). Evolutionary psychologists also point out that, consistent with their thesis, prostitution is predominantly for the benefit of males. The Kinsey report of sexual behaviour (Kinsey *et al.*, 1948; 1953), for example, indicated that about 70 per cent of American men had visited a prostitute at some time in their lives, while for women the incidence was negligible. The vast majority of prostitutes in all cultures are women and male prostitutes mainly service gay clients (Bullough and Bullough, 1987; McCormick, 1994). Most men who go to prostitutes are already in ongoing sexual relationships (Holzman and Pines, 1982). Evolutionary psychologists infer from such research that prostitution provides many male clients with an outlet for their need for sexual variety while enabling them to maintain an ongoing committed relationship; it thus offers them a way of coping with urges that evolutionary pressure has selected for in their behaviour.

The male preference for sexual variety is also manifested, evolutionary psychologists argue, in the extensive use of pin-ups in male magazines like *Loaded* and *FHM* and in the high sales of soft-porn men's magazines. Where similar attempts have been made to produce magazines for women with photos of nude men, they have either foundered (e.g. *Viva*) or have largely tended to be purchased by gay men (e.g. *Playgirl*). If anything, women's magazines are dominated by photos of women rather than men.

It is worth remembering that evolutionary psychologists do not deny that evolutionary urges are overlaid by the effects of contemporary social arrangements or culture. They would therefore acknowledge that it is too simplistic to argue that evolutionary pressures are the sole explanation for some men's propensity to visit prostitutes or buy pornography.

Another area of contemporary behaviour which is claimed to be in keeping with evolutionary predictions is the *features in potential partners that men and women seem to find especially attractive.* Particularly salient dimensions for men are physical appearance and youth, which would both relate to reproductive capacity. All questionnaire studies on the topic suggest that, while for women physical attractiveness may be desirable, for men it is especially important. This finding runs across generations and cultures (Buss and Schmitt, 1993). While there is considerable historical and cultural variation in appreciation of different body types, Singh (1995) has found with participants from a range of cultures that what is consistently attractive to men is a ratio of waist to hip measurements of about 0.70. This ratio, he argues, differentiates the woman from pre-pubertal females and males (whose comparable ratio is more in the order of 0.90). It would also signal that a woman was not already pregnant.

For women across cultures, in contrast, height seems to be a particular attractor (Gregor, 1985; Jackson, 1992; Wiederman, 1993). A preference by female ancestors for taller and more powerful males would have been more likely to ensure protection and support and to result in taller male offspring who could in turn hold their own in the competition for both resources and sex. But most salient for women appear to be the situation and status of the prospective partner. A study of over 1000 personal ads, for example, found that women advertizing for partners mentioned good financial position as a desirable characteristic about eleven times more than did males (Wiederman, 1993). A major cross-cultural study (Buss, 1989) involving 37 cultures and 10,000 participants found that in all the countries studied, women more often rated financial prospects as a desirable attribute in a potential mate than did men. (There was some cultural variation however. In Japan, for example, women valued good financial prospects 150 per cent more than men: in the Netherlands the male/female difference was only 36 per cent). It has been argued that such differences are not explicable simply in terms of unequal economic power because financially successful women show an even more marked preference for wealthy men (Wiederman and Allgeier, 1992), whereas poorer men show no greater preference for high income women (Buss, 1989).

In the Buss study, while the general trend is in the same direction across cultures there is some evidence of cultural variation. This would support the idea that the value placed on financial prospects reflects a complex interaction between biological predispositions and the particular social contexts of different cultures.

In most societies, social status is typically geared to the command of resources a person is likely to have (Betzig, 1986). So reasoning from evolutionary principles might lead you to think that women would also be more interested in the status of potential partners than males would be. This is indeed what Buss (1989) found in the cross-cultural study mentioned above. Numerous questionnaire studies in the USA (e.g. Langhorne and Secord, 1955) have also found that women value status and prestige in partners (as well as factors such as education and ambition that may signal future success) much more highly than do males. However, evolutionary psychologists accept that individuals and subcultures will vary in terms of which particular criteria (e.g. power, wealth, intelligence or popularity) they take as indices of status.

Evolutionary psychologists argue that all the criteria noted above (height, resource power and status of males) would have been related to the potential for protection and support; and thus, they reason, would have been selected for in the mate preferences of our female ancestors.

3.4 Concluding points

Evolutionary psychologists are not implying that the preferences and feelings discussed here are conscious strategies. Rather they are predispositions to respond and behave in particular ways which have been selected for in human ancestors, as in other species, because of the potential of these predispositions for facilitating reproductive success. However, note that it is not the goal of reproductive success in itself that has been selected for, but the kinds of behaviour that would have resulted in this in the past.

While the evolutionary approach outlined here may provide insights into certain differences in human sexual behaviour, sexual *relationships* generally involve a complex configuration of cultural and individual influences. Given this complexity, evolutionary psychology can provide only limited understanding of sexual relationships.

Finally, and importantly, evolutionary psychologists emphasize that there is no implication that because certain differences in sexual styles and preferences have an evolutionary underpinning they should therefore be regarded as desirable. Their argument is that human preferences evolved only because they were the optimal strategies for reproductive success in our distant past. Given the enormous success of human strategies for survival and reproduction, the further optimization of reproductive success is not a crucial or even desirable goal for humans as a species in the present time. In fact, Buss (2000) argues that the problem for contemporary humans is that this ancestral heritage of sexual styles and predispositions can impose considerable costs in feelings of rejection, jealousy and unhappiness. His view is that only by becoming aware of the origins of male and female sexual differences can we hope to alleviate their often painful consequences.

Summary   Section 3

- Evolutionary psychologists argue that sexual selection and the different optimal reproductive styles of our male and female ancestors have resulted in some differences in the behavioural predispositions of the two sexes.
- These are seen to be particularly apparent in the area of sexual behaviours and attitudes.
- Their explanations would appear to be consistent with research findings from cross-cultural differences in male and female sexual behaviours.

4   The social construction of gender

In this section, you will be introduced to an explanation of gender differences that emphasizes their social origins. We ask how gender differences get reproduced and changed in specific social settings and use the example of contemporary British schooling to illustrate the kinds of research and argument that social constructionists offer of boys' and girls' preferences, behaviours and achievements.

In Chapter 1 of Book 1 and Chapter 2 of this book, you were introduced to a social constructionist perspective that proposed that the ways in which we understand the world and the things we consider 'true' are not just 'natural'. This perspective suggests that all knowledge – even knowledge that looks as if it is obvious and about reality – is constructed by people within their own particular historical and social contexts.

4.1 The social constructionist perspective

There is a postcard that shows a nurse holding up a newly born baby for the just-delivered mother to see, with the words 'Congratulations! It's a lesbian!' underneath. Jokes often work by taking our everyday, 'natural' assumptions and turning them upside down, contradicting or gainsaying them. Here the joke is about sex and sexuality. When a baby is born we usually congratulate someone not only on having a lovely baby, but on having a lovely little girl or boy. From the first moment of life the appearance of a baby's genitals is taken as a biological (natural) given that defines their reproductive role, and hence the sexual relations and behaviours that accompany that role. Gay sexuality presents a deep challenge to this notion of a causal chain between 'natural' biological (or reproductive) sex and sexuality, because it is not possible to tell from a baby's genitals whether s/he will identify themselves as gay in later life or have same-sex sex.

This joke could also prompt us to query other characteristics or attributes assumed to follow from the biological, reproductive status assigned from a baby's earliest moments. Social constructionists would argue that when we say 'Congratulations, it's a girl' we are using a shorthand that refers to the western stereotype of femininity (see Box 3.1). Of course there is a biological, reproductive sex encoded into a baby's genes and this, in interaction with the hormonal and physical environment *in utero*, will find physical expression in the baby's body. However, social constructionists also argue that an individual's behaviour cannot be directly explained by their biological, reproductive sex status alone.

Social constructionists argue that we construct the world to have two basic types of people, men and women, who are then produced as different in all kinds of other ways. This is partly achieved by the social identity processes described in Chapter 1 of Book 1. Social Identity Theory suggests that, when we see ourselves as belonging to a group or category, we try to maximize our perceived similarity to others in the group, and minimize it with others outside the group. In this way we derive a sense of social identity from our membership of groups, and from the differentiation of those groups and categories from each other. Gender is one of the most important and powerful of social categories by which individuals define themselves.

Activity 3.4

In the context of social identity theory, how might social constructionists explain the notion of the 'opposite sex' – that each gender is defined in terms of being opposite to the other?

In Chapter 2 of this book you were introduced to the ideas of discourse and subject positions through which individuals, as they engage with daily activities, create identities for themselves. Social constructionists suggest that there are many discourses of masculinity and femininity that are socially produced and reproduced through media, social relationships, the rules of institutions, and practices like applying for unemployment benefit, going to see a doctor, or (as we shall see below) going to school.

If you are finding these terms and ideas hard to remember, look back at Chapter 2 Section 4.2 to the worked example of the subject position, 'good mother'.

Individuals can use these discourses to create their own gendered subject positions as masculine or feminine in a variety of ways. Discourses will change as they are used in different circumstances and in relation to different contexts, but they are always produced and reproduced through language. The social constructionist position, as you saw in Chapter 2, is that language is used to construct the world and accomplish particular actions within it, and in this section we will explore gender as one very powerful discourse through which this is done. In the context of our attempt to understand the process of becoming a man or woman, we shall look at how gendered subject positions affect how children understand achievement at school, and in their school subjects. In particular we shall explore the notion that the 'oppositeness' of sex has become a key part of these gendered subject positions. Social constructionists would argue that, in the process of becoming a man or a woman, school occupies a very powerful place, providing a set of highly differentiated discourses about gender-appropriate positions for girls and boys that are incorporated into every aspect of life. It is argued that these will influence career paths in terms of choices about occupation, the aims and goals of personal relationships and responsibility for child-rearing (and hence access to income, social position and expectations of the future), which will have an enduring effect throughout adult life.

3.5 Social construction of gender

In the social constructionist account of what it is to become a man or a woman, reproductive sex is seen as an easily identifiable sign of difference between the sexes that provides the basis for building a whole edifice of constructed gender differences. It is these constructed gender differences, not sexual or reproductive status or potential, which constitute what it is to be a man or woman and explain our behaviours and experiences.

In certain cultural traditions, this social construction of a man or woman is made particularly clear when biological females live as men under certain conditions. For example, in remote parts of Albania, if the male line in a family cannot take on its traditional masculine duties, a woman, who becomes known as an 'avowed virgin', takes the place of the absent son. 'They obey an unwritten rule which requires them never to marry or have children. When a girl adopts the mantle of 'paterfamilias', she cuts her hair short, dresses as a boy and takes on a man's job. The men and village elders accord the 'virgins' all the rights and privileges of fellow males.' (*Guardian*, May 7, 1996).

4.2 From gender as construct to constructing gender

Since the Second World War, Westerners have lived through a period of rapid social change in which women's and men's roles have been constantly transforming. Girls and women began to enter the workforce and higher education in increasing numbers and, in the 1960s, they gained access to a contraceptive pill that allowed control of their own fertility for the first time in history. Correspondingly some psychologists began to move away from seeing gender as simply the social expression of biologically grounded difference. Sandra Bem (1981) and others (for example, Spence, 1984) worked within an avowedly feminist framework to develop models of gender as related to identity construction. Bem's Gender Schema Theory proposed that individuals absorb culturally produced understandings of gender that they then use to interpret and make sense of themselves and their behaviour. These understandings are acquired as children learn to see the world through what Bem later described as the 'cultural lenses' of femininity and masculinity (1994). By this she means that masculinity and femininity are socially and culturally constructed dimensions that inform all the forms of our thinking, emotional experience and behaviour. In this analogy they literally condition and colour what we 'see' in our social and personal lives, constructing the world as a gendered place.

Social constructionists, however, do not see gender as a set of characteristics or properties that are acquired by the individual. They see it as something that exists only when it is being done or accomplished. Individuals establish and re-establish their gender continuously in actions, behaviours or experiences throughout their lives, both at the level of the individual and of the group or society. Gender therefore is an ongoing project, a construction of identity that is undertaken throughout one's life. It is dynamic because what is constituted as feminine or masculine will change with historical period or personal context and stage of life.

4.3 The (en)gendering of achievement and learning

From the age of two, children can identify clothes, toys and activities as designating gender, i.e. as 'girlish' or 'boyish'. As they get older, children play in increasingly gender segregated ways, with crossing of gender boundaries only allowed under particular circumstances (Thorne, 1993). This segregation is often explained as stemming naturally from the different reproductive roles of males and females, an argument which has been extended to explain the strong gender segregation of study and work. We discussed in Section 2 the claims that sex differences in visuo-spatial abilities were linked to differential brain lateralization. There have been similar claims about observed sex differences in olfaction (sense of smell), visual field attention and acuity, manual speed and skill performance. Some biological accounts of gender roles base these in differential development of the brain and processing of information between the sexes (Kimura, 1999) and claim this accounts for gender differences in academic subject achievement and occupational choice (Govier, 1998).

It is indeed the case that from early adolescence, children in the UK seem quite consistently to judge school subjects as either masculine or feminine. English and Humanities are preferred by girls, and PE and Science by boys (Colley *et al.*, 1994); French, English, Personal and Social Education and Religious Education are seen as most feminine and subjects like Information Technology, Design and Technology, Science and Maths as most masculine. There is an even stronger differentiation of vocational subjects where Typing and Cookery are seen as feminine and Metal and Wood Work as masculine (Weinreich–Haste, 1979; Archer and McCrae, 1991).

Social constructionists, however, propose that an important part of schooling is that children learn about the performance of masculinity and femininity, in terms of those things they can do to sustain their gender identity. In other words, the processes involved in schooling – the design of the curriculum, the apparent aims of learning and education, the way schools are organized and teaching is done, and how pupil interaction is regulated – act constantly to produce and sustain particular forms of masculinity and femininity.

Boys and academic achievement: 'real men' aren't girly
Social constructionists researching masculinity have used observation techniques and discourse analysis of interview material – a technique explained in more detail in Chapter 2 of this book – to explore how boys and young men understand their activities and achievements at school in relation to their gendered identity. In common with other social constructionist studies into adult masculinity (Mac An Ghaill, 1996), this research seems to indicate that, rather than there simply being one, there are several coherent masculine gender identities created within the school context (Connell, 1995;

Mac An Ghaill, 1994; Stainton-Rogers and Stainton-Rogers, 2001). Social
constructionists interpret the evidence as suggesting two common themes
across all masculinities. One is that they are relational: any particular gender
identity used by boys or men is defined in relation both to feminine identity
and also to the identities of other boys or men (see Chapter 1 of Book 1). The
second is that masculine identities are constructed through power relations;
that is, any masculinity is a privileged identity in that it is partly produced by
having control over others, access to resources of some kind, or special social
status or practices that others do not have (Wetherell, 1996).

UK primary school boys, as a group, achieve less academically than girls, and
are less likely to conform to the rules of the school and demands for particular
behaviours in the classroom. Because most teachers in the primary sector are
female, it has been argued that boys fail to identify with the source of authority
and that rebellion or rejection of authority – one of the defining features of
masculinity – becomes in this way a form of masculine identification. While
this relational production of identity is initially about being not-feminine, it
generalizes to sub-cultures that develop within schools as boys start to
identify consciously with particular groups or individuals representing those
masculinities. In primary as well as secondary schools, female teachers are
routinely exposed to sexual jokes and harassment from male pupils (Lloyd
and Duveen, 1992). Social constructionist approaches have argued that
experiencing power in relation to women is one way in which boys'
masculinity is produced and sustained in schools.

It has also been suggested that girls' increasing academic success has led
to a strengthening of an existing tendency to see academic achievement
as linked to femininity (Willis, 1977). In a study of boys in a secondary school in
the West Midlands, Haywood and Mac An Ghaill (1996) have identified four
different masculine identities and how academic achievement and gender
identity is constructed within them. The four groups were the 'Macho Lads',
the 'Academic Achievers', the 'New Entrepreneurs' and the 'Real Englishmen'.

> The Macho Lads rejected formal schooling. In contrast, the Academic
> Achievers legitimized and affirmed the schooling process, locating themselves
> within academic subjects. Meanwhile the working class New Entrepreneurs
> located themselves within the newly high status technical and vocational
> subjects as a resource to develop their masculinities. The Real Englishmen
> represented a group of middle-class students who, like the Macho Lads, rejected
> schooling but remained ambivalent as to its significance. Key elements of their
> masculinity included honesty, being different, individuality and autonomy,
> which they claimed were absent from the school's middle class culture.
>
> (Haywood and Mac an Ghaill, 1996, p.58).

In this study, boys generally positioned academic achievement as feminine –
as related to conformity and lack of self-assertion and individuality. Indeed the

Academic Achievers and the Real Englishmen groups involved in academic attainment were characterized by other groups as being literally feminized by it – turned into 'poofs' and 'ponces' i.e. feminized homosexuals. According to a social constructionist analysis of this situation, the way that boys can be involved in academic achievement is by being able to construct a gendered subject position that de-feminizes the activity, and reinterprets or reconstructs it in such a way as to fit with masculinity. In the case of the Real Englishmen group, this involved a sophisticated process of subverting and disrupting the teachers' authority and classroom activities while displaying an effortless academic achievement, which could not therefore be attributed to conformity and acceptance of the demands of formal schooling.

Girls and Information Technology: 'real women' relate to others

From a social constructionist perspective, the gendering of academic subjects does not lie in the subject itself, but in which types of knowledge, skills and activities are required by study (for example in the demands of the examinable curriculum). Properties like 'being about people' or 'technical' reflect choices that have been made about curriculum design. In other words, what a school subject is seen to be about, how it is to be used and the skills and abilities it involves, will be determined by the societal values and understandings of the wider culture at a particular point in history, using a particular lens of gender.

Despite the predominance of women in secretarial and clerical jobs involving Information Technology (IT) for word-processing or spreadsheet data, women and girls do not use computers as much for leisure as do men and boys. When they use computers in the domestic context it is more likely to accomplish specific tasks, like shopping, than the game-playing that men and boys do (Baines, 1991, cited in Kirkup, 1995; Cockburn and Furst, 1994). IT is one of the most segregated subjects in terms of voluntary enrolment and one of those subjects rated as most 'masculine'.

In their review of current research in the area, Littleton and Hoyles (2002) note that, at school, boys seem to feel more confident in monopolizing space and resources. Where for example that means occupying the computer terminal physically, it seems that girls do not assert equal access. However, they argue that giving girls more access to machines, or experience with them, is not the solution. They conclude from the literature review and their own classroom study that most girls working on computers appear to want to work collaboratively, creatively (in terms of defining their own tasks), and carefully (rather than competitively to make the speediest response). However, both the curriculum and the way that IT is taught reflect a construction of it as an individualistic, competitive and set-task oriented practice, which fits well within a variety of masculine identities. Since part of the construction of masculinity is that it is also 'not-feminine' (and vice-versa), the subject is shunned by girls who see it as demanding attitudes that they do not have and activities that they do not want. Support for this interpretation comes from a study that found that when the IT curriculum encourages thinking of computers as animate, reflecting a relationship with the user, and with connotations of friendliness and interactivity, girls are significantly less likely to drop out of a computer studies course. The reverse is true for boys (Nelson *et al.*, 1991).

Activity 3.5

Think about someone – perhaps yourself or someone you know – who has taken up an occupation, interest or course of study that is currently unusual for someone of their gender. How well do you think the social constructionist account explains their involvement?

4.4 Conclusion

Since feminism became influential in academic research in the 1970s, feminine gender identities have been well researched. However, although femininity is relational to masculinity in its construction (i.e. as 'not-masculine'), it is not as strong a defining principle as 'not-feminine' is for masculinity. The struggle for greater equality between the sexes has involved women seeking access to social and economic privileges and this has been achieved partly by women becoming more like men in terms of performance and behaviour. For this, femininities had to develop flexibly to encompass elements that previously constituted masculine gender identity, including academic achievement.

Some gender theorists argue that, as many boys are rejecting educational achievement as a worthwhile goal because of its feminization, so men will find it increasingly difficult to find a socially productive 'not-feminine' masculine identity in a society where women have diversified and incorporated so many aspects beyond traditional femininity. This has been labelled a 'crisis of masculinity' (Connell, 1995; Faludi, 1992).

Summary Section 4

- According to the social constructionist perspective, biological sex is not central to explaining what it is to be a man or a woman, rather it is a signpost to which a whole set of socially constructed gender differences are attached.
- In this account, socially created discourses about masculinity and femininity are used by individuals to create their own gendered subject positions.

- Sandra Bem developed the idea of the 'cultural lens' of masculinity and femininity. This lens is a way of perceiving the world that makes behaviour and experience gendered.
- In social constructionism, gender is seen as continuously produced throughout the lifetime, as people construct and interpret their behaviour and experience through the cultural lens of gender.
- The gendering of subjects of study is shown in the gender segregation of subject choice and achievement. This is created through both the way curricula and learning and assessment activities are organized, and the nature of student activity required.
- Academic achievement has become 'feminized'. Current masculinities, traditionally defined as 'opposite' to femininities, have therefore involved schoolboys in attempts to reject academic attainment.

5   Sex and gender: a psychoanalytic perspective

5.1 Becoming and being gendered

What does psychoanalysis contribute to understanding how men and women come to be, and experience themselves as, gendered and different from each other? Psychoanalysis has a strong developmental focus; it concentrates much of its explanation on how young children make sense of their early experience, in particular their early experience of sexual difference as they absorb it from the world around them. Although the main focus is on 'becoming', psychoanalysis uses this developmental process to build explanations about how adults experience being men or women. According to psychoanalysis, sexuality and gender relations play a crucial role in the development of the self and identity.

The main source of evidence for psychoanalytic theories is the clinical experience that psychoanalysts have with their patients. This clinical experience produces different insights from perspectives that depend on experiments or social observations.

In this section, we shall see that psychoanalytic accounts of sexual difference have shifted from a reliance on physical (genital) difference as the key explanation, to an emphasis on meaning. Children attribute meanings to the differences that they perceive between women and men, in particular within the family. The meanings that they attribute are highly influential in the early years. We will also consider the processes whereby these meanings become internalized, so as to make up a person's sense of themselves, their gendered identity.

The psychoanalytic approach to sex and gender should be seen as the product of a movement of ideas that occurred over more than a century. Psychoanalysis moved from drive theory towards understanding 'the self-in-relation-with-others' and an emphasis on the internalization of meanings concerning sexual difference. You will find these different accounts threaded through this section. They add up to a contribution that is distinctively psychological in its understanding of sex and gender, in the sense that it does not reduce to either a biological or societal explanation.

So what do these various psychoanalytic theories of sex and gender have in common? According to psychoanalysts of all persuasions, we acquire the characteristic parts of who we are through identification with parental (and other close) objects.

Why does psychoanalysis use the term 'object'? Look back to Section 2.4, Chapter 9 of Book 1 to find a definition.

Identification involves a modification of identity that takes place through an unconscious process called *internalization*. We imaginatively take in, or **introject**, parts of people, whole people and their relationships and make them our own, over time. It is not a conscious or intentional process and does not depend on language. It is an unconscious, dynamic process that occurs more through inchoate feelings than through thoughts. It is through insight into these processes, using clinical evidence, that psychoanalysis has come to explain the role of sexuality and gender relations in the acquisition of self.

Introject
To incorporate the characteristics of another person into one's own self-image, during the development of one's own identity.

5.2 Oedipal conflict according to Freud

Freud's theory of Oedipal conflict is where psychoanalysis first tried to explain how anatomically differentiated babies develop a psychological sense of being a girl or boy, that is how they become gendered. According to Freud, all children will feel rivalry with the father (or other sexual partner of the mother) because, in their fantasy, the mother is the source of all care, love and pleasure and they want to keep this to themselves.

Psychoanalysts believe, based on infant observation and clinical evidence, that babies have omnipotent fantasies; that is, in their imaginations, fuelled by pleasure seeking, they believe they can do and be and have everything.

His majesty the baby

The baby therefore imagines it can have its mother completely. Babies are dependent on the mother figure, not just physically but for their psychological survival. There is a difference between physical and psychological survival. Both adults and children can survive physically yet experience themselves as being shattered, no longer with a workable identity. The idea of psychological survival highlights the importance of psychological well-being in providing a person with feelings that they can trust the world around them. This contributes to a secure sense of their capacity to survive without undue pain and anxiety.

In this sense, both boys and girls initially desire the mother and find themselves in competition with the father. Take as an example the occasionally reported little boys' claim 'when I grow up I'm going to marry my mother and have a baby'. This claim is the product of intense wishes: never to separate from his mother and, like her, be able to create a baby. He does not yet know that he is breaking two taboos with his wishes; the incest taboo and the rule of sexual difference. In time, the **reality principle** will make inroads into this fantasy of omnipotence, as successive experiences of frustration are organized meaningfully in a way that involves understanding the difference between self and other. The reality principle means that individuals can respond in an adaptive manner, as opposed to acting as if their desires will be automatically gratified. In the process, *differentiation*, the distinction between oneself and others (who do not necessarily want what we want), is more firmly established.

The reality principle means that, sooner or later, we cannot avoid the realization that our mother is not completely at our disposal, that others make claims on her, and we are jealous. We also come to the realization that we cannot be both boys and girls. These realities face us with loss. How do we cope with these losses – loss of the loved other (or at least the loss of a fantasy of omnipotent control over her) and loss of part of our imagined selves? According to psychoanalysis, the ensuing conflict provides early answers to the question 'who am I (as a girl/woman; as a boy/man)?' and 'who do I desire? (a man; a woman)' The first question is about the achievement of a gendered self; the second about **sexual object choice**. These acquisitions are part of the process of coming to terms with loss in facing the reality of sexual difference.

> Reality principle
> The idea that, providing all goes well enough during the course of development, individuals are increasingly able to recognize the nature of the reality that they experience.

> Sexual object choice
> Whether we desire someone of the same or the other sex.

Consider the case of your own child or a child in a family you know. Think of an everyday example where that child has had to give up something it wants of the mother because of the father's (or father figure's) more authoritative demands. What lesson does the child learn about reality? Consider the common western arrangement whereby the parents sleep together in one bed and the baby sleeps on its own elsewhere. As a result, it is confronted with a disagreeable reality on a daily basis: namely, it is deprived of the comfort, reassurance and pleasure of sleeping next to the mother's body. In contrast, the father appears to have a right to just that position. When you come to ponder its significance, this arrangement is saying 'the father has rights and privileges over the mother that I do not have'. (It was all the more pronounced in the late nineteenth century heyday of patriarchal authority within which Freud worked and was a husband and father.)

According to Freud, boys and girls embark upon different psychic paths because of the dawning awareness of their own sex, defined for them anatomically by the presence or absence of the penis, a *visible* source of considerable pleasure. Freud believed that girls' and boys' different psychic routes to achieving their sense of gendered identity hinged on their different responses to the realization that the boy (like the father) possesses a penis and the girl (like the mother) does not. Through this realization, boys typically can *identify with* their father. This entails the rights and privileges that boys experience fathers as having, especially in relation to the mother: 'when I grow up I can be just like him (we are the same in this vital defining respect)'.

Girls have to acknowledge that they do not possess penises and they also know that their mothers do not. According to Freud, girls identify with their mothers, which is less gratifying because of the status and assumed greater pleasure that attaches to the penis. As a result, girls envy those who possess one.

In this account, there is simultaneously a biological explanation and a cultural one. At first Freud thought that the mere difference – whether the child possessed a penis or not – was sufficient to explain the different psychological development of boys and girls. Later, he began to recognize the importance of the *meaning* of this difference if he was to provide a properly psychological account of the acquisition of gendered identity. If children perceive that adult men have more rights and privileges than women and if they also come to realize that the defining characteristic of a man – the thing that makes him different from all women – is the possession of a penis, then the anatomical difference comes to hold particular social meanings. It holds *symbolic significance*. This argument moves from an exclusive reliance on biology to an inclusion of the significance of social arrangements for how biological difference is experienced. However, it still does not provide a psychological explanation of what it is *to be* a man or a woman. For this, psychoanalysis also needed to explain how the symbolic significance of biological difference affects the sense of who we are as men and women, rather than just influencing how we make sense of the world around us. This is where psychoanalysis uses the ideas of *internalization* and *identification*. These are largely unconscious processes and they are important processes in the child's resolution of the oedipal complex.

If you cannot remember the details of why the oedipal complex occurs and what it entails, turn back to Chapter 9 of Book 1 and reread Section 2.

5.3 Critical developments

Feminists and other women theorists rejected the demeaning of women implied in the claim that women's sex is just lack; that women are constituted through envy of what men have that they do not.

In particular, two arguments have been influential in developing the psychoanalytic understanding of gender development. First, the symbolic significance of the penis emphasized that the organ itself was not the central issue, but rather what it symbolized about the father's power, rights and privileges within the family, in particular his authority over the mother. In this light, the theory looks less like a patriarchal slight on women and more like a recognition of how patriarchal relations affect boys' and girls' experience of what it is to grow up one sex or the other. Further, it is argued that girls do not have to give up their mothers in the traumatic way that boys do: they can continue to have and be her.

The second argument has criticized Freud's failure to consider the significance of women's genitals. Just because the boy's genital is more visible, does that mean that the girl's is unknown or gives no pleasure to her? Challenging Freud, many argue that girls do have knowledge of their vaginas as well as their clitorises and get pleasure from them. Both boys and girls associate a girl's internal reproductive organs with their mother's capacity to give birth. Karen Horney, an early colleague of Freud, was struck, in her clinical practice, by her male patients' envy of women's ability to give birth. In *Flight from Womanhood* (1926) she commented:

A sculpture of the ecstasy of Teresa D'Avila, in the Santa Maria della Vittoria in Rome. Jacques Lacan, a French psychoanalyst, claims that it represents women's huge capacity for sexual pleasure, which radiates through their whole bodies, a capacity that rivals boys' pleasure in their penises and is accessible even to a celibate nun. The image also remains acceptable within the religious tradition of the time by ostensibly representing St. Teresa's ecstasy as she felt her heart pierced by 'the fiery arrow of Divine Love'

'When one begins, as I did, to analyse men only after a fairly long experience of analysing women, one receives a most surprising impression of the intensity of his envy of pregnancy, childhood and motherhood, as well as of the breasts and of the act of suckling' (Horney, 1926, pp.60–1).

Horney coined the idea of 'womb envy' and moreover pointed out that its neglect in psychoanalysis arose because, in a male-dominated cultural climate, the idea would more readily be repressed than the idea of penis envy.

Karen Horney's claim has wide-ranging implications. From a psychanalytical perspective it suggests that if an idea – such as womb envy – is uncomfortable for a whole category of individuals – men in this instance – and if that group is influential in producing the knowledge that is available at a given historical period, then that idea it less likely to be produced; it will have been collectively repressed as too threatening. Other ideas will be appealing because they are satisfying to a person's beliefs about themselves and their group.

It seems likely that Freud's theory of gender development was limited by his 'phallocentrism' (the view that the penis was the only significant genital and hence girls' development was determined by their lack and by their envy). Following Horney's account of womb envy, we can see girls' identification with adult women in a more positive light than Freud did: 'I may not have the advantages of a man, but I can do something even more valuable: I can create a child'.

Melanie Klein analysed very young children using her version of play therapy. Her evidence helped to show that the Oedipus complex isn't simply about loving the parent of the other sex and hating the same sex (rival) parent. She found very mixed feelings where both boys and girls could love and identify with the same-sex parent. She also found that 'children often show, as early as the beginning of their second year, a marked preference for the parent of the other sex and other indications of Oedipus tendencies' (Klein, 1926, p.129). This meant disagreeing with Freud's positioning of the Oedipus complex at age 4 or 5, the genital phase. Increasingly, psychoanalysis has moved away from talking about drives or instincts to seeing the developmental history of the baby in terms of the quality of its *actually experienced* object relations and the effects of these on its identifications. According to psychoanalytic theory, people internalize objects and object relations, and then may or may not identify with them. This means that the process of identification with significant others is not automatic but allows for fluidity and changes over time. The process of identification does not stop after childhood. Rather it is a mechanism that continues throughout life and helps to explain how our identities (including our gendered identities) are continually subject to change and modification.

5.4 Changing gender relations and cross-sex identifications

Most psychoanalysts now agree that identifications with the same-sex parent are neither exclusive nor unambivalent. Jessica Benjamin's writings (1990, 1995, 1998) demonstrate how contemporary psychoanalytic theory has transformed Freud's ideas in a way that recognizes the importance of the meanings of sexual difference, as experienced through relationships, and how these are internalized to shape gender identity. She argues that it is no longer convincing to suppose that boys identify with fathers who are unambiguously masculine and girls identify with mothers who are unambiguously feminine. Perhaps because of the profound unsettling of traditional gender relations, when contemporary psychoanalysts look at what it means to be a man or a woman, they see a more complex picture.

If the significance of the penis is symbolic (that is, it becomes a source of pride or envy or fear of loss because it stands for the advantages of being a man), this has implications for how social changes in gender relations are incorporated into psychoanalytic theory. A common criticism of Freud's ideas is that he was constructing a theory that made claims about human nature in general whereas his evidence was limited to the gender relations of a particular place and time (nineteenth century mid-Europe). If so, as gender relations change towards equality of the sexes, will not the unconscious significance of anatomical difference change?

The answer to this question can be both 'yes and no'. Yes, because, if babies grow up experiencing maternal-type care from both a father and mother, then the time when they have to acknowledge sexual difference and give up the fantasy of being both will not involve as much loss. If this were the case, the boy, in giving up the mother, would not be faced with losing his source of love and care. Likewise, if both parents are active and powerful in the world, the girl's identification with her mother would not entail losses of those potentials. Consider too that if each parent already combines plentiful feminine and masculine attributes, then identification with one parent is not going to limit that child's potential in the way that it would in an era in which gendered divisions of labour and character were rigid and mutually exclusive.

The 'no' side to the answer refers to the significance of anatomy. Anatomy is not destiny in the sense of determining our psycho-sexual characteristics: one of Freud's greatest achievements was to distinguish between biological and psychological characteristics when it came to explaining gender development. However, anatomical difference in reproductive organs was, for Freud, part of reality that every child has to come to terms with. It is the bedrock of unconscious experience of sexual difference; difference that will not be erased by gender equality, but can be changed by it.

Summary Section 5

- Psychoanalysis, starting with Freud but not limited to his work, has contributed a psychological way of understanding sexuality and gender that takes into account both anatomical difference and social factors like family structure and meaning.
- Gender and sexuality came to be seen, through Freud's and later psychoanalytic work, as having far-reaching implications for the development of self.
- The concept of identification is common to all forms of psychoanalysis and illuminates the way people unconsciously acquire their characteristic identities from significant (gendered) others, especially from their parents and their experience of how their parents relate.
- Central to the process of acquiring a differentiated self is the task of coming to terms with the reality of two kinds of loss: loss of the mother as

an extension of the child's desires, and loss of the possibility of being both sexes.

- Important critical developments in the psychoanalytic theory of sex and gender include: the symbolic significance of the penis (and penis envy) as a symbol of men's privilege; the significance of women's creative capacity to give birth in understanding how envy affects gender identifications; and emphasis on the complexity of identifications with parental figures, resulting in the incorporation of multiple-gendered characteristics in both women and men.
- The symbolic significance of anatomical sexual difference cannot be erased in human beings' experience of gender, but it can change with changing gender arrangements.

6   Conclusion

The above four perspectives provide very disparate accounts of sex and gender and inevitably raise the question of whether together they are more useful than any single account is on its own. How can we deal with such diversity? Might it be acceptable to 'add together' the convincing or preferred parts of each perspective? In other words, using the '3Cs' theme from the first book of the course, do these perspectives *complement* each other, *conflict* with each other or *coexist* with each other? And on what grounds do we evaluate their claims when seen in relation to each other?

In this concluding section we shall address this fundamental question in the following ways. A logical first step will be to evaluate the strengths of each perspective in its own terms, because these will clarify what it is we want to hold on to in a general psychology of sex and gender. In identifying strengths, we will also touch upon weaknesses, because these suggest what to be wary of and what we shall need from the other perspectives to compensate. If, as a result of identifying strengths, we wish to put together parts of each perspective, we shall then have to work out whether they can be combined together, that is whether they are complementary or not. The second part of this conclusion therefore discusses ways in which it may be possible to combine different perspectives. It emphasizes compatibility at the level of theory. There are many different grounds, however, according to which perspectives can be complementary, conflicting or coexisting. Having discussed theoretical compatibility, we shall move on to the question of conflict between perspectives. Here the focus will be on political or ideological differences and the way they often lead to theoretical conflict. Finally, under the heading

'Coexisting methodologies', we discuss forms of knowledge that, due to the fundamentally different methodologies that produced them, can do no more than coexist with one another, perhaps.

First, however, it will help you to clarify your own understanding of the various positions by working through the following activity.

Activity 3.8

Look back to the summaries of each of Sections 2 to 5. Identify – if you find it appropriate – one or two aspects of the perspective that you are convinced by and one or two aspects that you are unconvinced by. Put them in your own words and note your reasons for each, if you can.

6.1 Strengths and weaknesses

The *biological perspective* has the strength of referring to material characteristics, using material data. Assuming that the methods are dependable (and biological research aspires to the rigour that is most attainable in natural science), evidence from biology can demonstrate sex differences (and similarities) in genetic make-up, hormones and brain regions. Section 2 made it clear just how complicated it can be to establish the relationship between biological processes, for example the effects of genes on hormones and of these on the sexed bodies of babies or adolescents. By carefully documenting these separate effects, biology shows us that biological difference between the sexes is not a simple fact, even before we take into consideration life history and experience. Biology's actions and effects are always in interaction, not just with other biological processes, but also with physical and cultural environments. Biological study can highlight developmental changes, for example, Hofman and Swaab found that sex differences that appear in certain regions of the adult brain are not found in the younger brains of children (see Section 2). The interpretation of this kind of finding is quite complex and the underlying causal sequence is not straight forward. In this case, changes in certain brain regions between childhood and adulthood could be a result, for example, of experience interacting with hormones that do not get triggered until puberty. An important message of biological psychology is that biological differences between the sexes can be a *product* of psychological experience as well as a *cause* of differences in behaviour.

However, although biological psychology can demonstrate the complexity of connections between biological mechanisms and behaviour, it cannot (and does not attempt) to say anything about the realm of human experience, or 'being' as this was defined in the introduction. By itself, then, it does not provide us with a psychology of sex and gender.

Evolutionary psychology has the strength of keeping in view the basic principle that the genetic make-up of human animals, like non-human animals, has evolved according to the principles of natural and sexual selection. The question that follows from this widely accepted principle is a valid and important one: can differences in sexual behaviour between men and women be explained – or partly explained – by genetic differences selected for in the course of evolutionary survival? It is a very ambitious question, because, to answer it, evolutionary psychology has to demonstrate ways in which contemporary behaviour is influenced by genetically programmed behaviours that were laid down many generations ago, notwithstanding all the other influences on the species during that time. Consequently, evolutionary psychologists do not address the detail of how particular forms of sexual behaviour have evolved among humans, but restrict their research to trying to show that contemporary differences in human sexual behaviour are consistent with their theoretical argument.

The difficulty with this is that the evidence gathered to support the argument cannot readily discount other explanations for the behaviours in question nor can it explain how other factors may influence and modify the behavioural outcome. Take as an example Clark and Hatfield's finding (see Section 3) that 75 per cent of American college men, as opposed to none of the women, consented to sex with an 'attractive stranger' of the other sex. This is consistent with the evolutionary psychology argument (always supposing that these men would have followed through on their claim, an outcome that was not tested). The finding would also be consistent with a social constructionist claim that men are motivated to position themselves in a discourse that constructs men as being 'properly masculine' provided that they are seen to be constantly in pursuit of heterosexual sex. Some evolutionary psychologists (e.g. Dunbar *et al.*, 1999) have proposed that evolved behavioural predispositions underlie many of the cultural patterns that we observe. So one possibility here is that evolution may have shaped cultural practices that in turn serve to reinforce patterns of evolved behaviour. In this way, evolutionary psychologists acknowledge social influences on sexual behaviour. However, their methods provide no systematic way of taking these into account in explaining the behaviour observed in their experiments with contemporary, culturally-situated, meaning-making human beings.

The strength of a *social constructionist* explanation of gender difference is its capacity to take into account the historical and cultural situation of human beings, and in particular their unique capacity, in the animal world, for meaning-making and communication of intentions. Its methods focus almost exclusively on the meaning-making activities of humans. Social constructionists would argue that the cultural lenses through which men and women filter their own sexual behaviours would be strong enough to account for Clark and Hatfield's findings. Many of them would probably argue that an evolutionary or biological account is superfluous because genetically-selected or hormonal influences would be comprehensively overlaid by the importance of cultural practices, meaning and intention in shaping human sexual behaviour.

Evolutionary psychology's rejoinder would probably be in terms of social constructionism's failure to explain the origins of these gender differences. How did the cultural lenses of gender come to construct the differences in men's and women's sexual behaviour in the first place? They point to the cultural universality of such human behaviours and argue that they cannot be explained entirely in terms of social influences. When evolutionary psychology considers genetic selection in human animals, how are the arguments modified to accommodate the unique features of human beings such as language and the existence of culture that survives through countless generations?

Psychoanalytic psychology's challenge would be different, namely that social constructionism over emphasises the role of external influences (identities being constructed by discourses and discursive practices) in determining people's behaviour. Consequently, it does not explain their agency and capacity for resistance and change.

The strength of *psychoanalytical psychology* is in addressing the question of 'becoming' and the processes involved in this: how the baby, sexed by its biology and gendered by society, takes on a *psychological* gender that becomes intrinsic to its later identity as a person. In this perspective, the social constructionist account (that social discourses concerning gender are consciously taken on board to comply with social pressures and group identity) is insufficient. For psychoanalysis, these meanings are transformed by unconscious and creative fantasies, born out of anxieties, desires and defences. These are unique to the human species. Meanings, then, are a crucial interface between the social environment that exists before any given individual, and the becoming of that individual. This can provide an explanation for how people resist and change the cultural meanings around them, so that people's gender is not seen as *determined* either by social discourses or by biology.

The criticism from most other perspectives would be to argue that psychoanalysis cannot demonstrate the validity of its claims. Critics point to its exaggerated or unlikely emphasis on unconscious experiences such as castration anxiety that cannot be empirically demonstrated, and its disregard for people's conscious explanations of their behaviour. This challenge raises questions about evidence and methods to which we shall return below.

In summary, as a result of considering the strengths and weaknesses of our four perspectives, it is possible to conclude that each has a valuable point of view, one that should not be lost sight of in a psychology of sex and gender. At the same time, no one perspective has the necessary breadth to provide a full explanation. Why, you may be asking, can we not combine these four to provide a full explanation? Would they not together take account of the full range of influences that make up being a man or a woman: biological, evolutionarily selected, social and psychic-developmental? Do not all these factors contribute?

6.2 Complementary perspectives

Most agree that there is necessarily some interaction among these influences. But how would such an interaction work? The idea of an interaction does not solve the problem if it is just a matter of combining theories that do not share any common theoretical ground. The challenge is to build a theory that *explains* how the different influences interact to produce some aspect of human behaviour.

So we need to establish whether the perspectives in this chapter are indeed complementary or not. Are there ways in which they can be combined to provide a better, fuller picture of human sex and gender differences or are they completely incompatible? Let me give an example in which biological and social explanations are rendered theoretically compatible within a psychological account: the *experience* of a girl's menarche (the onset of menstruation), which is a significant time in her experience of herself as becoming a woman. We have established that a properly psychological explanation must accept that hormonal and bodily changes take place in adolescence, because these impinge in some way on experience and are also affected by it. Likewise we must accept that the social context in which adolescents grow up is already awash with gendered meanings about adolescence that circulate in families and schools (and vary between cultures). It has also been argued that a psychological explanation needs to explain in detail how these social meanings become internalized and impinge on gendered 'being'.

The analysis would need therefore to examine the meanings that are made in the psyche of the experience of bodily and hormonal change, in the context of available social meanings. Some of these social meanings will have an effect, not just on the psyche, but on biological processes. If a girl starts her periods at an unusually early age, this will have been affected by genetic inheritance, triggering hormones into action that are expressed in the physical changes of puberty. But early periods have social significance that could well make them more anxiety-provoking. If – at whatever age – a girl absorbs from her mother or peer group the idea that menstruation is something to dread, or from her father that it is dirty or taboo, the anxiety can take a biological form that arguably can modify the biological processes giving rise to painful periods. Once biology is understood to be a two-way process, not just acting on individual behaviour, meaning and experience, but also being affected by it, then we can begin to see a way in which ovulation, for example, can be affected by social meanings.

However, we are not just combining hormonal change and social meaning (biological and social factors). The way that a particular girl experiences the social meanings concerning menstruation is *mediated* by her psyche. The psyche is not just a mirror of social meanings. We need to include the dimension of psychic development to make this 'bio-psycho-social' explanation properly psychological: that is, a girl's unique past experience and how she has, consciously and unconsciously, transformed its significance when it comes to an event that is central to becoming a woman. The meaning that menstruation has for her is not just dictated by the culture that surrounds her at the time, but by the inner meanings that her body, her gender and her sexuality have already acquired, meanings that are unique to her. Although related to those available in her culture, these have been creatively modified during her development through unconscious anxieties (for example about becoming like her mother) and desires (for example to have children of her own.)

6.3 Political conflict among explanations

Throughout the twentieth century, biological and social explanations ('nature' and 'nurture') have been at loggerheads because of what has been seen as their opposite political implications. Those who were in favour of changing what they saw as women's disadvantaged position in society tended to favour social explanations because social influences can be changed. They saw biological explanations as dangerously deterministic: for example if women's caring capacity was naturally given, not socially given, would women ever win equal rights in the workplace? The kind of biology represented in this chapter, with its emphasis on plasticity and becoming, does not lend itself to this kind of political conclusion.

More recently, evolutionary psychology has been accused of the same politically conservative tendencies. Now, as then, it is difficult to separate out what responsibility lies in the explanation itself and what lies in the use to which it has been put by popularizers who oversimplify. One notorious example of such a conflict is the claim that evolutionary psychology 'excuses' rape by suggesting that sexually predatory behaviour is a genetically selected strategy because it maximizes male reproductive advantage by enabling them to inseminate as many women as often as possible.

In a book entitled *A Natural History of Rape: Biological Bases of Sexual Coercion* (2000), Thornhill and Palmer argue that rape is an adaptive strategy in animal species – and by extension in human males – which enables males who otherwise might be sexually unsuccessful to propagate their genes. The authors reported studies on forced sex in mallard ducks and scorpion flies. Supporters of evolutionary psychology do not accept the charge that this application of the evolutionary perspective 'excuses' the behaviour of men who rape. However, critics take issue with Thornhill and Palmer's failure to make the necessary conceptual distinctions between animals and humans in their use of the term 'rape'. Hilary and Stephen Rose (2000) point out that forced sex in animal species is always with fertile females, hence the reproductive potential. An account that omits the human capacity to make meaning (in this case out of violent intrusion of the body) is guilty of a serious conflation of humans with non-human animals. Some other criticisms are that Thornhill and Palmer's argument does not account for the behaviour of the vast majority of men who do not rape and who wish to be monogamous. Nor does it account for gang rape. However, evolutionary psychology *does* assume some individual (inherited) differences. Indeed, they are the very features on which natural selection operates. Moreover, as we have acknowledged, it accepts that environmental and social influences modify behaviour by operating on, or overlaying, existing genetic variation. Nevertheless, within this framework, evolutionary psychology as a perspective does not theorise about how individual differences arise. It considers universals as its object of knowledge.

There is one issue that it is important to disentangle when trying not to get sucked into a political argument that could be as unproductive as the history of the nature-nurture debate. Put simply, it is not acceptable to dismiss a theory on the grounds that it appears to legitimate behaviour that is morally repugnant to us. On the other hand, it would be surprising if morally repugnant arguments were not first in line for a very close examination of their assumptions, logic of argument and methods. As we saw in the introduction, feminists have long been suspicious of conclusions about 'natural' differences between women and men that male scientists discovered on the basis of so-called 'scientific evidence'. Many, especially social constructionists, have concluded from historical research that values inevitably underpin all knowledge. This should not mean, however, either that distasteful ideas are rejected out of hand, or that an equally partisan new set of ideas should be advanced that claims to explain the whole psychology of sex and gender.

6.4 Coexisting methodologies

Psychological methods have traditionally been based on scientific principles, derived from the natural sciences, that rely on systematic observation and measurement of phenomena. Such research derives testable hypotheses from current knowledge and theory, and draws on empirical data to test it.

Both biology and evolutionary psychology embrace this scientific approach. Evolutionary psychology constructs theoretical models concerning the origins of human behaviour, and seeks empirical evidence from the behaviour of contemporary humans and other species to support them. There is controversy about whether this conforms to the rigorous procedures of science (see Herrnstein-Smith, 2000). Evolutionary psychology seeks to counter criticisms that it cannot provide 'direct' proof for its theories, arguing that the availability of different kinds of converging scientific evidence provides a suitable alternative.

Another criticism that has been levelled at evolutionary psychology is that it invokes the notion that particular patterns of behaviour are genetically selected without providing any evidence at the *genetic level*. Certainly we are a long way from identifying genes that might determine sexual behaviours. However, the existence of some genetically transmitted disorders, such as Huntingdon's disease, is well documented. In this case, as well as distressing degenerative effects, quite specific behavioural patterns are documented. For instance, patients seem unable to experience and recognise in others the emotion of disgust, while retaining the capacity to recognise emotions such as anger, happiness and fear. Animal models suggest that groups of genes can determine quite complex patterns of behaviour. It is highly unlikely that sexual behaviour in humans will be determined solely by genes; however, intricate interactions between inherited and acquired characteristics are to be expected. Thus, there will not be a gene for 'human females to have a predilection for wealthy men', but it could conceivably be that a gene complex, interacting with cultural determinants of 'high rank', predisposes some females to choose wealthy men.

The group of methods that are usually contrasted with scientific approaches are based on the hermeneutic (or interpretative) principle (see Chapter 1, *Exploring Psychological Research Methods*). Social constructionism and psychoanalysis are both based on the interpretation of meaning (symbolic data in the typology of data given in the Introduction to Book 1) and therefore, it is argued, cannot comply with natural science principles. Some psychologists regard this as 'special pleading' while others contend that the very criteria for what is scientific should be modified for psychological research to accommodate meaning-based interpretations of human behaviour.

Different psychologies use different methods, and this fundamentally affects what they can study and the knowledge that they produce. Such radical differences between different psychological approaches *can* lead to conflict but more usually result in coexistence. If two perspectives share some methodological principles, they have something specific to argue about, as when biologists, such as Herrnstein-Smith, argue that evolutionary psychology is not rigorous in its hypothesis testing, and evolutionary psychologists counter that hypothesis testing about evolution must necessarily take a different form. However, when the methodological principles are radically different, like those of natural science-based psychology and psychoanalytic psychology, useful debate is more difficult because they start from different principles and follow different procedures. For example, we saw that psychoanalytic psychology has been accused of being speculative and that psychologists have argued that concepts like repression and the unconscious cannot be tested according to scientific principles. Psychoanalysts counter that their methods derive from the clinical situation, where, they argue, the patient's free associations allow access to unconscious conflict and the way that, unintentionally, personal meanings influence behaviour.

Unlike natural science-based psychology, psychoanalysts, in common with social constructionist psychology, believe that the researcher's subjectivity is inevitably involved in research (see Chapter 8, *Exploring Psychological Research Methods*); that its influence should be recognized rather than denied. It is not surprising then that this model of research has difficulty entering into meaningful debate with the natural scientific approach, either consensual or conflictual. Neither is it surprising that psychoanalytic methodology has generated such different knowledge from scientific psychology.

Where does this 'failure to engage' at the methodological level leave our nicely complementary theories of the menarche? Is such complementarity an illusion if theorists from different perspectives cannot agree on the status of each other's evidence? There is no easy answer to this question.

6.5 Last words

In the introduction to this chapter, we said that the topic of sex and gender illustrates many of the difficult and contentious questions that psychology faces. We have seen how these include the challenge of putting a range of very diverse perspectives alongside each other, of reckoning with the inevitable political dimension of psychological knowledge, of taking into account the importance of method to what knowledge can be generated. Above all, we must try to produce an account that convincingly does justice to the complexity of our experience as gendered human beings. All of these challenges are typical of those faced in the social sciences, although psychology faces the extra difficulty of incorporating the broad span of theories and methods entailed by biological and social accounts.

Is it reasonable to expect psychology to be able to solve all of these problems in its account of sex and gender? There is a lively debate in the social sciences as to whether an overarching explanation, a 'grand narrative', is either possible or desirable. At the moment the climate has shifted from those who believed in the possibility of dependable scientific knowledge to those who celebrate the multiple, unruly, often conflictual nature of different perspectives as they jostle for space in contemporary academic and cultural life. Certainly you should not expect, or try to produce, a single explanation of the psychology of sex and gender. It is also helpful to develop a critical capacity when confronted with the many accounts that are available. We hope that this chapter has helped you in this important area of academic study. It is a theme pursued throughout this book.

Summary Section 6

- The objects of knowledge of each of the four perspectives are all valid and useful in a general psychology of sex and gender.
- No perspective on its own can tell the whole story.
- Any explanation of human behaviour that draws from non-human animal behaviour must include a good understanding of specifically human characteristics.
- Perspectives and levels of analysis and explanation cannot just be combined without an account of how they interact.
- The experience of menarche provides an example of the potential complementarity of biological, psychoanalytic and social constructionist perspectives.
- Political differences are often exposed when conflicting accounts of sex and gender differences occur.
- The major differences between psychological methods based on natural science principles and those based on hermeneutic principles means that perspectives based on these methods may have difficulty achieving more than an uneasy coexistence.
- Don't worry if you cannot come up with a single psychological explanation of sex and gender. It might be more productive to enjoy the diversity. But cultivate your critical faculties.

Answer to Activity 3.2

female; male; male; female; female; female; male; male; female; female

Further reading

Buss, D.M. (2000) *The Dangerous Passion*, London, Bloomsbury.

This book focuses on sex differences in jealousy and is based on the findings of a large cross-cultural study. The book provides a readable up-to-date account of the evolutionary origins of sexual desires.

Minsky, R. (ed.) (1996) *Psychoanalysis and Gender: An Introductory Reader*, London, Routledge.

This is an accessible introduction that covers several important psychoanalytical theorists and includes significant extracts from their own work, with commentaries.

Rogers, L.J. (1999) *Sexing the Brain*, London, Weidenfield and Nicolson.

Stainton-Rogers, W. and Stainton-Rogers, R. (2001) *The Psychology of Gender and Sexuality*, Buckingham, Open University Press.

An accessible introduction to a range of perspectives on gender and sexuality, ranging from biology and evolutionary psychology to anthropology, psychoanalytical and feminist and critical perspectives.

Trew, K. and Kremer, J. (1998) *Gender and Psychology*, London and New York, Arnold (Hodder).

An edited collection with chapters by specialists in every area, including cognition, biology and emotion.

 # References

Allen, L.S. and Gorski, R.A. (1990) 'Sex difference in the bed nucleus of the stria terminalis of the human brain', *Journal of Comparative Neurology*, vol.302, pp.607–706.

Archer, J. and McCrae, M. (1991) 'Gender perceptions of school subjects among 10–11 year olds', *British Journal of Educational Psychology*, vol.61, pp.99–103.

Baines S. (1991) 'Personal computing, gender and distance education', paper given to the International Federation of Information Processors (IFIP) conference, Helsinki, June. Cited in Kirkup, G. 'The importance of gender as a category of Open and Distance Learning', *Teaching and Consultancy Centre Report no.90*, Milton Keynes, The Open University.

Baker, S.W. and Erhardt, A.A. (1974) 'Pre-natal androgen, intelligence and cognitive sex differences', in Friedman, R.C., Richart, R.M. and van Deeds, R.L. (eds) *Sex Differences in Behavior*, New York, Wiley.

Beach (1938) 'Sex reversals in the mating pattern of the rat', *Journal of Genetic Psychology*, vol.53, pp.329–34.

Bem, S. (1981) 'Gender Schema Theory: a cognitive account of sex-typing', *Psychological Review*, vol.88, pp.354–64.

Bem, S. (1994) *The Lenses of Gender*, London and New York, Yale University Press.

Benjamin, J. (1990) *The Bonds of Love*, London, Virago.

Benjamin, J. (1995) *Like Subjects, Love Objects: Essays on Recognition and Sexual Difference*, New Haven and London, Yale University Press.

Benjamin, J. (1998) *The Shadow of the Other: Intersubjectivity and Gender in Psychoanalysis*, London, Routledge.

Betzig, L.L. (1986) *Despotism and Differential Reproduction: A Darwinian View of History*, Hawthorne, NY, Aldine de Gruyter.

Bishop, K.M. and Wahlsten, D. (1997) 'Sex differences in the human corpus callosum: Myth or reality?', *Neuroscience and Biobehavioral Reviews*, vol.21, pp.581–601.

Broverman, J.K., Broverman, D.M., Clarkson, F.E., Rosenkrantz, P.S. and Vogel, S.R. (1970) 'Sex-role stereotypes and clinical judgements of mental health', *Journal of Consulting and Clinical Psychology*, vol.34, pp.1–7.

Bullough, V.L. and Bullough , B. (1987) *Women and Prostitution: A Social History*, Buffalo, NY, Prometheus.

Buss, D.M. (1989) 'Sex differences in human mate preferences: Evolutionary hypotheses testing in 37 cultures', *Behavioural and Brain Sciences*, vol.12, pp.1–49.

Buss, D.M. (2000) 'The evolution of happiness', *American Psychologist*, vol.55, pp15–23.

Buss, D.M., Larsen, R.,Westen, D., and Semmelroth, J. (1992) 'Sex differences in jealousy: Evolution, physiology, and psychology', *Psychological Science*, vol.3, pp.251–55.

Buss, D.M. and Schmitt, D.P. (1993) 'Sexual strategies theory: An evolutionary perspective on human mating', *Psychological Review*, vol.100, pp.204–32.

Caplan, P.J., Macpherson, G.M. and Tobin, P. (1985) 'Do sex-related differences in spatial abilities exist – a multilevel critique with new data', *American Psychologist*, vol.40, pp.786–99.

Clark, R.D. (1990) 'The impact of AIDS on gender differences in willingness to engage in casual sex', *Journal of Applied Social Psychology*, vol.20, pp.771–82.

Clark, R.D. and Hatfield, E. (1989) 'Gender differences in receptivity to sexual offers', *Journal of Psychology and Human Sexuality*, vol.2, pp.39–55.

Cockburn, C. and Furst, D. (eds) (1994) *Bringing Technology Home*, Buckingham, Open University Press.

Colley, A., Comber C. and Hargreaves, D.J. (1994) 'Gender effects in school subject preferences', *Educational Studies*, vol.20, pp.379–85.

Cooke, B., Hegstrom, C.D., Villeneuve, L.S. and Breedlove, S.M. (1998) 'Sexual differentiation of the vertebrate brain: principles and mechanisms', *Frontiers in Neuroendocrinology*, vol.19, pp.323–62.

Connell, R.W. (1995) *Masculinities*, Cambridge, Polity Press.

Dunbar, R., Knight, C. and Power, C. (eds) (1999) *The Evolution of Culture*, Edinburgh, Edinburgh University Press.

Eagly, A.H. (1994) 'On comparing women and men', *Feminism and Psychology*, vol.4, no.4, pp.513–22.

Faludi, S. (1992) *Backlash: The Undeclared War against Women*, London, Chatto and Windus.

Fausto-Sterling, A. (2000) *Sexing the Body*, New York, Basic Books.

Fielding (1997) *Bridget Jones's Diary*, London, Picador.

Fielding (2000) *Bridget Jones: The Edge of Reason*, London, Picador.

Fitch, R.H. and Denenberg, V.H. (1998) 'A role for ovarian hormones in sexual differentiation of the brain', *Behavioral and Brain Sciences*, vol.21, pp.311–27.

Geary, D.C., Rumsey, M., Bow-Thomas, C.C. and Hoard, M.K. (1995) 'Sexual jealousy as a facultative trait: evidence from the pattern of sex differences in adults from China and the United States', *Ethology and Sociobiology*, vol.16, pp.355–83.

Giedd, J.N., Blumenthal, J., Jeffries, N.O., Castellanos, F.X., Liu, H., Zijdenbos, A., Paus, T., Evans, A.C. and Rapoport, J.L. (1999) 'Brain development during childhood and adolescence: a longitudinal MRI study', *Nature Neuroscience*, vol.2, pp.861–63.

Govier E. (1998) 'Brain, sex and occupation', in Radford, J. (ed.) *Gender and Choice in Education and Occupation*, London, Routledge.

Gray, J. (1993) *Men are from Mars, Women are from Venus*, London, Thorsons.

Gregor, T. (1985) *Anxious Pleasures: the Sexual Lives of an Amazonian People*, Chicago, University of Chicago Press.

Halpern, D.F. (1994) 'Stereotypes, science, censorship, and the study of sex differences', *Feminism and Psychology*, vol.4, no.4, pp.523–30.

Haywood, C. and Mac an Ghaill, M. (1996) 'Schooling masculinities', in Mac an Ghaill (1996).

Herrnstein-Smith, B. (2000) 'Sewing up the mind: the claims of evolutionary psychology', in Rose, H. and Rose, S. (eds).

Hofman, M.A. and Swaab, D.F. (1991) 'Sexual dimorphism of the human brain – myth and reality', *Experimental and Clinical Endocrinology*, vol.98, pp.161–70.

Holzman, H.R. and Pines, S. (1982) 'Buying sex: The phenomenology of being a john', *Deviant Behavior: An Interdisciplinary Journal*, vol.4, pp.89–116.

Horney, K. (1926) 'Flight from womanhood', *Feminine Psychology*, New York, Norton.

Hyde, J. (1990) 'How large are cognitive differences? A meta-analysis using ω^2 and d', in Nielsen, J.M. (ed.) *Feminist Research Methods: Exemplary Readings in the Social Sciences*, Boulder, CO, Westview.

Hyde, J. (1994) 'Should psychologists study sex differences? Yes, with some guidelines', *Feminism and Psychology*, vol.4, no.4.

Jackson, L.A. (1992) *Physical Appearance and Gender: Sociobiological and Sociocultural Perspectives*, Albany, State University of New York Press.

Johnson (1970) 'Some correlates of extramarital coitus', *Journal of Marriage and the Family*, vol.32, pp.449–56.

Kimura, D. (1999) *Sex and Cognition*, Cambridge, MA, MIT Press.

Kinsey, A.C., Pomeroy, W.B. and Martin, C.E. (1948) *Sexual Behavior in the Human Male*, Philadelphia, Saunders.

Kinsey, A.C., Pomeroy, W.B. and Martin, C.E. (1953) *Sexual Behavior in the Human Female*, Philadelphia, Saunders.

Klein, M. (1926) 'The Psychological Principles of Early Analysis', *The Writings of Melanie Klein*, vol.1, London, Hogarth Press.

Langhorne, M.C. and Secord, P.F. (1955) 'Variations in marital needs with age, sex, marital status, and regional composition', *Journal of Social Psychology*, vol.41, pp.19–37.

Levay, S. (1991) 'A difference in hypothalamic structure between heterosexual and homosexual men', *Science*, vol.253, pp.1034–7.

Littleton, K. and Hoyles, C. (2002) 'The gendering of information technology', in Yelland, N. and Rubin, A. (eds) *Ghosts in the Machine: Women's Voices in Research with Technology*, New York, Peter Lang.

Lloyd, B.B. and Duveen, G. (1992) *Gender Identities and Education: the Impact of Starting School*, New York/London, Harvester Wheatsheaf.

McCormick, N.B. (1994) *Sexual Salvation*, Westport, CT, Greenwood.

Mac an Ghaill, M. (1994) *The Making of Men: Masculinities, Sexualities and Schooling*, Buckingham, Open University Press.

Mac an Ghaill, M. (1996) *Understanding Maculinities. Social Relations and Cultural Arenas*, Buckingham, Open University Press.

Maccoby, E.E. and Jacklin, C.N (1974) *The Psychology of Sex Differences*, Stanford, CA, Stanford University Press.

Money, J. and Erhardt, A. (1972) *Man and Woman: Boy and Girl*, Baltimore, Johns Hopkins University Press.

Nelson, C.S. and Watson, J.A. (1991) 'The computer gender gap: children's attitudes, performance and socialization', *Journal of Educational Technology Systems*, vol.19, pp.345–53.

Rogers, L.J. (1999) *Sexing the Brain*, London, Weidenfield and Nicolson.

Rose, H. and Rose, S. (eds) (2000) *Alas Poor Darwin*, New York, Harmony.

Schneider, F., Habel, U., Kessler, C., Salloum, J.B. and Posse, S. (2000) 'Gender differences in regional cerebral activity during sadness', *Human Brain Mapping*, vol.9, pp.226–38.

Singh, D. (1995) 'Ethnic and gender consensus for the effect of waist-to-hip ratio on judgement of women's attractiveness', *Human Nature*, vol.6, pp.51–65.

Spence, J.T. (1984) 'Masculinity, femininity and gender-related traits: a conceptual analysis and critique of current research', in Maher, B.A and Maher, W.B. (eds) *Progress in Experimental Research in Personality*, vol.13, pp.1–97, Academic Press, New York.

Stainton-Rogers, W. and Stainton-Rogers, R. (2001) *The Psychology of Gender and Sexuality*, Buckingham, Open University Press.

Swaab, D.F. and Fliers, E.A. (1985) 'A sexually dimorphic nucleus in the human brain', *Science*, vol.228, pp.1112–5.

Thorne, B. (1993) 'Gender play: girls and boys in schools', Buckingham, Open University Press.

Thornhill, R and Palmer, C. (2000) *A Natural History of Rape: Biological Bases of Sexual Coercion*, Cambridge, MA, MIT Press.

Trivers, R.E. (1972) 'Parental investment and sexual selection', in Campbell, B. (ed.) *Sexual Selection and the Descent of Man*, Chicago, Aldine.

Weinreich-Haste, H. (1979) 'What sex is science?', in Hartnett, O., Boden, G. and Fuller, M. (eds) *Women: Sex-Role Stereotyping*, Tavistock, London.

Wetherell, M. (1996) 'Life histories/social histories', in Wetherell, M. (ed.) *Identities, Groups and Social Issues*, Sage, London, Thousand Oaks, New Delhi in association with The Open University.

Wiederman, M.W. (1993) 'Evolved gender differences in mate preferences: evidence from personal advertisements', *Ethology and Sociobiology*, vol.14, no.5, pp.331–51.

Wiederman, M.W. and Allgeier, E.R. (1992) 'Gender differences in mate selection criteria: sociobiological or socioeconomic explanation?' *Ethology and Sociobiology*, vol.13, pp.115–24.

Wiederman, M.W. and Kendall, E. (1999) 'Evolution, gender, and sexual jealousy: investigation with a sample from Sweden', *Evolution and Human Behavior*, vol.20, pp.121–8.

Willis, P. (1977) *Learning to Labour: How Working Class Kids get Working Class Jobs*, Aldershot, Saxon House.

Young, W.C. (1964) 'Hormones and sexual behaviour', *Science*, vol.143, pp.212–8.

Commentary 3: The psychology of sex and gender

This chapter has introduced four main theoretical perspectives, biological, evolutionary, social constructionist and psychodynamic perspectives, to examine the complex question of which factors influence our emergence as men and women. These perspectives have helped us to explore the varying meanings of the terms 'sex' and 'gender' and to examine the role of biological, social and cultural factors which influence people's perception of sex and gender. No single perspective provides a full account of sex and gender.

Theory

1   The perspectives focus their enquiry in different ways and hence have different objects of knowledge. These include the influence of biological processes, how evolution shapes thinking and behaviour, the social constructions of sex and gender and their influences, and the psychic development and the internalization of meanings concerning sexual difference.

2   These perspectives ask different questions, use different methods and data, and produce different theories. It is therefore difficult to establish whether the perspectives are complementary, conflicting or coexisting; the methods can be coexisting, the objects of knowledge can be complementary, but the theoretical explanations provided can be conflicting.

Methods

3   The psychoanalytic and social constructionist perspectives use methods based on the hermeneutic principle, and consider people's beliefs and experiences, and focus on the interpretation of meaning. The biological and evolutionary perspectives use methods like those of the natural sciences and adopt a scientific approach to sex and gender. There is however controversy about the kinds of proof evolutionary psychology uses to substantiate its theories.

Themes

4   The study of sex and gender is concerned with the complex interplay of nature and nurture in shaping similarities and differences between women and men. The biological and evolutionary perspectives include an emphasis on the contribution of nature to our experience and behaviour by examining genes and biological structures which relate to sex. The social constructionist perspective looks at the importance of culture and context in the construction of ideas about gender. The psychoanalytic perspective acknowledges both the importance of biological difference and the social and cultural meanings of this difference. We have seen that there has been political

tension between these approaches in relation to their implications about the fixity of men's and women's social roles and personal relationships and behaviour.

5   In this chapter you have been introduced to the theme of what it is that makes us unique as individuals and as humans and therefore different from other animals.

■ Thinking about theory

As you will recall from Book 1, psychologists may explain human behaviour or experience using very different theoretical perspectives, and these perspectives can be viewed as complementary, conflicting or coexisting. It can be a complex task to decide how perspectives relate to each other as they can be compared using a variety of different dimensions, such as the methods they use or their position in relation to fixity and change. In this chapter, a central debate is around the terms 'sex and gender' – what each different perspective construes these terms to mean and the priority they give to each term in explaining the differences between men and women, boys and girls.

The biological perspective offers theories which consider the relationship between genetic and physiological aspects of sex and their implications for gender; and the evolutionary perspective underpins theories which see sexual behaviour and partner choice as determined by behaviours and dispositions that have been selected for in evolutionary history and coded for within genes. These two perspectives complement each other, in that gender is viewed as a consequence primarily of biological sex and both perspectives take the view that differences between men and women arise largely from biological features which have been selected for during evolution.

In direct contrast is the social constructionist perspective which argues that biological sex is not central to explaining what it is like to be a man or woman. Instead biological sex is seen as a 'signpost' to which socially constructed gender differences of masculinity and femininity are attached. Here the biological and social constructionist perspectives juxtapose ideas about the relationship between sex and gender which directly challenge each other.

The psychodynamic perspective takes a different approach from the other perspectives as it combines both biological and cultural explanations of gender. This perspective has a strong developmental focus, and underpins theories which suggest that our early relationships with parents and other significant individuals determine our progression through a series of psychosexual stages and our consequent sex and pleasure-seeking behaviours. According to this perspective, children become gendered through realization of anatomical differences, notably the possession or non-possession of a penis and of the meanings attached to this anatomical difference in terms of power and status with society. We have seen that post-Freudian theorists such as Karen Horney,

Melanie Klein and analysts including Jessica Benjamin have developed the psychoanalytic understanding of gender and criticized Freud's phallocentric approach. The psychodynamic perspective can be seen as contradicting the other perspectives presented in the chapter as it is unique in providing an explanation which takes into account both family dynamics and anatomical difference.

Levels of analysis

In studying sex and gender we have a good example of how perspectives can consider the same topic at different levels of analysis. We have seen that perspectives pursue different objects of knowledge and therefore guide how questions about subject matter are formed. So a biological psychologist might be expected to formulate a theory and ask questions about differences between men and women at the level of hormones, genetic inheritance, or in terms of the structure of the brain. An evolutionary psychologist would look to understand how differences in behaviour between men and women might have evolved and the evolutionary functions they might have served (i.e. functional explanations) in relation to reproductive fitness. The issue of how far psychology can be reduced to biology has been and continues to be the subject of considerable debate within the discipline.

Other perspectives attempt to understand the relationship between sex and gender at a different level of analysis. Social constructionists look at the social and cultural context to examine how knowledge about sex and gender has been constructed within a particular historical and social context. The psychodynamic perspective can be seen as distinctly psychological in its attempts to understand how girls and boys acquire a sexed and gendered sense of themselves as they are growing up within the context of family life. This approach does not reduce sex or gender to biological or societal explanations but acknowledges the importance of both of these in understanding how children acquire a gendered sense of themselves.

We can see that each of these perspectives frames its questions about sex and gender in different ways such that they might appear to be complementary perspectives; however, some of the explanations that have been generated have conflicted.

■ Thinking about methods

In this chapter you have been introduced to a range of psychological research methods using both insider and outsider viewpoints. The methods used directly relate to the questions asked by the perspectives and their 'objects of knowledge'. For example, the biological perspective asks what effect biological processes have on behavioural differences between women and men and goes on to investigate this through scientific procedures. The methods used by the biological perspective include comparison of areas of brain size and function through scanning techniques such as PET which produce material data. These methods have the strength of being highly scientific but we have also seen that the search for biological correlates of behavioural and cognitive differences is a complex and a confusing one and that the results can often be understood only in the light of context and environmental influences. The biological approach can also be criticized for telling us little about the experience of being female or male in a particular cultural or historical context.

The evolutionary perspective makes use of varied methods including experimentation (Clark and Hatfield, 1989) and questionnaire-based studies which seek to establish indicators of physically attractive attributes for men and women. However, an evolutionary explanation for the findings of such studies is often not the only explanation. For example, female choosiness, in terms of which male to mate with, might have evolved and this may be linked to reproductive fitness, but it can also be interpreted in the light of cultural influences. Evolutionary explanations do not lend themselves to being tested in the same way as other scientific explanations, and instead evolutionary psychologists have to seek converging scientific evidence to support their hypotheses.

The group of methods that are usually contrasted with scientific approaches are based on the hermeneutic principle. Social constructionism and psychoanalysis both rely on the interpretation of meaning or symbolic data. The psychodynamic perspective uses clinical experiences and observations of infants as main sources of evidence. Here the emphasis is on the meaning of the biological differences between men and women and how these become internalized in the child's mind. Much of the explanation focuses on unconscious processes such as internalization and identification which cannot be investigated using traditional scientific procedures.

The social constructionist perspective does not see sex and gender as a set of characteristics within or acquired by the individual, but as something which exists only when it is being 'done' through actions, behaviour and experience. As a consequence, social constructionists examine how knowledge about sex and gender has been constructed within particular historical and social contexts using as evidence what people say and write. The social constructionist perspective uses methods that yield qualitative data; for example, the use of observational techniques and discourse analysis to examine different types of masculinities in young men within a school environment (Haywood and Mac an Ghaill, 1996).

It is important to see here how methods are closely linked to the objects of knowledge sought by the four perspectives in the chapter. The social constructionist and psychodynamic perspectives can also be seen as largely complementary with each other in terms of methods, as both use approaches based on the hermeneutic principle to understand the meanings and experiences of being 'gendered'. The biological and evolutionary perspectives largely complement each other by taking a scientific approach derived from the natural sciences using systematic observation of phenomena and experimentation.

■ Thinking about themes

In this chapter you have been introduced to the theme of what it is that makes us unique as individuals and as humans and therefore different from other animals. Gender is clearly a human issue and closely linked to our sense of identity. The study of sex and gender focuses on what makes us unique individuals as well as being an important feature which separates us from other animals.

The relative contributions of nature and nurture have also been explored. Both biological influences and social and cultural influences have been considered in relation to differences between men and women. We have seen that, throughout the twentieth century, biological and social explanations have been at loggerheads because of their political implications, and that the four perspectives covered in the chapter take different stances on this issue.

The biological perspective largely frames questions about the role of nature in sex-role development, asking about the importance of hormones and brain structures. This explanation acknowledges that biology is a two-way process, not just acting on individual behaviour but also being affected by it. Biological psychology can help us to understand sex differences (which are usually established at birth) but does little by way of explaining gender differences as our bodies and brains may become gendered over a lifetime. The evolutionary perspective attempts to identify predispositions to respond in particular ways that have been selected as they promote reproductive success and convey potential reproductive benefits to men and women. Like the biological perspective, the evolutionary approach acknowledges that cultural and social influences modify behaviour, but over a much longer period of time by operating on and overlaying genetic variation. This provides us with some insights into differences in human sexual behaviours but does not explain how sexual relationships are influenced by many cultural and individual factors. We have noted also that is difficult to separate out the role of factors such as genetics, motivation and environment as they work closely together.

In contrast, the social constructionist perspective argues that gender cannot be explained by reproductive sex status but is a production of culture (i.e. nurture). Gender involves two categories, male and female, constructed partially through processes of social identification and viewed as different (the opposite sex). Gender categories are created and maintained through discourses (particularly those relating to the 'opposite' rather than 'other' sex) which provide highly differentiated accounts of gender-appropriate behaviours for girls and boys in relation to toys, activities and school subjects. Gender is therefore seen as dynamic, existing when it is being enacted and re-established continually though actions as an ongoing project. What constitutes masculine and feminine changes within historical periods and at different stages of an individual's life, thus emphasizing the importance of social and cultural influence on our perceptions and understanding of gender.

The psychodynamic perspective is unique in the approach it takes in acknowledging the contribution of both social and biological forces, and hence both nature and nurture. It considers the starting point for gender to be biological sex and discovery of anatomical differences which then leads to different psychic paths for girls and boys. It is the meaning of this difference which is important and which holds symbolic significance to the child who discovers that possession of a penis brings rights and privileges to the male. This perspective differs from the social constructionist one in that this meaning is then shaped by unconscious forces and desires. This account is simultaneously biological and cultural.

We have shown in this chapter that gender is far too complex an issue to be understood without taking account of biological, social and cultural factors. Each perspective presented in the chapter acknowledges to a greater or lesser extent the importance of both biological and social factors, and hence both nature and nurture, to the development of our sense of gender.

References

Clark, R.D. and Hatfield, E. (1989) 'Gender differences in receptivity to sexual offers', *Journal of Psychology and Human Sexuality*, vol. 2, pp. 39–55.

Haywood, C. and Mac an Ghaill, M. (1996) 'Schooling masculinities', in Mac an Ghaill, M. *Understanding Masculinities: Social Relations and Cultural Arenas*, Buckingham, Open University Press.

■ Epilogue

Troy Cooper

We hope that you have enjoyed reading this book. It may be that having read these chapters you are somewhat confused by how psychology goes about its business, since in looking at any one topic it can come up with so many different answers. One issue which has emerged, and which you had not really encountered in Book 1, is that of different 'objects of knowledge'. Different perspectives introduced in Book 1 suggested a different way of seeing something, but you could be forgiven for thinking they were different views of the same thing. In terms of memory, for example, the cognitive perspective on memory might be interested in short-term recall of three- letter triads and the social constructionist perspective might be interested in collective memories – but 'memory' as the object of knowledge appears the same in each case.

However, in the chapters on language and on sex and gender, you encountered perspectives which were very obviously not looking at the same object. For example, the cognitive view of language was that people use language to reflect internal thinking; the social constructionist view of language was that language is a tool for mediating social interaction and shaping the social world. These different views of language have different implications – the cognitive view implies that language underpins human thought, that is its function, and, as Steven Pinker would propose, that is how it evolved. The social constructionist view on the other hand has no particular implication for the relationship of language to thought. These are therefore very different ideas of what language 'is' – reflected in the chapter in terms of the debate about where meaning is created.

These differing views of the nature of the topic under consideration inevitably direct how they are looked at, or what is considered valid and useful evidence. This is the province of epistemology, or the theory of knowledge. The types of evidence, and hence also the method of evidence (or data) collection, that a perspective considers valid will be directly related to what it considers its 'object of knowledge' to be. If these objects are viewed as objectively constituted – with an existence outside the social and cultural world – they are open to scientific investigation; but if they are subjective and a product of the social and cultural world, then they have to be investigated with hermeneutic or interpretative methods. It is worth noting here, because it can be confusing, that this is quite distinct from the issue of insider or outsider methods of data collection. An insider method, for example using interviews to reflect the inner experience of depression, can be used to gain evidence which is then interpreted to support an underlying objective and biological 'object of knowledge'. An outsider method like psychometrics can be used in a study of perception of femininity to gain evidence that is interpreted as reflecting an underlying subjective and socially constructed 'object of knowledge'.

With these thoughts in mind, and having read these chapters, you should now be able to revisit the three Cs from Book 1 – complementarity, conflict or coexistence of perspectives – in order to realize that they can be applied at several different levels in considering any set of perspectives or theories. Accordingly, it is not just a theory or perspective which can come under the analysis provided by the three Cs – analysis in terms of the three Cs can also be applied to the focus of investigation, the assumptions about the nature of the 'object of knowledge', the methods, the implications for perspectives other than those under comparison, and indeed to any underpinning of the larger perspective on which the perspectives or theories under consideration stand. Undoubtedly, this does rather complicate the business of understanding and analysing theories and perspectives in psychology! However, recognizing that complication is also a sign of growing sophistication and deeper understanding and analysis. Psychology is a very interesting discipline, but as you have progressed further in the course you will have realized it is not an easy one. It requires an appreciation of the scientific and hermeneutic traditions and of epistemology – psychology as a whole is a diverse, multi-perspective discipline. There are clearly no uncomplicated answers to be had – rather, there are a series of debates and discussions to which we have begun to introduce you in this book. We hope that you will continue to enjoy engaging with these challenging issues as you progress further in your studies in psychology.

Index

Acknowledgements

Book 1 Chapters 1-5

Grateful acknowledgement is made to the following sources for permission to reproduce material in this book:

Chapter 1

Text

pp.39-40: From Lemme, B.H. *Development in Adulthood*, Copyright © 1995 by Allyn & Bacon. Reprinted/adapted by permission of Allyn & Bacon; p.57: Ford, D.H. and Lerner, R.M. (1992) *Developmental Systems Theory – An Integrative Approach*, Sage Publications, Inc. Copyright © 1992 by Sage Publications, Inc. Reprinted by permission of Sage Publications, Inc

Figures

Figure 1.1: Maylor, E.A. (1996) 'Older people's memory for the past and the future', *The Psychologist*, October 1996, British Psychological Society; Figure 1.2: Adapted from Baltes, P.B. (1987) 'Theoretical propositions of life-span developmental psychology: on the dynamics between growth and decline', *Developmental Psychology*, vol.23, no.5, American Psychological Association. Adapted with permission; Figure 1.3: Adapted from Schaie, K.W. and Willis, S.L. (1991) *Adult Development and Aging.* Copyright © 1991 by K.Warner Schaie and Sherry L. Willis. Reprinted by permission of Pearson Education, Inc., Upper Saddle River, NJ; Figure 1.4: Adapted from Ford, D.H. and Lerner, R.M. (1992) *Developmental Systems Theory – An Integrative Approach*, Sage Publications, Inc. Copyright © 1992 by Sage Publications, Inc. Reprinted by permission of Sage Publications, Inc.

Chapter 2

Figures

Figure 2.1: From J.L. McClelland (1985) 'Putting knowledge in its place: a scheme for programming parallel processing structures on the fly', *Cognitive Science*, 9, 115, Ablex Publishing. Reprinted by permission of Cognitive Science Society, Inc.; Figure 2.2: From 'An interactive activation model of context effects in letter perception: Part 1. An account of basic findings' by J.L. McClelland and D.E. Rumelhart, 1981, *Psychological Review*, 88, p.380. Copyright © 1981 by the American Psychological Association. Reprinted with permission; figure 2.3: Picture context for the 'balloon story' from J.D. Brandsford and M.K. Johnson, 'Consideration of some problems in comprehension', in *Visual Information Processing*, p.396, edited by W.D. Chase. Copyright © 1973 by Academic Press, reproduced by permission of the publisher.

Illustrations
p.79: Copyright © Language Research Center, Georgia State University

Chapter 3

Illustrations
p.160: Copyright © Science Photo Library; p.163: Detail of sculpture by G.L. Bernini, The Ecstasy of Saint Teresa, 1647-1652. Photo: Alinari Archives, Florence

Every effort has been made to trace all the copyright owners, but if any has been inadvertently overlooked, the publishers will be pleased to make the necessary arrangements at the first opportunity.